THEORY AND PRACTICE
WITH ADOLESCENTS

D1132063

Also Available from Lyceum Books, Inc.

Advisory Editors: Thomas M. Meenaghan, *New York University*
Ira C. Colby, *University of Houston*

The Ethics of Practice with Minors: High Stakes, Hard Choices
Kim Strom-Gottfried

Social Work with Families: Content and Process
Robert Constable and Daniel B. Lee

Therapeutic Games and Guided Imagery: Tools for Mental Health and
School Professionals Working with Children, Adolescents, and Their Families
Monit Cheung

Secondary Traumatic Stress and the Child Welfare Professional
Josephine G. Pryce, Kimberly K. Shackelford, and David H. Pryce

Social Work Practice with Families: A Resiliency-Based Approach
Mary Patricia Van Hook

Straight Talk About Professional Ethics
Kim Strom-Gottfried

Working with Children, Adolescents, and Their Families, 3E
Martin Herbert and Karen V. Harper-Dorton

School Social Work: Practice, Policy, and Research, 6E
Robert Constable, Carol Rippey Massat, Shirley McDonald, and John P. Flynn

THEORY AND PRACTICE
WITH ADOLESCENTS
AN APPLIED APPROACH

Fred R. McKenzie
Aurora University

LYCEUM

BOOKS, INC.

Chicago, Illinois

© Lyceum Books, Inc., 2008

Published by

LYCEUM BOOKS, INC.
5758 S. Blackstone Ave.
Chicago, Illinois 60637
773+643-1903 (Fax)
773+643-1902 (Phone)
lyceum@lyceumbooks.com
http://www.lyceumbooks.com

6 5 4 3 2   11

ISBN 978-1-933478-22-7

Library of Congress Cataloging-in-Publication Data

McKenzie, Fred R.
    Theory and practice with adolescents : an applied approach / Fred R. McKenzie.
        p. cm.
    Includes bibliographical references and index.
    ISBN 978-1-933478-22-7
    1. Social work with teenagers. 2. Teenagers—Counseling of. 3. Teenagers—Family relationships. I. Title.
    HV1421.M45   2008
    362.7—dc22
                                                            2007042995

To my son Sam, for teaching me what it means to be the parent of an adolescent, and to my loving wife Tamela, my soul mate, constant support, and love of my life!

Contents

About the Author

Fred R. McKenzie, PhD, LCSW, is associate professor and director of the School of Social Work at Aurora University in Aurora, IL. He received his MSW from George Williams College in Downers Grove, IL, in 1982, and his PhD in clinical social work from Loyola University of Chicago in 1995. Professor McKenzie has been working with adolescents and their families in a myriad of professional practice venues since the mid 1970s. He has been a full time faculty member at Aurora University since 1991.

Foreword

A friend of mine was recently talking on the telephone within earshot of her adolescent daughter. In making plans for lunch with the person on the other end of the line, she said, "Let's hook up at —" and suggested a meeting place. After the call had ended, the daughter felt compelled to inform her mother what the term "hooking up" meant in modern teenage parlance. Such is the world of adolescence both parents and therapists encounter today.

Fred McKenzie's book, *Theory and Practice with Adolescents: An Applied Approach,* fills an important void in the professional literature and offers an invaluable tool for those who have the courage to enter into this scary realm occupied by adolescents today. Drawing on over thirty years of practice experience and distilling and integrating a wide and often disparate literature, Professor McKenzie has written a book that should be on the shelf of every practitioner working with this age group.

The book is organized in a logical progression that begins with a thorough review of the seminal thinkers and theorists in the area of physical, psychological, and emotional development including Piaget, Kohlberg, Gilligan, Erikson, and Blos, as well as Bowlby and other attachment theorists. This chapter introduces the reader to two valuable devices that McKenzie uses throughout the book, a closing discussion of the research basis of the material presented and a presentation of films/television/other media and Internet sources that augment and enhance the discussion. The first chapter, for example, recommends *Rebel Without a Cause, The Breakfast Club,* and *Boyz in the Hood* as essential viewing in helping understand the chapter.

Chapter 2 discusses biopsychosocial assessment and intervention planning and provides a series of questions to guide the practitioner in conducting a thorough assessment and developing an intervention plan. The third chapter on practice skills develops McKenzie's concept of the "the clinical practice template," and in chapter 4 he presents the "Big 5" theoretical models guiding intervention: cognitive behavioral therapy, family systems theory, psychodynamic/attachment/relational theories, narrative and solution-focused theory, and neuroscience. Each of these theories is accompanied by a case example that demonstrates the theory in practice. This introduction of case material also signals a subtle shift in the text. Having done, to this point, an outstanding job in summarizing and presenting a vast amount of the literature, McKenzie now begins to draw upon his long clinical experience.

Chapter 5 discusses the context of the family, and in chapter 6, McKenzie introduces an area of research and practice of particular interest to him, the use of self and the meaning of transference and countertransference in the context of practice with adolescents. This chapter includes a revealing view of McKenzie's own adolescent experience as a way of highlighting the material. The text concludes with a discussion of nontraditional work with adolescents. McKenzie once again draws upon his own experience to discuss outreach and "street work" with adolescents and also discusses play and experiential learning. This chapter is augmented with an extensive case example.

In his preface, McKenzie states that he was drawn to write this book in part because there was no single source for the practitioner to refer to and draw upon in his or her work with adolescents. He has solved that problem admirably with this publication.

Kenneth I. Millar
Florida Gulf Coast University

Preface

I have been working with adolescents and their families since my professional career began in 1974. I have been teaching courses on practicing with adolescents since the mid 1980s. Over that period of time, there have been many changes in culture, family, and the nature and type of services that adolescents and their families receive. Adolescents are probably the most challenging and rewarding group of clients that one can work with. Working with them successfully requires an essential combination of developmental, theoretical, and empirical knowledge combined with the ability to skillfully apply that knowledge in practice. Adolescents and their families receive services from a variety of agencies and institutions, staffed with professionals from diverse disciplines such as psychology, social work, criminal justice, and human services in general. Each of these disciplines has its own ideology and approach to understanding and working with adolescents. Professional education in these disciplines prepares students to work with teens in many ways. Yet each of these professional disciplines relies on similar theoretical and empirical knowledge and practical application skills in order to train competent practitioners. I am writing this book to provide a comprehensive approach to working with adolescents and their families that cuts across all professional disciplines.

Over my many years of teaching graduate practice courses on working with adolescents, I have come to realize that there are many gaps in the professional textbooks written for that purpose. I have found myself using a variety of texts from psychologists, social workers, and psychiatrists, each emphasizing its own particular philosophy of practice with adolescents. This information has always been of limited use because of the inherent gaps in theoretical, empirical, and applied knowledge specific to each discipline. It has been extremely difficult to find a professional text that at the same time embodies a comprehensive and inclusive theoretical approach, supplies relevant empirical information, and demonstrates the practical application of those elements to work with teens and their families. More often than not, a text ends up being in the "either/or" category. Either they are rich with theoretical material and sparse in the specific application of it, or they provide detailed application principles but fail to ground them in explanatory theory or empirical studies. Even when I have found the occasional text that attempts to do both, it has never included the more nontraditional approaches to working with adolescents, such as recreational therapy, games, and play. Practitioners working nontraditionally with teenagers in youth and family service agencies are not in a position to write such a text. In fact, I have never found a text that has grounded nontraditional approaches with adolescents in specific developmental and clinical theory. This is unfortunate because professional students end up not knowing why they are drawn to these approaches, why they work, and why they are essential to adolescent development. Furthermore, if funding sources, parents, teachers/principals, supervisors, and so on understood that these approaches are not only effective but grounded in empirical theories, there would be greater recognition, support, and use of them with the clinical adolescent population. This dilemma has troubled me for many years.

Professional practice with adolescents also requires the ability to work with parents, families, groups, communities, hospitals, schools, the courts, and many other institutions. Yet again, my experience as a professor has been that the literature and texts fail to include these important areas in a comprehensive approach to practice. As a result, I am sure I am not the only professional educator who must rely on multiple textbooks to cover the subject matter comprehensively. After many years of unproductive searching for *the* comprehensive text to address work with adolescents and families, I decided that I would need to write it. *Theory and Practice with Adolescents: An Applied Approach* is that effort.

In this text, I will address the important fundamental developmental theories of adolescence, as well as the clinical theories and applications that are derived from them. This is a book dedicated to an inclusive approach to this important topic. It has been many years in the making in my own mind as well as continually developing in the theoretical and practice literature. Effective practice with adolescents demands that the practitioner be knowledgeable about theories of development, cutting-edge empirical research, and comprehensive clinical theory and also possess the hands-on ability to apply this knowledge in a useful way with clients. All too often I have found that my students read and hear the discussion of this important information but are unable to apply it because they have not fully understood it from an application standpoint. This text will use hands-on practical examples from my own ongoing work with teens and their families to assist in this process.

The book will focus on four main areas: theory, practice, case examples, and a general discussion of the basis for the practice. Classic and contemporary developmental and clinical theories as well as the practices associated with them will be included based upon their validity. Thus I hope the book will help to provide the reader with a professional rationale for differential decision making in his or her work with adolescent clients and their families.

Theory and Practice with Adolescents: An Applied Approach is not a research text, nor is it a book of simple recipes of technique. It is also not a text of theoretical overviews of adolescent development and clinical theories. This text is essentially a theory and practice book designed for those who teach how to conceptualize and carry on clinical work with adolescents in a disciplined and empirically informed fashion. It is also a book for students and practitioners on all levels who are hungry for material that truly addresses the theoretical, technical, applied, and empirical aspects of complex practice with adolescents.

It has taken me many years of professional experience, three degrees, and nearly twenty years of teaching to be able to understand and impart this knowledge to my students. It is my hope that students, teachers, and professionals using this text will benefit from that experience.

Acknowledgments

First of all, I want to thank Ken Millar, without whose guidance and mentorship this text would never have happened. Ken saw in me the author that I failed to see in myself. His encouragement and guidance enabled me not only to recognize my strengths but to have the courage to persevere throughout this process.

Chuck Zastrow has been a strong supportive consultant, particularly as I entered into the revision and copyediting phase of this work.

I want to thank Lisa Gebo from Thomson/Brooks/Cole for her initial acceptance of my prospectus and for her help in steering it to David Follmer at Lyceum Books, Inc., in Chicago.

David Follmer, my publisher, has been a never-ending source of support and guidance in this journey. David connected me with Tom Meenaghan, whose extensive experience and wisdom helped me to streamline the revision process.

Finally, I would never have been able to embark upon or finish this book if it had not been for the loving and unconditional support of my primary editor—my wife, Tamela! Her strong encouragement, love, patient ear, and gentle critique were absolutely essential in this lengthy process.

1

Theoretical Underpinnings of Applied Practice with Adolescents

The phenomenon of adolescence has existed since the early Greek philosophers (Muuss, 1996). There have been many philosophical, theological, and psychological ideologies used to explain the nature of adolescence. Each of these schools of thought has attempted to capture the physical, mental, spiritual, and psychological elements of that developmental time period somewhere between the ages of twelve and twenty-one. Contemporary theories of adolescence tend to focus on physical development, which includes cognitive and emotional/psychological development, and on social development, which includes peers and the family, moral development, and the development of gender identity.

Adolescence has been characterized as a stormy time in which the teenager rebels against adult authority in order to establish emotional independence. Although this viewpoint has changed considerably in recent years, one finds it difficult to argue against the notion that adolescence in general is a period in which the teenager is coming to terms with his or her identity and beginning the process of becoming an adult. What then are the theoretical conceptualizations that are most useful to the practitioner who works with adolescents and their families?

Clinical practice with adolescents demands that the practitioner be well versed in a comprehensive matrix of developmental theories and possess competent skills and interventions, empirically valid research information, and a creative and flexible approach. Adolescents as a group are not easily categorized. Even when considering them as a general group, one must take into consideration whether they are in early adolescence (11 to 14 years of age), mid-adolescence (15 to 16), or late adolescence (17 to 20). Each of these relative time periods brings with it a very different type of teenager with respect to temperament, cognition, social ability, sexual identity, and so on. When one adds diversity to the picture, it becomes even more complex.

This book will offer the beginning practitioner as well as the seasoned veteran a wide range of theories and application principles that are relevant

1

in working with adolescents of any age, gender, and background. What is most crucial in examining these concepts is the question of differential diagnosis and application. In other words, which theory or approach is most appropriate for the client, under what circumstances, and with what type of clinician?

One of the advantages of having many years of clinical experience working with teens and their families is that one benefits from one's inevitable mistakes. All good practitioners learn from their successes and failures and develop an approach to practice that utilizes a combination of their personalities, life experiences, and a pragmatic clinical orientation. This means that most clinicians get better as they get older and more experienced. Professional education is a part of that process, but ongoing personal growth and examination are also key to it. The clinician who possesses knowledge of a wide range of theories and skills is better able to draw from that internal "practice template" (McKenzie, 1995) in order to provide the optimal form of treatment. Practice with adolescents and their families should come from an informed, eclectic approach. This book will help provide the background for such an approach, whether the practitioner is working in the schools, a youth and family service agency, a mental health facility, the child welfare system, the courts, detention, hospitals, or private practice. Different theories and skill sets are needed for different types of settings as well as clients.

DEVELOPMENTAL THEORIES OF ADOLESCENCE

In order to fully appreciate the complexity of the adolescent growth process, it is helpful to get a basic understanding of some of the major developmental theories associated with it. The following theories are crucial to developing a well-rounded knowledge base in which to make informed judgments about treatment with adolescents and their families.

Physical Development

Physical development in adolescents is triggered by the release of certain hormones in the brain that signal areas of the body to grow. It is the hormones that are released from glands within the body that guide this process. The timetable for this process may be very different in different teenagers. Some believe it depends upon nutrition and other key environmental factors. In childhood, boys and girls have very similar bodies except for their sexual organs. The onset of adolescence changes this drastically. Girls usually develop earlier than boys. There is a dramatic increase in height for both sexes. Boys lose body fat and develop more muscle, whereas girls gain more body fat in preparation for reproductive development. Both sexes develop sexual characteristics. This is reflected in the growth of pubic hair around the genitals, as well as a substantial change in the nature of the sex organs in general. In girls, there is also the development of breasts and rounded hips, as the body prepares for the possibility of childbirth. Girls also begin to menstruate, which signals the ability to become pregnant. The tremendous surge of hormones in both adolescent boys and girls accounts for much of the wide range of moods and emotions so characteristic of adolescence (Rice & Dolgin, 2005).

What is probably the most important implication of the tremendous shift in physical development from a clinical standpoint is the way in which it affects the adolescent emotionally and psychologically. The rapid and unpredictable rate of growth can have a far-reaching effect on the adolescent's sense of self, particularly her body image and self-esteem. Although there are a variety of other influences on these elements, teens' perception of their own body and how others perceive them can strongly affect their future development.

In particular, the more consistently the adolescent's physical growth parallels the growth of his peers, the less troublesome it will be from a psychological standpoint. The clinician should be aware of how this part of the teen's development may have affected his total adolescence. Freud (1960) once said, "The ego is first and foremost a body ego" (p. 26). Nowhere is this more important than in adolescence. Although quoting Freud may seem antiquated in a twenty-first-century text on adolescents, I do so to illustrate that even in the late 1800s psychological theorists recognized the intimate and inseparable connection between the mind and the body. Freud's statement not only captures that premise but also emphasizes the manner in which the self/identity (Freud calls it "Ego") comes from the interaction of the mind and body with the external environment.

Jean Piaget's Theory of Cognitive Development

Perhaps the most well known theory of cognitive development came from Jean Piaget (1896–1980). Through a series of rigorous empirical tests, Piaget was able to show that cognition as a process moves through a sequence of stages, each built upon the last, which ultimately result in the capacity for abstract thought in adulthood. His theory has also generally been accepted as a universal paradigm for all cultures.

For the purposes of the clinician working with teenagers, it is important to remember that children move from the stage of *concrete operations* (7–11 years of age) to that of *formal operations* in early adolescence (11–15). Piaget also suggested that there is perhaps a stage of adult thinking that comes after formal operations, in which the young adult may be capable of even greater abstraction and theoretical analysis (Rice & Dolgin, 2005).

The stage of formal operations heralds the onset of the adolescent's ability to engage in abstract thought, in other words, to play with ideas, imagine complex scenarios, question the logic of adult ideas, and even critique her own thought. This new ability enables the teenager to debate adults and others in a way that was impossible just a few years earlier. This is one of the reasons why adolescents argue with adults so much: because they can! This newfound ability is both a curse and a blessing. On the one hand it allows them to enjoy their own minds to a much greater extent, but it also allows them the opportunity to question themselves, their peers, their family, and others in ways that may become anxiety provoking and lead to emotional challenges. In other words, the complexities of life are now apparent to the adolescent. The future is more evident, and their part in it more clear. Combine this newfound ability with the physical changes mentioned above, and one can imagine that body image and self-esteem take on a whole new meaning.

Lawrence Kohlberg's Theory of Moral Development

Lawrence Kohlberg (1927–87) enhanced Piaget's theory by suggesting that there are stages of moral development that are roughly equivalent to Piaget's stages of cognitive development. In other words, children and adolescents progress in their ability to comprehend and hypothesize abstractions in moral reasoning. The process according to Kohlberg moves the individual from a more self-centered, reward-and-punishment view of morality in childhood to the ability to comprehend universal principles of morality in adolescence. Ultimately the adolescent is able to make independent moral choices based upon a complex examination of universal morality and contextual situations involving issues of diversity, socioeconomic status, gender, and so on (Muuss, 1996). This ability, however, is undoubtedly influenced by the individual's emotional development.

Carol Gilligan's Theory of Sex Differences

Carol Gilligan (1936–) helped to further enhance and elaborate Kohlberg's theories by suggesting that women's experience of morality is different from men's. Women, Gilligan argued through her research, are also initially concerned primarily with self but develop a moral standard in which the interdependence of all becomes the guiding principle of moral decision making. This finding has implications not only for Kohlberg's theory but for all developmental propositions that tend to generalize male and female growth. Girls should be seen as different from boys in their development, Gilligan argues (Muuss, 1996; Rice & Dolgin, 2005).

Erik Erikson's Theory of Identity Development

Most clinical practitioners are familiar with Erik Erikson's theory of identity development. Erikson (1902–94) expanded Freud's basic psychosexual developmental timetable into a major life stage theory that emphasized not only individual emotional development but also society's role in pushing the individual from one stage to the next. Erikson's theory has withstood the test of time because of its parsimoniousness as well as its relevance to all cultures (Franz & White, 1985). Erikson studied not only Western European society but diverse cultures from around the world. Clinicians working with children and families should be informed by Erikson's "eight stages of man" as a major explanatory base from which to understand the psychosocial development of individuals throughout the life cycle (Erikson, 1950).

Erikson's theory posits that the individual moves through eight major life stages, each stage building upon the successful completion of the developmental tasks of the previous stage. Modern-day theorists and clinicians alike recognize that these discrete stages are relative to the individual's overall life circumstances, background, resilience, and strengths (Gilgun, 1996; Saleebey, 1997b). In other words, the child is compelled to move through the eight stages in life, her competence and emotional stability dependent upon the extent to which the tasks of each previous stage have been adequately achieved. However, moving on to a new stage does not mean that there is not still unfinished business left over from previous stages. Individuals may continually be working through or revisiting previous stages as they work on the new tasks of the present one. For example, an individual's ability to successfully negotiate Erikson's sixth stage, intimacy vs. isolation, is strongly influenced by the success with which he has accomplished a sense of self in stage 1, trust vs. mistrust. Another way to look at it is to say that the challenge of the intimacy vs. isolation stage may positively (or negatively) influence further development in the trust vs. mistrust stage.

All of Erikson's eight stages are crucial to understanding and working with adolescents, but stages 4 and 5 in particular are worthy of some further discussion. The first three stages—trust vs. mistrust, autonomy vs. shame and doubt, and initiative vs. guilt—all are crucial to the development of the child's ability to experience the world as a safe place and begin to see she has the ability to influence her surroundings. One can also not discount the importance of both environment and constitutional makeup as key factors in that process. Any comprehensive clinical assessment must take these first three stages into consideration.

Stage 4, industry vs. inferiority, is a stage whose importance in life and as a precursor to adolescent development is often misunderstood. Freud suggested that this time period was a "latency" stage, in which the intense drive struggles of the previous years were sufficiently repressed so that the child could begin to sublimate his instinctual needs into the forms of skills and talents, both physically and socially. The intense focus on both academics and behavior in the first half dozen years of education emphasizes this concept. The young child's elementary teacher is as much concerned about how the child gets along with others and behaves in class as with the child's ability to read and write.

It is, however, what is happening in the development of that ability to manage their behavior with adults and peers that is of so much importance diagnostically for the practitioner working with adolescents. The young child is learning to control her impulses, manage her emotions, delay gratification, get along with others, respect authority, work in groups, and begin to develop a sense of self. These elements are the beginnings of the development of more mature ego defenses, and the origins of immature identity formation. If the young elementary school child is able to successfully complete this industry vs. inferiority stage, she is able to have not only a sense of her own skills and abilities but, more importantly, the emotional skills with which to enter into the next stage, identity vs. identity confusion. Difficulties in the industry vs. inferiority stage can be diagnostic indicators of more serious problems in adolescence. Clinicians would be wise to explore this area of development in their overall assessment of any adolescent client, especially keeping in mind issues of diversity, gender, socioeconomic status, strengths, and the general impact of the environment.

Erikson's fifth stage of identity development, identity vs. identity confusion, is the one most crucial to understanding and working with adolescents. According to Erikson, it is this stage in which the adolescent begins to develop a sense of who he is in relationship to family, peers, himself, and society in general. This of course is possible only through the development of Piaget's *formal operations cognitive stage.* Identity is an abstraction that would be impossible to achieve at an earlier stage of life. Only when the adolescent is able to question and critique herself, others, and the world is she able to conceptualize an identity.

How does the adolescent do this? To understand it fully, we will need to visit sections further on in this chapter. However, from Erikson's viewpoint, the adolescent must negotiate a comfortable sense of self through a process of personal interaction with peers and adults, as well as a personal introspection. Erikson would often mention the word *fidelity* when speaking of the outcome of identity vs. identity confusion. Fidelity according to Erikson meant honesty about one's identity. It is being true to oneself. One of the most horrible things that a teen can be accused of today is to be inauthentic, fake, or phony. Why would that be? It is because the innate and instinctive goal of all adolescents is to know themselves and be true to that identity.

Many teenagers practitioners see are in the midst of some form of this search for identity. For some it is more obvious than others, and for those who have had a more challenging time in completing previous life stages, it can be agonizing. The problems can represent themselves in the form of poor academics, behavioral acting out, depression, isolation, family problems, and a myriad of other complex social and environmental issues. The goal, as in all work with children and teens, is to help them get back on the developmental track. Fortunately, most adolescents are generally moving away from dependent caretaking (parents/family) and searching for others who can help them find themselves. The most obvious choice is peers, but idealized adults, including therapists, can also serve that important function.

Peter Blos's Second Separation-Individuation Process

Peter Blos (1904–97) was an ego psychologist and psychoanalyst whose main contribution to the understanding of adolescent development lies in his conceptualization of the "second individuation" process. Blos hypothesized that teenagers move through a second process of emotional separation-individuation in which the ultimate end is a sense of autonomy and relative separation from family. The first separation-individuation process happens in the first few years of life, during which the infant develops a sense of self apart from the primary caretaker(s). Attachment and psychodynamic theories provide a comprehensive description of that earlier process (Blos, 1967).

Blos believed that after the child has achieved object constancy (the internal ability to self-soothe during times of stress and to tolerate being alone) through the successful negotiation of the first separation-individuation process, the stage is set for the final part of that process, which involves a move toward adult autonomy and mature adult relationships. Adolescents accomplish this emotional task through emotional attachment to their peers and other significant relationships outside the family. The choice of others outside the emotionally dependent circle of the family helps the teenager to invest their dependency needs in others who do not represent infantile attachments. Peers serve that purpose quite well in the adolescent's world. Blos proposed that the ultimate act of emotional independence considered as a part of ego development resided in the adolescent's ability to form a sexual/romantic attachment with another. This relationship signaled the teen's ability to invest emotional energy and attachment in a mature relationship with another. It is the first true adult attachment in life. The ability to accomplish this feat lies in the successful resolution of the second separation-individuation process according to Blos (1967).

Attachment, Psychodynamic, and Relational Theories and Neuroscience

Attachment theorists and researchers as early as John Bowlby and Mary Ainsworth emphasized the importance of early attachment as a foundation for all future development. The recent *Psychodynamic Diagnostic Manual (PDM)* is replete with comprehensive contemporary empirical studies emphasizing that fact (Greenspan & Shankar, 2006).

There are numerous attachment and psychodynamic theories and theorists to draw from in understanding the importance of early development for the adolescent. Object relations theory is one of the more powerful and empirically viable ones. In particular, Margaret Mahler (1897–1985) and

D. W. Winnicott (1896–1971) independently contributed conceptually intricate and comprehensive theories of *object constancy* with which to understand the development of self from the successful internalization of the emotional aspects of primary caretakers early in life. Object constancy, they theorized, is the development of the ability to self-soothe and in the process attain the rudimentary ability to become emotionally independent (Mahler, Pine, & Bergman, 1975; Winnicott, 1953).

Neuroscience would describe this process as the solidification of multiple neural networks in the brain through repetitive physical, emotional, and cognitive experiences in a safe caretaking environment. This process allows the infant to draw from its own self-soothing abilities in order to function securely in life. It has been documented through empirical research with infants. In fact, Mahler's separation-individuation stage theory is the result of extensive empirical studies with mothers and their young children. An interesting aspect is the fact that most of what was merely theorized about fifty years ago regarding infant development is now becoming validated through infant research and neuroscience studies (Lyons, 1991). It appears as if our clinical intuition and practice wisdom have been empirically valid all along (Cozolino, 2004).

Winnicott developed the concept of the *transitional object* as a crucial element in the process of initial separation-individuation and later competence in adult life. He theorized that once the infant had achieved a "good-enough" holding environment in life, it was primed to develop or create the transitional object as an emotional substitute for adult self-soothing until it became able to internalize that ability for itself. This elaborate yet simple process is contingent upon the right combination of physical and emotional constitution, environmental safety, and "good-enough" caretaking provision. A transitional object can be anything. It is found or created by the infant once it has the ability to trust and be spontaneous or play in its world. Transitional objects are utilized by infants when they experience anxiety, especially when they are alone. The use of a blanket, doll, sound, touch, and so on to soothe themselves in times of stress not only alleviates the tension but reinforces the infants' sense of competence in life. This competence, Winnicott would say, forms the basis of creativity and the ability to feel that one can influence the world.

What does this have to do with adolescence, you might ask? Social work author Jeffrey Applegate has applied Winnicott's concept of the transitional object or phenomenon to the adolescent's separation-individuation process. As adolescents move through the process of separating from their families, they are often filled with anxiety, depression, and other conflicted emotions. Applegate posits that teens who have successfully developed the ability to utilize transitional objects in childhood resort to that same emotional phenomenon in their move toward emotional independence. This regressive process is adaptive and allows the teen to be independent, even while she sits at home in her room. For example, many adolescent boys and girls spend hours alone listening to their music. The music itself is a transitional phenomenon that assists them in the emotional process of self-soothing while still living with family (Applegate, 1984, 1989).

Winnicott also addressed the need for love and structure in the adolescent's development in his article "The Anti-social Tendency" (1971). In it Winnicott suggested that much of the defiance and quasi-delinquent behavior that many adolescents demonstrate can be understood as a reaching out for love and structure from their environment. The inability to achieve the good-enough love and structure from their infantile environment leads adolescents to seek it out as they negotiate their sense of independence in the adult world. This unique perspective on adolescent acting out can help to inform some of the clinician's efforts in working with teens and their families.

Winnicott emphasized the environment extensively in his writings. The antisocial tendency in a present-day context must be understood through the complex social and environmental situations that many of our adolescents struggle with in their day-to-day lives. Saleebey (1997b) would also caution us as practitioners to recognize and work with the strengths and resilience with which many of our clients thrive in an oppressed environment.

Heinz Kohut's (1913–81) theory of self psychology is pivotal in understanding a crucial element of adolescent development. The theory states that the infant's sense of self develops through the incorporation of what Kohut calls *self-objects.* Self-objects are the emotional aspects of key human interactions. They provide mirroring, idealizing/merging, and twinship needs first to the infant but later to adolescents and adults throughout life. Kohut believed that self-objects were needed in much the same way that food, air, and water are needed by the young infant. Eventually the child develops the ability to provide self-objects for themselves from their own inner resources. *Mirroring* is the self-object need to be validated, admired, and made to feel that one is special. This happens through early attunement experiences with caretakers and continues throughout life. *Merging/idealizing* is the self-object need for others that one can idealize, merge with, and internalize to help develop a sense of self (Kohut, 1971).

Twinship is perhaps the self-object need that is most crucial to adolescents as they negotiate their search for identity and separation-individuation. The self-object need for twinship reflects the child's need to have experiences with others who are like her. The child must be able to draw emotionally from her relationship with key individuals or groups who possess similar qualities, attitudes, interests, and so on. Nowhere is this more relevant than in the adolescent's move toward her peer group to help solidify her identity and reinforce a sense of self as someone who is like others but different from family. Of course this distinction may be a bit of an illusion since so much of what one becomes is influenced by one's family of origin, either genetically or from a relational standpoint. Regardless, the very real identification with peers in adolescence can be much better understood in the context of Kohut's self-object concept of twinship. The need for twinship can also help to explain why it is that so many adolescents in treatment demand self-disclosure from their therapists. It reflects perhaps a developmental need for identification with the clinician as well.

Stephen Mitchell in his classic 1988 book *Relational Concepts in Psychoanalysis: An Integration* emphasized the crucial and invaluable fact that identity development is an interactional and relational process. The unique combinations and contributions of all key participants in a human being's life form the basis of that identity. They include primary, secondary, and tertiary relationships. Environmental, societal, and personal elements are part and parcel of this dynamic developmental process.

Systems Theory and Sociology

The teenager is going through a tremendous amount of individual changes during adolescence. However, integral to this process are the systems in which the adolescent finds himself. Human beings do not function in a self-contained vacuum. We are all social beings. Systems theory helps to explain the interactive process by which the adolescent relates to family, school, and community. Each of these areas is an important aspect of any diagnostic evaluation of the adolescent.

Socially and academically, the adolescent's world is drastically altered in the move from elementary to junior high and high school. Academically, school becomes harder. There is more homework. There are projects to do. The work often demands abstract thinking. For the first time, perhaps, teenagers must begin to think about their future. Will they go to college? What trades are they interested in pursuing? Do they want to consider marriage and family? Will they finish school? Will they live at home past high school? These are just a few of the issues that an adolescent must begin to face.

Socially, most teenagers begin to experience a tremendous pressure, internally and externally, to belong to a certain group of peers. This process, although natural and most often helpful in the move toward independence, also brings with it intense self-doubt, as well as possible anxiety and even depression. Many of the teenagers we as clinicians see in practice suffer from the consequences of this important dilemma. Of course, this challenge may not be difficult for many adolescents, but few negotiate it without some sort of ambivalence.

Another element of social importance during adolescence is gender development and the beginnings of adolescent social sexuality. There is far greater recognition and acceptance in this society for a gay and lesbian lifestyle than there was even fifteen years ago. However, adolescents struggling with their gay and lesbian identities face a severe emotional challenge.

The teens who are at the highest risk for suicide are those who are gay and lesbian. Even today, the word *gay* often connotes all that is awkward, weird, or bad to many teens.

Even if an adolescent is not struggling with gender identity issues, coming to terms with one's sexual identity as a heterosexual is difficult. The dating process can be awkward, and the adolescent usually acquires this ability through trial and error. The emotional impact of dating on the growing adolescent is tempered by many of the factors mentioned above, especially the adolescent's level of emotional maturity. Becoming sexual with another has a profound impact on self-esteem, identity formation, body image, and many other facets of adolescent development. As a result it is not uncommon for many teens to postpone this developmental task (consciously or unconsciously) until later in life. In many cultures, people do not become sexually active until they are older.

Family systems theory also helps to explain the developmental process of the adolescent. Family life stage theory would suggest that most families move through a process in which the child is born, becomes relatively independent, attends elementary school, goes on to junior high/high school, and eventually leaves home one way or another. Each of these stages brings with it certain shifts in the functioning and ongoing relationships in the family. Terms such as family boundaries, family communication, subsystems, family hierarchy, rules, roles, enmeshment, differentiation, triangulation, and so on help to characterize these processes. Each family life stage brings with it changes in all parts of the system. A system is affected by a change in any of its members, and the process is circular, not linear. For example, if little Tommy beats up the next-door neighbor, the reverberations may be felt throughout the neighborhood as well as within the family itself (Nichols & Schwartz, 2006).

The adolescent stage of family life is characterized by the teen's move toward physical and emotional independence, as well as shifts in the way in which the family relates not only to the teenager but to one another as well. In fact one of the most common times that families seek help from professionals is when they are raising an adolescent. Why might that be? One of the reasons is that as the adolescent emotionally moves away from the family, he abandons or shifts the roles that he has been accustomed to playing. This may mean that there is now a gap in certain family functions or relationships. For instance, if the adolescent as a young child helped to provide emotional support for a caretaker, that source of support is now modified or gone. The teenager may be ambivalent about this role and from time to time return to provide the kind of relationship that he did as a child, but in general he is no longer the little boy that the caretaker could count on. As a result, the caretaker may experience a loss in his emotional life and find it difficult to replace the relationship. Some couples experience a tension in their marital relationships when this happens. The role the teenager played for the parent is now vacant, and the couple is forced to look to each other for that need. This often can result in tension in the couple's relationship.

In addition, the way in which the family treats the teenager may be a result of the shift in these roles. The teenager, for example, is now no longer a good, loving, and responsible child but one who is seen as distant, uncaring, and self-centered. The unfortunate fact is that adolescence is a time of self-centeredness. Adolescents are narcissistic. It is part of their development task to be so.

Finally, any responsible practitioner must be well aware of the community in which the adolescent lives. The socioeconomic factors in any adolescent's life are profound influences on her family's culture, values, morals, and viewpoints on life. In addition, factors such as racial, ethnic, spiritual, and gender diversity have the potential to dramatically alter the adolescent's development in the areas mentioned above. It is incumbent upon the clinician to learn above the adolescent's world and use that knowledge to practice in a culturally competent manner.

BASIS OF PRACTICE

For each topical area covered in this book, there will be a discussion of the basis of practice, whether in intuitive knowledge, practice wisdom, theoretical knowledge, or validated knowledge. The overall emphasis here will be on the concept of *informed practice,* that is, a range of empirical processes by which the clinician attempts to plan and carry out interventions and evaluate their success or failure, thereby determining if they should continue to be utilized or whether some modification or entirely different approach is in order. Gerald T. Powers, Thomas M. Meenaghan, and Beverley G. Toomey (1985) describe this process as "practice-focused research." Their very powerful argument is that there are different types of knowledge and a range of processes by which they can be examined, understood, and utilized to help the clinical process. First is intuitive knowledge and common sense. All human beings rely on common sense to function every day. It is indispensable knowledge for life. It is also, however, highly subjective.

There is also assumptive knowledge and practice wisdom. This type of knowledge is based upon the clinician's practice experience, as well as the understanding she has been able to acquire based upon that experience. It is not knowledge that necessarily has been validated by an empirical research process. Simply put, most clinicians have learned what works for them.

Theoretical knowledge comes from the use of developmental and clinical theories. The hypotheses derived from such theories as cognitive-behavioral theory, family systems theory, and psychodynamic theories are utilized by the clinician in order to help him develop his view of the practice situation and ultimately decide upon a practice approach. Every competent clinician should base his practice decisions upon some form of practice theory. The process of deciding upon one or several theories, implementing them in the clinical process, and evaluating the relative success of each is part of the development of practice wisdom. Theories should not be applied randomly, nor should they be adhered to if they are not working. In that sense, clinical practice is a research process.

Finally, according to Powers, Meenaghan, and Toomey, there is validated knowledge. This is knowledge that has been gained through a more formalized and rigorous process of research. To date, there has been relatively little validated knowledge about the clinical process. The clinical situation is a complex environment with multiple variables that are difficult not only to operationalize but also to measure. How does one fully capture the concept of transference, for instance? How is hope defined so that it can be measured and studied? These are challenging issues for the clinical researcher and the clinician. The ongoing debate about whether clinical practice is an art or a science continues (Heineman, 1981).

There have been some remarkable strides in clinical research, and this text will cite and address some of these studies in each chapter. The onset of "evidence-based" practice research will also be presented. There appear to be some interventions that have been successful with certain types of clinical situations. Unfortunately even the evidence-based research has not been able to generalize its findings to the larger population. They tend to be situation specific.

The theoretical and practice concepts in each chapter will be examined and discussed from the perspective of the four levels of research knowledge indicated in Powers, Meenaghan, and Toomey's text: (1) assumptive practice knowledge, (2) practice wisdom knowledge, (3) theoretical practice knowledge, and (4) validated practice knowledge. This text is designed to focus primarily on the first three types of knowledge: intuitive, assumptive/practice wisdom, and theoretical. Validated knowledge will be addressed as well, especially with regard to some of the contemporary research related to each chapter topic. This is, however, not a research book. It is a theory and practice book that will address practice-focused research on all four levels.

Having set the parameters for this aspect of the text, let us assess the status of the developmental theories described above. The physical and cognitive development that takes place in adolescence is well documented and considered to be common knowledge throughout the world. The reader is encouraged to pick up any textbook on physiology to review and further understand the physical, hormonal, and cognitive changes that occur in adolescent development. These studies have been going on for hundreds of years.

Piaget's studies on cognitive development are also widely accepted throughout the world as one of the standards by which to predict and monitor the evolving growth of the mind. The recent advances in neuroscience theory and research have further validated the sequential nature of cognitive development, which Piaget postulated many years earlier. This work falls into the category of validated knowledge, given the extensive nature of the research that has been done (Cozolino, 2002; Rice & Dolgin, 2005; Santrock, 2006; Siegel, 1999).

Kohlberg's and Gilligan's work have helped to expand Piaget's research on cognitive development. Gilligan's research methodology has been questioned, casting doubt for some on the validity of her findings about the differences between women and men (Muuss, 1996). Kohlberg has expanded Piaget's cognitive findings and premises to include a phase-specific development of morality. His work, like Piaget's, has generally been accepted as theoretical knowledge, with the caveat that factors such as gender, race, and culture may modify these phases to some extent (Muuss, 1996; Rice & Dolgin, 2005).

Erik Erikson's life stage theory has received both praise and criticism for its validity and applicability across the cultural spectrum. However, life stage theory is still utilized as one of the primary standards in developmental education throughout the world. Erikson's work probably falls somewhere between theoretical and validated knowledge. From an intuitive and commonsense perspective, most clinicians would agree that human beings progress through some sort of stage or phase process throughout life. One might quibble with the particulars of whether or not there are discrete stages and specific goals that must be met. However, few would agree that development is totally random or chaotic in nature.

Erikson did study many cultures in arriving at his conclusions regarding a life stage process. His work is not simply a matter of intuitive notions or practice wisdom. Nor does it lie entirely in the realm of theory. The difficulty in validating a developmental theory such as Erikson's is that one must take into consideration variables such as gender, race, culture, socioeconomics, and a myriad of intervening factors (Erikson, 1950; Muuss, 1996; Santrock, 2006).

Peter Blos's work falls directly into the area of theoretical knowledge. Although certainly very sound in its intuitive and practice wisdom principles, the notion of a second individuation has not reached the level of validated knowledge. However, the separation-individuation process in childhood has been researched and validated by Margaret Mahler (1975), as well as highly influenced by the attachment research of John Bowlby (1969). Blos's premise that adolescents revisit and rework this phase in development certainly has considerable merit.

Attachment theories and research have reached the level of validated knowledge, beginning with John Bowlby's work (1969, 1973, 1980). The relationship between attachment in infancy and childhood and adolescent development has not been proven, but it has a basis in intuitive, practice wisdom, and theoretical knowledge (Johnson & Whiffen, 2003; *PDM,* 2006).

Psychodynamic and family systems theories are solidly in the realm of theoretical knowledge. These important practice paradigms have evolved from a core of intuitive knowledge and years of practice wisdom, case study research, and clinical observation. At the present time, various forms of both psychodynamic and family therapy approaches have been researched, as have cognitive-behavioral, narrative, client-centered, and many others. Even the latest evidence-based research has examined various forms of many of these models with varying degrees of validity (Hubble, Duncan, & Miller, 1999; O'Hare, 2005; *PDM,* 2006; Prochaska & Norcross, 2003; Rogers, 1965). Please refer to the extensive list of recommended readings at the end of this chapter for further study.

Summary

This opening chapter has given the clinician a comprehensive background in many of the main theories and concepts essential in assessing and working with adolescents and their families. Much of this material will be revisited and expanded upon as the book progresses. This initial chapter serves as a basic review or foundation summary with which to approach all subsequent chapters. The stage is now set for a comprehensive approach to understanding and working with adolescents from an informed contextual basis.

Recommended Resources

Readings

Joan Berzoff, Laura Melano Flanagan, & Patricia Hertz, *Inside Out and Outside In* (New York: Jason Aronson, 1996). This text examines traditional developmental theory from a contemporary standpoint.

Peter Blos, *The Adolescent Passage: Developmental Issues* (New York: International Universities Press, 1979). Blos examines one of the most pivotal concepts in the developmental literature on adolescence, revisiting the separation-individuation stage of development from early childhood and its implication for successful identity formation and mature object relations.

Erik Erikson, *Childhood and Society* (New York: Norton, 1950). Erik Erikson's work is still considered to be one of the most important sources of theoretical knowledge on development.

Rolf Muuss, *Theories of Adolescence,* 6th ed. (New York: McGraw-Hill, 1986). Muuss's collection of theoretical writing from various authors offers a comprehensive examination of most of the traditional literature on adolescence.

Michael P. Nichols & Richard C. Schwartz, *Family Therapy: Concepts and Methods,* 7th ed. (New York: Allyn & Bacon/Pearson, 2006). This book is considered by many to be *the* source for family therapy history and concepts.

Philip F. Rice & Gale Kim Dolgin, *The Adolescent: Developmental, Relationships and Culture*, 11th ed. (Boston: Allyn & Bacon/Pearson, 2005). This is an excellent source for examining adolescence in light of contemporary cultural issues.

D. Saleebey, "Is It Feasible to Teach HBSE from a Strengths Perspective, in Contrast to One Emphasizing Limitations or Weaknesses? (Yes)," in M. Bloom and W. C. Klein, eds., *Controversial Issues in Human Behavior in the Social Environment*, pp. 16–23 (Boston: Allyn & Bacon, 1997). It is important to understand adolescence from the perspective of both strengths and deficits. Saleebey's book is a definitive examination of this issue.

Film/Television/Media

Rebel Without a Cause (1955). This classic film is based on a book by Robert Lindner, a renowned psychotherapist. The depiction of the adolescent's struggle for identity through interactions with family and peers is powerful.

The Breakfast Club (1985). This film is considered by many to be the definitive depiction of the adolescent's identification with his peer group and its implication in identity formation.

Boyz in the Hood (1991). This film captures the challenge of identity formation for African American youth in the urban setting.

2

The Practice Formulation for Biopsychosocial Assessment and Intervention Planning

Chapter 1 presented the fundamental theoretical base with which to understand adolescent development. When a clinician finds herself working with an adolescent, his family, and/or other key players in the teen's life, how does she approach the issue of assessment and intervention planning? Part of that process necessitates the use of all of the theories and empirical information presented in chapter 1. However, finding a format for such an inclusive assessment can be daunting. John Meeks, in his now classic adolescent text *The Fragile Alliance*, developed what he called the *diagnostic evaluation* to do just that (Meeks & Bernet, 2001). Meeks proposed a series of questions to guide the practitioner in gathering and formulating a clinical picture of the adolescent. Although his guidelines were relevant, they were also in some ways incomplete. Specifically, Meeks's work was predominantly psychoanalytic in nature, which limited his contributions to a narrower realm of knowledge. In order to fully understand, assess, and formulate a comprehensive understanding of the adolescent, Meeks's model needs to be broadened.

This chapter will present the *practice formulation for biopsychosocial assessment and intervention planning* as a method by which to comprehensively evaluate the adolescent, his family, community, and resources. This formulation is a dramatic modification of Meeks's "diagnostic evaluation," as it expands and elaborates the assessment process to include a broader range of theoretical, social, and cultural variables. This assessment enables the practitioner to understand the adolescent much more contextually, as well as incorporating some of the more contemporary theoretical paradigms.

Depending upon the particular practice setting in which the clinician is seeing the client, a full diagnosis using *The Diagnostic and Statistical Manual of Mental Disorders,* 4th edition, text revision *(DSM-IV-TR)* may be included, as well as the more recent and expanded *Psychodynamic Diagnostic Manual (PDM)* axes. The *PDM* is a particularly compelling addition to a diagnostic formulation because of its broader and more strengths-oriented view of pathology (e.g., it includes a diagnosis of a healthy personality). In addition, the *PDM* has been developed through the extensive utilization and incorporation of contemporary neuroscience and attachment theory research.

THE PRACTICE FORMULATION FOR BIOPSYCHOSOCIAL ASSESSMENT AND INTERVENTION PLANNING

The practice formulation consists of twelve questions, each of which will be discussed here.

1. *Is there any evidence of constitutional factors that may have contributed to the present situation? If so, how have they affected the adolescent?* Constitutional factors are an important element in the diagnostic assessment of the adolescent. In most circumstances, it is difficult to say with certainty that there are definitive hereditary or constitutional predispositions that will have a strong bearing on the developmental functioning of the adolescent client. But gathering a preliminary family history, even informally in initial discussion with parents, can help the clinician understand and work with the adolescent in a more informed and effective manner. Constitution is just one of many contributing factors to the therapeutic relationship, and it can certainly be modified by the nature and quality of caretaking as well as by environmental factors. Nonetheless, constitution is one of the most important variables in clinical work and must not be overlooked.

Constitution can be a generic term for any type of physiological condition that may have affected the adolescent. There are many examples. Attention deficit disorder (ADD) or attention deficit hyperactivity disorder (ADHD) might be one of them. The adolescent with ADD or ADHD is not as able to process his thoughts or manage his behaviors as effectively as the teen that is born without ADD/ADHD. We will revisit these diagnostic categories later in this book, but for now suffice it to say that ADD and ADHD could be a constitutional hindrance to normal adolescent development. The genetic predispositions to depression, bipolar disorder, anxiety, schizophrenia, or alcoholism are all constitutional variables in the development of any individual. In short, any type of physical, mental, or emotional condition that may have a hereditary or prenatal etiology can seriously affect the development and ongoing functioning of the adolescent.

It is imperative that the clinician to the best of her ability explore or be on the lookout for any behaviors, thoughts, or emotions on the part of the adolescent that might signal some type of constitutional challenge or problem. This information is crucial in order to make the most competent and ethical evaluation possible. Failure to take this type of information into consideration can have far-reaching consequences in not only the assessment process but also the types of interventions that are planned for the teenager and his family. For example, the teenager who does not pay attention in school can be understood in a much different light if we know she is having difficulty with ADD rather than being oppositional. Not only is the diagnosis completely different, but the treatment as well.

It should be standard ethical practice for clinicians to refer an adolescent and her family for a medical evaluation if there is any indication that the presenting issues or concerns may have a physical cause. The examples are far too numerous to cite in this text, but some of them might include symptoms of depression (tiredness, lack of motivation, irritability, lack of appetite, sleeping problems) and of bipolar disorders (moodiness, irritability, heightened creativity). There are many other similar situations that warrant a thorough medical evaluation in order to rule out physical and constitutional factors before proceeding with a course of counseling.

Each of the formulation questions must be understood in the light of factors such as the environment, diversity, and the adolescent's own unique strengths and resilience that may alter the outcome. Far too often, clinicians fail to recognize those key factors and plunge ahead in a misguided fashion (Gambrill & Mason, 1994; Saleebey, 1997b).

2. *What level of psychosocial development do you believe the adolescent has achieved? Do you believe the adolescent is fixated or regressed at all? What factors lead you to believe this may be the case?* A tremendous amount of information is imbedded in these highly pertinent questions. The clinician may make use of several different theoretical frames of reference in evaluating the adolescent's level of development. For the purposes of this text, Erikson's psychosocial stages will be the main general source. It is a useful, pragmatic, and relevant theory with which to understand the adolescent's social and emotional life (Marcia, 1966). According to Erikson, the individual will most probably look a certain way socially and emotionally if she has successfully negotiated the tasks previous to the adolescent stage of identity vs. identity confusion. But what do the terms fixated and regressed mean, and how do they figure into the diagnostic picture?

Fixation is a psychodynamic or psychoanalytic term that describes the process of being stuck in one's emotional development. In other words, the child never moved beyond a particular emotional stage and is still behaving in a manner that would be expected of a child at that stage. It means that the adolescent is emotionally immature and needs to do some social and emotional work in order to move into the adolescent stage of development. This fixation can be the result of a variety of things. Failed attachment, physical and sexual abuse, and neglect are all factors that contribute to a child's being stuck in earlier stages of development. Reactive attachment disorder, in which a child has failed to achieve a secure attachment with primary caregivers, is a good example of this type of challenge. In order to move into the adolescent stage of development, the teen must first be able to work on the emotional challenges from earlier in life. Ongoing intensive therapy and perhaps medication are usually indicated for problems of this nature. However, there are a wide range of fixation problems that a clinician may encounter in working with adolescents. Many teens are not severely stuck but only mildly delayed; working with adolescents like this is much less difficult and usually has a good outcome. Not all children are on the same timetable in their emotional and social development. The adolescent practitioner will see many children who need professional support in order to move ahead in development.

Whether one is comfortable with the psychodynamic term fixation is not the issue here. In the most general sense, fixation can be understood as a delay in emotional development due to any number of factors. Usually this delay is contextual and environmental. Children of all racial, ethnic, and economic backgrounds can be delayed in their development. For some, that delay is a strength and source of resilience given the oppressive and threatening environments in which they live. For others, it may be the result of inadequate caretaking, abuse, or neglect. It is the astute clinician's job to make a thorough and nonbiased assessment of the factors that may have contributed to a particular delay in development.

In *regression,* another psychodynamic concept, the adolescent may have been able to accomplish some of the tasks of the appropriate stage of development but for some reason has backslid to an earlier stage. Some of this regression is a normal part of the emotional ambivalence inherent in adolescent development. It is not uncommon, for instance, for parents to experience rather dramatic swings in their teenagers from childhood dependence to adolescent autonomy. One minute your teenager wants to sit on your lap, hug you, have you tuck him in at night, and the next he wants nothing to do with you. Don't dare walk near him at the mall or talk with him about anything personal if his friends are around. Is this the same child? Is he disturbed? The answer is no. Most teenagers fluctuate in their dependency needs and behaviors throughout adolescence. That process is fairly normal. It should be understood and tolerated. Regression is different.

Regression is a pervasive pattern of emotionally immature behavior reminiscent of early development that can ultimately be traced to some type of psychosocial stressor(s) in the teenager's life. It is not fleeting or ambivalent; it is rigid, inflexible, and stuck, much like fixation. The difference is that the regressed child was demonstrating age-appropriate emotional and social behavior, and something happened that caused her to revert back to an earlier form of emotional and social behavior because it is familiar and safe. Regression can be adaptive. In fact, one of the most adaptive ego functions is "adaptive regression in the service of the ego" (Goldstein, 1995).

Most healthy adults are able to do childlike things in order to soothe themselves in times of stress. Even as I write this book, I often need to get away from it in order to alleviate the stress and take care of myself. I take a nap, watch TV, or engage in my favorite activity . . . playing computer games.

Does it mean I'm irresponsible? No, because it is not chronic and does not interfere with what I should be doing but in fact enables me to reinvest in the project at hand. This ability allows human beings to manage life therapeutically. Regression that is a problem in adolescence is usually debilitative. The teenager does not feel safe as an emotional adolescent and reverts to earlier forms of emotional functioning in order to survive. For example, a fourteen-year-old girl in the early stages of adolescent development may experience a setback when her best and only friend moves away. This young girl was beginning to embark on social activities outside the home, as well as engaging in activities at school with her best friend. As a result of the abrupt move of her friend and the subsequent emotional loss that it entailed, this young teen isolates herself at home, reverting back to interacting only with her family, much as she did prior to the onset of adolescence, and behaving the way she did as a ten-year-old. This type of behavior is regressive, inflexible, and serves to emotionally protect the young girl from anticipated disappointment or loss in the future. It is, however, also a problem because it is holding the teenager back from moving ahead in her natural social and emotional development. Regression can come in many forms and be related to a variety of emotional challenges. Depending on the extent to which the behaviors interrupt the adolescent's ongoing development, therapeutic efforts are aimed at helping to identify the stressors and finding appropriate solutions in order to help the adolescent get back on the developmental track.

The factors involved in fixation and regression are many and include family trauma, divorce, death in the family, or the inevitable stress of entering high school. These conditions can also be the result of unresolved physical, sexual, or emotional abuse. Only a thorough exploration of the teen's life will yield that information. The answer to this question also may take time. In fact, each new meeting with any client configuration brings a further modification of the clinician's ongoing assessment process. In other words, assessment is tentative and evolving. Both fixation and regression are contextual; issues of diversity, culture, gender, and environment must all be taken into account in understanding the reasons and, more importantly, the meaning of fixation or regression. The crucial factor is the extent to which the client's behavior is interfering with normal life.

In conclusion, Erikson's theory of identity development can help us answer the question of which level of psychosocial development fits the adolescent best. According to Erikson, this outcome of successfully managing the identity vs. identity confusion stage or challenge is a beginning sense of self and autonomy. As mentioned in chapter 1, Erikson used the word *fidelity* to describe the successful completion of this stage. In the most general sense, an adolescent who has been able to achieve a healthy degree of identity formation is relatively comfortable with who he is, his friends, his plans for the future, and his overall ability to manage his emotions in a relatively autonomous manner. This sense of self or identity is, of course, relative to gender, family constellation, diversity, and many other factors. However, a relative sense of emotional independence and identity solidification is a universal concept across all cultures. It is one of the hallmarks of adult life.

3. *What type of attachment did the adolescent have with her primary caretakers, and how did these early developmental periods affect her present relationships with family, peers, and significant others, especially the therapist?* The way in which any human being engages in interactions with another can be understood in part by attachment theory. As mentioned in chapter 1, how an infant/toddler is soothed and nurtured by its primary caretakers has a tremendous influence on its ability to manage emotions throughout life. Many attachment theories specify particular types of attachment styles that originate at birth but are modified and influenced in early childhood by caretaking, environment, and constitution (Johnson & Whiffen, 2003). The continuum can range from secure to disorganized types of attachment. A secure attachment is obviously a generic term for what Winnicott might call the "good-enough" development. The child has learned to manage life emotionally in a fairly positive manner. The other types of attachment—avoidant, dependent, disorganized, and so on—demonstrate a range of difficulty in handling dependency, anxiety, and self-soothing and in achieving autonomous behavior. These character styles are embedded in the young child's neurobiology and have strong implications for the way in which she will approach each successive stage of development (Cozolino, 2002; Greenspan & Shankar, 2006). The extent to which an adolescent is able to interact with others in his life is highly influenced by his attachment style and early development.

What does this look like to the clinician? One of the most general ways to evaluate an adolescent's level of attachment is to get a sense of how she interacts with the key people in her life, namely, family and peers. It is useful to think of this key diagnostic area as a continuum from utterly anxious and dependent to extremely chaotic and disorganized. The picture of emotional health is somewhere in the middle, where the adolescent can strike a balance between dependency and autonomy. It is the clinician's job to assess this ability over time, through a careful examination of and dialogue about the teen's life. Key factors, as mentioned earlier, include the nature and amount of peer relationships, any romantic ties and how these are handled by the teen, and the way in which he relates to his family. The combined understanding of these crucial areas helps the practitioner assess the adolescent's level of attachment contextually (Beasley, Thompson, & Davidson, 2003; Garmezy, 1991; Lyons, 1991).

4. *Why is the adolescent in need of service right now? Is he self-referred, or does someone else believe he needs help?* This is perhaps the most obvious part of the assessment, but an important question nonethe-

less. Most adolescents are not self-referred. Whether it is the school setting, juvenile courts, detention, child welfare, mental health, youth and family agencies, or private practice, most teenagers come to counseling because someone else has suggested it. Of course this is not always the case. In fact, older adolescents, sixteen years of age and up, will often seek out help. What is important to remember is that therapy can be very different when it is voluntary from when it is mandatory. Engagement, trust building, goal setting, and working on issues can be much more tedious if the teen is forced to come to treatment.

The question of why the adolescent is in need of help right now is an important one. Usually, teenagers come to the attention of clinicians of all types because they are off track in the developmental process, and it is the clinician's job to help them get back on track. In assessing the teenager, it is crucial to have a thorough understanding of the needs and expectations of all parties involved in the referral. This understanding sets the tone of the treatment planning and work ahead.

Again, being off track may sound like an indictment of the adolescent client. Remember that key intervening and contextual issues such as culture, diversity, gender, and environment can be mitigating factors in understanding the presenting concern and the reason for treatment.

5. *Does the adolescent see herself as being conflicted or in need of help, despite the fact that she may not be self-referred? To what extent can she see her part in the situation? Does the adolescent have the capacity to be introspective and/or to view herself objectively? What is the extent of her observing ego?* Adolescence is a time of self-absorption. It is the rare teen that can have mature objectivity about his situation. However, the degree to which an adolescent can see his part in a particular problem, or imagine how others may see him, is diagnostically important for the clinician in her assessment and treatment planning. The terms *ego syntonic* and *ego dystonic,* as well as the term *observing ego,* shed important light on this area of assessment. Ego-syntonic character traits, thoughts, and behaviors are those that an adolescent feels comfortable with and accepts as a part of her personality. Ego-dystonic traits are those that are unacceptable to the teen and amenable to change. A problem develops when behaviors that are unacceptable to parents, school, or society are ego syntonic to the adolescent. The teen who believes that vandalism, stealing, or using profane language with authority figures is perfectly acceptable has a difficult problem (Goldstein, 1995). Another way to pose the question would be to ask: Does the adolescent own the problem (when she clearly should), or does she blame others (when she clearly shouldn't)? Most good clinicians know the difference.

The observing ego is another concept from ego psychology that is very useful in the diagnostic process with adolescents. As mentioned earlier, teens develop the ability to become more objective and self-aware as they mature emotionally and cognitively. A clinician would not expect a thirteen-year-old to have the same degree of objectivity as a nineteen-year-old. A person's observing ego allows him to metaphorically stand outside himself and imagine how others might see him. It represents the extent to which an adolescent has perspective on her interactions with others. Such perspective is considered to be a mark of emotional maturity and has implications for all types of human interaction, be it school, work, or play. This kind of emotional ability also has profound implications for adult life. The clinician should be aware of the range of the adolescent's observing ego ability and how it affects the presenting concerns as well as the teen's life in general. This diagnostic feature has important implications for the nature and style of interaction the clinician decides to use with the adolescent client. The further along an adolescent is in the development of an observing ego, the more introspective and direct the therapy process can be (Blos, 1967).

6. *Is the adolescent's defensive structure adaptive or maladaptive?* The defensive structure refers to an individual's ability to manage his emotions and impulses when alone and in the presence of others. This ability can come from an individual's inherent constitution, attachments, social learning, culture, and other key areas of life. There is, of course, a relative range of functional defenses; all behavior is to be considered contextually. However, some behaviors pose a greater problem than others, and many adolescents find themselves in trouble or conflict owing to an inability to manage their feelings, impulses, and behaviors in appropriate ways. From a psychodynamic perspective, defenses are considered on a continuum from primitive to mature functioning. A primitive defense is one in which the individual distorts reality, for instance, in denial ("I didn't say that" when they just did), or projection ("You're angry, aren't you?" when it's the adolescent who is actually angry). Mature defenses are ones that are more adaptive. The epitome of maturity in defensive functioning is *sublimation,* in which a destructive or maladaptive impulse of behavior is channeled into something constructive. In adolescence, an angry teenage boy might sublimate his aggressive tendencies by becoming the most fearsome defensive linebacker on his high school football team. The extent to which a teenage boy or girl manages his or her interactions, impulses, and emotions should be examined on a continuum of adaptive to maladaptive defensive functioning.

Whether the clinician is comfortable with the use of the word *defenses* is not as important as her recognition that there is a range of emotional capabilities that all human beings possess. Some styles of interacting are more adaptive and helpful than others. Emotional functioning becomes a problem when the adolescent—or adult, for that matter—is unable to be flexible in his interactions with others, which interferes with his life. This question is meant to gather a general sense of that ability in order to gauge the adolescent's strength and resilience in his relationships with others.

7. *How would you assess the adolescent's family system, and how does it affect her present situation?* Family systems theory is one of the cornerstones of clinical work (Nichols & Schwartz, 2006). It has been a useful paradigm for working not only with children, adolescents, and families but with adults as well. The structure, functions, rules, roles, values, and culture of any family system have a tremendous impact on the development of the child. The astute clinician working with teenagers and their families must be able to understand the extent to which the family system has affected the teen and perhaps contributed to the presenting concerns. In particular, it is important to get a sense of family type (nuclear family, single parent, divorced, step-family, blended family), family makeup (who is in the family and what are their roles?), family structure and hierarchy (how are decisions made? who is in charge? what are the implicit and explicit norms and values?), family culture (what are the unique qualities of this family based upon issues of diversity and especially socioeconomic factors?). Finally and most importantly, the clinician must determine how this family system has influenced the past and present development of the particular adolescent that has been referred for treatment.

Key to this question is how the family system has understood and approached the notion of adolescent development in the upbringing of their children. How knowledgeable are they about general adolescent development, and how have they handled their relationships and parenting with this particular teen? What is the discipline structure like in this family, and how has it affected the developing adolescent? All of these questions and many others are an important part of the overall assessment of the adolescent and whatever difficulty she may be having in her life.

Once again, the key intervening factor in this question is context. I cannot stress enough the necessity of developing a sense of cultural competence, as well as openness to understanding the unique culture, strengths, and resilience of every family that one sees in practice (Boyle & Springer, 2001).

8. *Are the adolescent's parents/caretakers invested and willing to recognize there might be a problem and help work on it?* Again, this may sound like an obvious question, but the extent to which parents and family are motivated to become involved in the clinical work with their child, the more likely it will be successful. It is not uncommon for parents and family to view their child as the problem, with no willingness to examine their contribution to the situation. This is an unfortunate dilemma not only for the family but for the adolescent as well. The presenting concern that accompanies the adolescent client is usually multifaceted. Family, school, peers, the community, and society at large are often an integral part of the problem. A family that is willing to work with the clinician can only help the situation. In fact, it is difficult to imagine working with an adolescent without to some extent

involving the family and perhaps other key systems in the teen's life. If at all possible, the practitioner must try to involve the family in working with a teen that is still a dependent.

9. *Are there particular issues of diversity that heavily influence the adolescent's situation?* Diversity is one of the most overlooked factors in not only assessment but ongoing work with the adolescent and her family. It is imperative that the practitioner working with adolescents be culturally competent (Chung & Bemak, 2002). This means doing your best to be aware of your own biases and prejudices (we all have them) and also being committed to learning from your clients. The key areas to be aware of in assessing and formulating a treatment plan with adolescents are race, ethnicity, culture, gender, spirituality, physical challenges, and socioeconomic issues. All of these can heavily influence the adolescent's worldview, upbringing, and identity formation. It is important never to take anything for granted but rather to explore thoroughly any issues of diversity in order to better understand the adolescent and her family.

Perhaps the most crucial of these areas are the socioeconomic factors. Socioeconomic issues influence racial, ethnic, cultural, spiritual, gender, and physical factors. Income and available resources are crucial to how one sees the world and approaches life. Far too often we as clinicians attribute factors to a client or family based upon race, ethnicity, or other key diversity factors alone. Socioeconomic issues are the modifiers of all of the others. It should be an important part of any comprehensive clinical assessment of adolescents to scrutinize diversity issues as important factors in shaping development on all levels.

10. *What environmental factors are relevant to this situation?* This question is in some ways related to question 9. Socioeconomic factors are of course directly related to the kinds of resources available in the adolescent's environment. However, the abundance of resources in general is also a key factor regardless of what socioeconomic background one comes from. The practitioner working with adolescents and their families must take into account the nature of the environment and how it has affected the adolescent's early development as well as his present situation.

For example, I recently began seeing a fourteen-year-old boy who, because of his parents' divorce, had to move to a new town and school just when he was entering middle school or junior high. In his old school environment, he was well liked, had many friends, and was considered one of the *popular* kids. This all changed when he moved. Now he is unknown and has had to negotiate an environment in which he is an outsider. This is especially complicated because of the importance of group membership in adolescence. My young sensitive client is now feeling isolated, disconnected, and insecure, particularly because of his environment. This factor becomes a driving force in assessment and treatment planning.

11. *What resources are available to the adolescent in dealing with this situation? What are the adolescent's strengths?* These questions encompass a wide range of factors. In deciding what type of plan to initiate for a particular teenager, the clinician must take into account resources in the community, family, peer group, as well as the innate strengths of the adolescent herself (Saleebey, 1997b). Is the family a supportive factor in the adolescent's treatment? Is there a sibling within the family that can help with the client's depression, for instance? Is there an abundance of resources in the community that can be drawn from in developing a comprehensive treatment plan for the teenager? In the case I mentioned earlier, the new high school the boy is going to is rich in academic and social activities. This may become part of the plan in helping him adjust to a new world. Does the adolescent have a peer group that is helpful and constructive, or as is often the case with teens with chronic drug dependence, is her peer group a destructive factor in her life?

What kinds of inherent strengths, resilience, and abilities does the adolescent possess that can be incorporated into the treatment? Some teens journal as a way of dealing in solitude with their issues. Is the adolescent able to be introspective, and can this strength be utilized successfully in the clinical work? The client mentioned above, although only fourteen, is very able to verbalize his feelings of inferiority and actually wants to be in therapy. This is a real strength. It is the clinician's job to be able to ascertain client strengths and types of resources available and necessary to develop a successful intervention plan.

12. *Based upon all of the factors above, what is your intervention plan, and what do you think the outcome might be?* Once a thoughtful and thorough assessment has been done, taking into consideration all of the questions above, the clinician can begin to develop a comprehensive intervention plan. This plan will be based upon a wide range of theories and other key factors crucial to understanding the adolescent in context. Based upon this assessment, the practitioner will be able to get a diagnostic sense of how optimistic the prognosis may be. I am not suggesting that the clinician presume to know that outcome or potential progress of the case. However, given a comprehensive biopsychosocial assessment, the practitioner should be able to formulate some tentative assumptions that may guide the initial intervention planning. Assessment is an ongoing process. Many of the questions in this formulation may be impossible to answer quickly, but the informed clinician will be on the lookout for information and factors crucial to a successful working relationship with the adolescent and his family.

This formulation may appear to be useful only in long-term work with teenagers. However, all of the questions above can be adapted to brief treatment, crisis intervention, group work, family therapy, nontraditional recreational approaches, and many other types of adolescent work. The formulation presented in this chapter helps to set the stage for the informed use of differential therapeutic approaches in the effective treatment of adolescents.

BASIS OF PRACTICE

Throughout this text, the practice formulation for biopsychosocial assessment and intervention planning will be utilized as a multidimensional assessment tool. The practitioner working with the twelve questions of the practice formulation is incorporating intuitive knowledge, practice wisdom, and theoretical knowledge into her assessment of the adolescent client. The practice formulation approaches the level of validated knowledge in its use of multidimensional assessment. Thomas O'Hare, in his recent book *Evidence-Based Practices for Social Workers* (2005), emphasizes the strong need for multidimensional assessment in working with all client populations. Specific theories and frameworks with which to assess clients must be used differentially in order to capture the unique factors necessary to develop a functional approach to treatment with a specific client (Franklin & Jordan, 2003). The practice formulation does just that through specific questions aimed at exploring a variety of areas of functioning and resources, including the adolescent's inner emotional life, capacity for insight, family systems information, life stage/phase information, environmental circumstances, resource capabilities from within (strengths/resilience) and without, and issues of diversity (Gambrill & Mason, 1994).

SUMMARY

In this chapter the reader has been introduced to a comprehensive assessment formulation that will enable him or her to thoroughly evaluate multiple developmental, systemic, environmental, and diversity frameworks in order to develop an appropriate intervention plan in working with an adolescent. An expanded and diversified variation of John Meeks's "diagnostic evaluation" from his classic book *The Fragile Alliance,* the practice formulation for biopsychosocial assessment and intervention planning delineated in this chapter goes far beyond Meeks's criteria to encompass a wider range of theoretical, systemic, and environmental factors in the process. This framework will serve as the basis for many of the discussions that will take place in the following chapters. Comprehensive case examples will be utilized in order to demonstrate the application of this intricate yet user-friendly formulation.

RECOMMENDED RESOURCES
Readings

M. Beasley, T. Thompson, and J. Davidson, "Resilience in Response to Life Stress: The Effects of Coping Style and Cognitive Hardiness," *Personality and Individual Differences*, 34 (2003): 77–95. This article emphasizes the importance of the notion of resilience in development.

Diagnostic and Statistical Manual of Mental Disorders, 4th ed., text revision *(DSM-IV-TR)* (Washington, DC: American Psychiatric Association, 2000). This is the international standard manual for diagnosis of all mental disorders.

Eileen Gambrill and Mary Ann Mason, eds., *Debating Children's Lives: Current Controversies on Children and Adolescents* (Newbury Park, CA: Sage, 1994). This excellent text focuses on the ability of children to succeed despite their unfavorable circumstances.

R. Lyons, "Rapprochement on Approachment: Mahler's Theory Reconsidered from the Vantage Point of Recent Research on Early Attachment Relationships," *Psychoanalytic Psychology* 8, no. 1 (1991): 1–23. This research article adds some key validated knowledge and credibility to Margaret S. Mahler's developmental theory.

J. E. Marcia, "Development and Validation of Ego Identity Status," *Journal of Personality and Social Psyhology* 3 (1966): 551–558. This is a classic article on development.

John E. Meeks and William Bernet, *The Fragile Alliance*, 5th ed. (Malabar, FL: Krieger, 2001). This book is considered by many to be *the* text on theory and practice with adolescents.

Psychodynamic Diagnostic Manual (PDM) (Silver Springs, MD: Alliance of Psychoanalytic Organizations, 2006). This work sets a new standard in diagnostic assessment and research information on development.

Film/Television/Media

Ordinary People (1980). This classic film depicts family dysfunction.

Stand by Me (1986). This film captures the experience of early male adolescence.

Welcome to the Dollhouse (1995). This film offers an excellent portrayal of adolescence.

American Beauty (1999). This film captures the complexity of adolescence and the family.

Girl, Interrupted (1999). This film is a realistic portrayal of adolescent personality disorders.

Six Feet Under (HBO, 2001–2005). This series about a family-owned funeral home portrays powerful individual, family, couples, and adolescent issues.

3

Use of Practice Skills: Engagement and Ongoing Work with Adolescents

Part of a successful assessment and intervention plan with an adolescent client involves the clinician's ability to development a strong therapeutic relationship. The practitioner's ability to answer the formulation questions proposed in chapter 2 hinges on the extent to which she has been able to form an empathic connection with the teenager and his family. This chapter addresses the intricate and challenging task of doing just that. Engagement with adolescents can be a very different process from engaging with children, families, or adult clients. The developmental and theoretical information presented earlier speaks to this phenomenon. In addition, as when working with children, the successful clinician must develop trust with the family or caretakers if she is to be successful in helping the adolescent. What are the key factors, techniques, and skills necessary in order to accomplish this task?

THEORETICAL UNDERPINNINGS OF THE DEVELOPMENT OF LISTENING SKILLS

The most important element in the development of a therapeutic relationship in any form of clinical treatment is the use of effective listening skills. Empathic communication is essential whether the practitioner is using CBT (cognitive behavioral therapy), solution-focused approaches, crisis intervention techniques, narrative therapy, family therapy models, or psychodynamic forms of therapy. This is a commonly agreed upon assumption in all clinical work. In fact, much of the clinical research on therapy has demonstrated that it is the therapeutic relationship that is crucial to a successful outcome (Chung & Bemak, 2002; Gurman, 1977; Hubble, Duncan, & Miller, 1999). However, not much of the clinical literature explains from a developmental or theoretical standpoint why it is that we must be empathic with our clients or how it is that empathy helps in the process of developing a therapeutic relationship.

In early development, the way in which an infant is mirrored or empathically responded to helps to shape its sense of self and its ability to emotionally soothe itself and respond to others throughout life. From a neuroscience standpoint, the young infant is developing neural networks of cognition, emotion, and physical experience that, with repetition over time, solidify an ability to manage itself emotionally, correctly read others' emotions and behavior, and become competent in life tasks (Greenspan & Shankar, 2006).

Daniel Stern (2004) has recently suggested that perhaps this intersubjective need to be understood is in fact a primary motivational need throughout life. It is through this kind of empathic validation with significant others throughout life that one develops a sense of meaning and purpose to existence. Many of the problems in life at all developmental stages may in some ways be examples of a breakdown in our ability to make sense of ourselves or our situations. This can be particularly salient for adolescents, whose task it is to discover who they are and to find meaning and a sense of true identity. When a clinician can successfully make a therapeutic connection with an adolescent client in therapy through the use of empathic listening skills, it sets the stage for the development of trust and a willingness on the part of the client to engage in treatment. This is why empathy and understanding are so important in therapy.

Carl Rogers (1957) and his colleague Eugene Gendlin (1969) can perhaps be credited with developing the foundational listening skills and techniques that are used in almost all clinical training programs. Rogers is best known for developing client-centered therapy, a theory of the self, as well as a set of techniques for listening empathically to clients. Rogers (1961, 1965) believed that empathy was curative and that the use of a prescribed set of listening skills and techniques was integral in successful work with clients. Gendlin (1978) expanded these core principles even further to include an emphasis on inner exploration and awareness called focusing. The ability to focus on one's own feelings and ideas especially in relationship to interactions with clients helps the therapeutic process. Terms and techniques such as summarizing, reflection, clarifying, open-ended questioning, and paraphrasing, are all forms of active listening developed by Rogers and his associates. These techniques along with many others form the basis of the practitioner's clinical repertoire. They also serve as a foundation for clinical work with adolescents and their families.

In order to engage successfully with an adolescent client, the clinician must be able to develop a trusting, nonjudgmental relationship through the use of empathic listening skills informed by clinical and developmental theories. This means that the clinician needs to be adept not only at making a good emotional connection with the teenager through listening skills but also at discerning what skills and approaches will be necessary based upon the ongoing differential assessment of the adolescent. This is a complex process that goes on intuitively and perhaps even unconsciously on the part of the practitioner.

THE CLINICAL PRACTICE TEMPLATE

The internalized clinical self is similar to a template. It will be called here the *clinical practice template*. Through her educational and practical experience, the practitioner begins to form a series of mental representations of clinical knowledge. In life we all learn and remember certain thoughts, feelings, and experiences through repetition and reinforcement. Those elements of experience (thought, emotion, activity) that are useful, adaptive, and rewarding become more solidified in our minds. Over time we come to use them almost automatically. Some of our most basic ways of functioning in the world are referred to as implicit processes (Cozolino, 2002). While the clinician working with adolescents does not operate totally out of awareness, much of our practice interventions and activity goes on somewhat automatically. For example, the clinician, even a fairly experienced one, is not consciously aware of why he is saying certain things to a client all of the time. However, after a session, or upon reflection in supervision or consultation, most clinicians do understand why they intuitively interacted the way they did in session. This is the clinical practice template in action. In the beginning of most practitioners' careers, there is a great deal of uncertainty, insecurity, and doubt not only about what to say next but about what is happening in the session, how to understand it theoretically, and where to go next. One might say that the clinical practice template is just beginning to be formed. It is tentative and not solidified through clinical experience and reinforcement. However, an experienced adolescent therapist does or should understand the process much more fully and feel a sense of comfort and competence in proceeding with the clinical work. His mental/emotional/ experiential template is well developed and reinforced through many years of trial and error and success in treatment.

ENGAGEMENT TECHNIQUES AND CONSIDERATIONS

But what specific techniques are necessary in working with adolescents? All adolescents are different, but there are some common principles that seem to hold true when working with teens. First, the clinician must remember that most adolescents are not self-referred. This means that they have not chosen to come for therapy. Whether they are being seen in school by the social worker or school psychologist or in a group home, psychiatric or residential facility, or in detention, or whether they have been brought to counseling by their families, they are more often than not involuntary clients. This means that the clinician will have to work much harder to engage and develop a trusting, nonjudgmental relationship. In order to do that, the practitioner needs to take into consideration the developmental factors that have been mentioned in previous chapters. Adolescents as a group are developing a sense of self and growing physically, cognitively, socially, and morally. They are also emotionally separating from their primary caretakers. They are defining their identity through association with people outside the family. These people are mostly peers but also key adult figures that they can identify with and idealize. A helpful clinician can provide this important function, even if the teen is not self-referred.

Experiencing a safe, trusting, and nonjudgmental relationship with an idealized adult can truly help the adolescent work through many difficult developmental issues. The clinician does not have to agree with or approve of everything the teenager thinks, feels, or does, but he must withhold or suspend judgment in order to help the adolescent explore important areas of life without fearing punishment, criticism, or blame. There may be areas in therapy in which the clinician must become more actively involved, such as suicide or dangerous self-destructive behaviors, but by and large it is not the practitioner's role to be another parent or authority figure in the adolescent's life. It cannot be emphasized enough how important it is for the therapist to be a developmental ally in the adolescent's life journey.

The language that a therapist uses in therapy is different with all clients. The effective clinician learns to vary her style to fit the client's developmental needs, personality, cultural affiliation, and so on. The clinician must in many ways speak to the adolescent on his level. She must also be genuine in her language and style in interacting with the teenager. This is a tricky proposition. However, with a little trial and error, the therapist learns to develop a style of communication that is conducive to therapeutic trust. Most teenagers do not use the same words that sophisticated adults do. Over time the therapist working with teenagers learns their language and interacts reciprocally using her own version of the teen's language. Some of the teen's vocabulary may feel natural or appropriate for the therapist to use in interacting with the adolescent. Other words or phrases may sound extremely awkward or even insincere coming out of the therapist's mouth. Developing a common language for ongoing interaction is one of the first tasks of the therapist working with adolescents. Over time this becomes part of the template with this teen.

Mark A. Hubble, Barry L. Duncan, and Scott D. Miller's book *The Heart and Soul of Change: What Works in Psychotherapy* (1999) is an excellent empirical examination of the therapeutic need for flexibility and individuality in developing the relationship and deciding upon which type of interventions will be most beneficial and effective with different clients.

Another crucial part of the development of a successful and trusting relationship with an adolescent is to know what to talk about. Many involuntary teens do not respond very well to the direct approach of asking them about the problem. This approach often leads to silence. This silence might seem like resistance, but it could also mean that the adolescent does not feel that the problem as defined by others is his problem. It is not something he truly agrees with or is interested in or willing to talk about in therapy; at least initially. There are a variety of topics that the therapist working with teenagers can use in developing a trusting and therapeutic relationship. Of course the presenting concern must be addressed in the first session, but the way it is approached is crucial to developing trust. Whether the therapist first meets alone with the teenager or in a joint session with the primary caretakers, some discussion of the presenting concern must occur. If it is determined that the adolescent will be seen in individual therapy, the presenting concern can be discussed further in private with the teenager. It is usually important to try to help the adolescent talk a little bit about his perspective on the problem. It may be very different from the parent's or family's viewpoint, but it is important to get the teenager's view of the situation. Doing so is part of the process of building trust as well as formulating a diagnostic impression of the adolescent and his family. If a therapist is going to help an adolescent, she must be able to empathically relate to the teenager's worldview. Only through this vicarious identification with the teenager can a working therapeutic relationship develop. This is also the essence of a nonjudgmental approach to treatment.

If the adolescent seems interested in discussing the presenting concern at length, the practitioner should pursue this line of discussion. There are some adolescents, even involuntary clients, who are more than willing to engage in an insight-oriented, problem-solving discussion from the onset of therapy. This process resembles therapy with many adults. However, most teenagers, especially those brought forcefully to therapy, tend to avoid any overt discussion of the presenting concern. How then does a therapist engage with them?

Manifest and Latent Content

In all forms of clinical work there is what is known as the manifest, or surface, and latent, or underlying, content of therapy. Manifest content is that verbal material that is direct, conscious, and clear-cut. The teenager doesn't like a teacher, says he/she is unfair, boring, and so on. This is a clear-cut, conscious, or surface-oriented problem. The latent content related to that concern is the deeper emotional meaning or symbolism that may be a contributing factor to the manifest problem or even the problem's source. The client is usually not aware of this meaning initially. Over time the additional meaning may become evident through further discussion and perhaps resolution. For instance, one of the latent issues that may fuel this adolescent's problem with the teacher is the fact that he/she represents parentified authority, an issue that is especially troublesome given this teen's development history with a controlling parent. It becomes the therapist's job to be able to listen not only to the manifest content but also to the latent emotional issues that may exacerbate it. This holds true whether the practitioner is practicing a more conscious direct form of treatment such as CBT or longer term psychodynamic therapy. The clinician's adeptness at recognizing underlying emotional concerns gives him the ability to intervene with much greater awareness and confidence at any level of discussion with any type of problem (Gurman, 1977).

Given the fact that adolescents may discuss concerns on both the manifest and the latent level, and that they are just beginning to develop the ability to think and communicate on more sophisticated adult levels, approaches to engagement can be varied. There are a multitude of issues in the adolescent's life that are a source of diagnostic and developmental significance in therapy. Rather than force a discussion exclusively around the presenting concern, the practitioner can begin to build a therapeutic relationship through nonjudgmental discussion of many other important areas of the teen's life. Each of these may hold greater significance for the adolescent than the presenting concern, while at the same time shedding important diagnostic light on the teenager's life. Most, if not all, adolescents clinicians see are in school. An adolescent's interest and involvement in school can be an important diagnostic indicator of her life in general. In addition, it is a source of discussion that can be relatively benign in therapy. The practitioner can ask about teachers, classes, school activities, as well as classmates and friends. Each of these areas will help to give insight not only into how the teenager views the world but into how he functions academically, socially, and behaviorally in this setting. These are important manifest and latent content areas that can be approached in discussion even in the first session.

DISCUSSION OF FAMILY, PEERS, SCHOOL, AND OTHER INTERESTS

Family is another important yet safe discussion topic with adolescents. Adolescents are often very willing to give their opinions about their family; parents and siblings to an adult clinician who they feel might understand and not criticize them. These types of discussions help the practitioner get a true sense of the teenager's view of family while at the same time shedding important light on other diagnostic factors mentioned earlier. Again, the notion of manifest and latent content is instructive here. How the teenager views his role in the family can be useful material for work with that adolescent. The adolescent's relationship with siblings and other extended family can also be a source of important diagnostic information. Not only is this type of discussion helpful in gathering information and expanding the clinician's diagnostic formulation in the first session, but it can set the stage for areas of discussion later in the therapeutic relationship. Family issues, especially with parents, can often be at the core of a teen's difficulties.

Issues of culture, diversity, and gender are essential to the understanding of the adolescent client. However, the clinician needs to move slowly and build trust before discussing these potentially crucial life-stage issues (Chung & Bemak, 2002; Morrow, 2004; Zayas, 2001).

The adolescent's relationship with peers is a pivotal area of discussion in the therapeutic relationship. The adolescent peer support group is a phenomenon that has remained constant for many decades. Adolescents often define themselves by virtue of what peer group or clique they are in or identified with. The developmental significance of this social dynamic is an important element in the treatment situation.

As adolescents move through a process of solidifying an identity, they utilize others outside the family to help them incorporate aspects of an identity. The seeds of that process have been sown early in life through the internalization of emotional, cognitive, and physical aspects of the primary caretakers. However, the onset of adolescence heralds an emotional move away from the infantile dependency of childhood and a conscious rejection of parental influences. The teenager looks toward her peers for some sense of belonging as well as character traits that she can identify with and incorporate into a sense of identity. The choice of peer group or clique has tremendous emotional and symbolic significance to the adolescent in her journey toward identity formation. Although the names and style of dress may have changed over the years, the symbolism and meaning of most cliques have not. There are still some versions of preps, jocks, nerds, gang bangers, goths, and so on in most school settings today. In addition, racial, ethnic, and gender variables must be seriously taken into consideration in the formation of identity (Floyd et al., 1999; Phinney, 1991; Zayas, 2001). It should be the task of any practitioner attempting to engage in a therapeutic relationship with a teenager to explore the nature, type, and extent of her peer group. Its significance has both manifest and latent aspects, as well as important emotional symbolism for the adolescent. Many teens are more than willing to discuss this part of their lives with a therapist whom they trust.

Clinicians also should explore the nature of the teenager's peer relationships. This means how the adolescent gets along with others, how dependent or independent he is in relationships, and whether he feels that he can really be himself with others. Some teenagers have difficulty making many friends or even any friends at all. This is a very sensitive area in life and one that needs to be addressed in therapy. A sense of social isolation can be an indication of earlier attachment issues or more severe family dynamics. However, discussion of isolation issues can be an ongoing way to help engage and work through overall attachment issues over time.

If the adolescent happens to be in a romantic relationship, that too can be a source of discussion that can provide useful diagnostic information. What is the nature of the relationship? How can the teen's behavior be characterized in terms of the dependency/independence continuum? Is the relationship sexual? What does that mean to the teenager? Does the relationship help to make him happy or enhance his search for identity? All of these questions and others are important sources of information for the clinician. Remember that from a psychodynamic viewpoint, the move toward a true love relationship with a peer is the first emotional separation from the primary caretakers or family. It is an important landmark in the teenager's move toward emotional autonomy and identity formation.

Hobbies, sports, and other outside interests are another key area of safe discussion that the practitioner can utilize in developing a secure therapeutic relationship with an adolescent. Most, if not all, teenagers are interested in some type of hobby or personal activity. These may be social in nature, such as text messaging, instant messaging, or rave, or more solitary activities such as journaling or even listening to music. The discussion of these areas of an adolescent's life can yield important information about the inner life of that teen. It is the symbolism and latent meaning of the activity or interest that are useful for the clinician in her ongoing diagnostic assessment and intervention planning with a teenager. In fact, many of these activities can serve a useful purpose in helping the teenager work through his difficulties. Journaling is a wonderful example of this process. A more withdrawn, depressed, or socially isolated adolescent can make good use of his journaling interest by sharing it with his therapist as part of the clinical work.

The list of topics to explore with any teenager cannot be exhaustive. The point to remember is that there are a multitude of topics that can be discussed with teenagers in the engagement stage that will be viewed by the teenager as safe topics while at the same time yielding important diagnostic information to the educated clinician. It is the clinician's job to develop a safe, trusting, empathic, and nonjudgmental atmosphere in order to get to know the adolescent and be able to help him get back on the developmental track. Addressing the topics mentioned above not only enables the practitioner to develop a good diagnostic sense of the teenager but also helps to form a mutual language and basis of discussion. The teenager feels he is understood and recognizes that the therapist is genuinely interested, empathic, and nonjudgmental. This sets the stage for the trust that is needed to work on the presenting concern.

CASE EXAMPLE

The following case example helps to illustrate the material above. Peter is a fourteen-year-old referred by his school social worker for therapy because he was caught cheating on one of his final eighth-grade English papers. Peter comes from a recently divorced middle-class family. Both of his parents are remarried. Peter lives with his mother and stepfather and spends weekends with his biological father. Peter is the youngest of a sibship of two. His older brother, Paul, is a freshman away at college. Peter's biological father has two young children with his new wife. Peter gets along very well with his two stepbrothers and enjoys the fact that they both look up to him. Peter does not get along with his new stepfather. He describes him as extremely critical and negative in his relationship with him. Peter gets along well with his mother, who always brings him to therapy. Peter is willing to come to therapy and was initially very open in his discussion about his feelings, but since the first session he has found it difficult to talk about much of anything.

Although the presenting concern according to Peter's mother and school social worker was his cheating at school, Peter had an entirely different view of his life difficulties. I first met with Peter and his mother to explore the presenting concern. Peter's mother, Mary, expressed her deep concerns about Peter's academic work and the fact that he blatantly cheated on a major assignment. She also was concerned about Peter's habit of taking his older brother's clothes and wearing them without his permission. It seemed as if Mary was worried about Peter's lack of honesty and ability to follow through appropriately with his responsibilities. When I asked Peter to comment on the concerns of his mother, he refused to talk in front of her and stated that he wanted to see me alone. I agreed to do so.

Mary left the therapy room, and Peter immediately began to sob uncontrollably. He told me without any prompting that he takes his brother's clothes because he feels good about himself only when he is wearing something of his brother's. With very little encouragement, Peter went on to discuss the fact that he has been miserable ever since the divorce. Ever since his mother and stepfather moved the family to another town, Peter has not been able to be popular or make any friends who are popular. He was very popular at his old school, before the move, but he now is in the least popular group of kids. In fact, Peter sees himself as "the lowest of the low." Peter feels that his brother Paul is someone very special, and he idealizes him. Only by wearing his clothes can Peter feel that he is popular. When I mentioned that the way he feels drawn to taking and wearing his brother's clothes seems almost like an addiction, Peter said, "Yeah, that's it, it really is like an addiction!" Peter continued to be very open to discussing this issue and felt that his situation was completely hopeless. He is going into high school and knows that things will not get any better. He also knows that it's too late to move back home because too much time has gone by and he would be an outsider there as well. Peter expressed a true sense of hopelessness regarding his situation.

I next began to explore some possible ways in which Peter might begin to develop a greater sense of popularity, but he did not seem optimistic about any of them. He definitely wants to feel better about himself and his social situation but does not know how to do it or feel that anything will get much better soon or ever. I explored whether Peter was depressed or even suicidal. He clearly was sad and perhaps was experiencing some depression, but he did not feel suicidal or have any thoughts or plans along those lines.

I told Peter that if he wanted to continue therapy, we would work on these things together, and that I felt confident that things could get better. Peter agreed to continue but did not want me to tell his mother about his compulsion to wear his brother's clothes or how badly he felt about being unpopular. I assured him that our relationship was confidential and that together we would decide what to share with his mother about his concerns and progress in therapy. Peter seemed a bit more optimistic when he left.

After that very first session, however, Peter was much more hesitant or unable to discuss the issues he first raised. I did not believe that he was consciously avoiding the discussion; it seemed as if he did not know where to go next. Any attempts that I made to overtly discuss Peter's insecurity were not fruitful. I decided that I would need to find another means to engage Peter in the therapeutic process. Clearly he still wanted to be there, but it seemed as if he did not have the ability or means to discuss his presenting concerns in any greater depth.

I had already explored Peter's families. His peer group was virtually nonexistent and a dead-end topic of discussion. I decided to talk with him more about his other interests. He didn't really like music, he wasn't into video or computer games, and he certainly didn't have anyone to email or chat with online. What did this adolescent enjoy? I noticed that he had some scrapes on his arms. It crossed my mind that he might have self-injured, so I thought that I would casually explore where they came from. Peter told me that he got them from falling off his bike. He went on to talk about how he loved to take risks and would love to be a sky diver, stuntman, or even an actor. As we talked further, Peter mentioned that in his old school he used to be in plays. He said that he really enjoyed the attention and liked to get into being other characters. Peter demonstrated an enthusiasm for this area that I had not seen before in him. He enjoyed acting because it felt real to him and made him feel good. He also loved movies and saw some of them ten times or more if he really liked them. We went on to discuss some of his favorite films and what he enjoyed about them. Peter said he liked comedies and action films the best, but he wasn't sure which he liked better. I mentioned in passing that perhaps high school plays or drama club might be something he could pursue this year at school. Peter seemed interested but cautious about committing to that idea at the present time.

CASE DISCUSSION

This initial attempt at engagement illustrates the complex and multifaceted process of working with adolescents quite well. On the surface it appears as if Peter is capable of in-depth insight-oriented therapy to explore his thoughts and feelings as well as problem-solve about the possible solutions to the problem. His initial overwhelming anxiety, isolation, and possible depression compelled him to express some surface emotions. However, it is clear that at the present time Peter is not able or willing to go much further with that type of discussion. Maybe a better way to say it is that discussion of that nature has become a dead-end topic because of Peter's anxiety, fear, hopelessness, or inability to endure the topic for any length of time. It appears as if he's stuck.

Using the concepts and techniques mentioned above, the clinician was able to develop a language and trust level with which to begin to help Peter feel a greater sense of confidence in himself and his abilities. As time unfolds, perhaps after a month or two, he will feel confident enough to begin to test out some of his abilities in order to improve his social status. There may be other areas of discussion that originate in therapy that can help shed light on Peter's issues and abilities. The key is for Peter to feel they are his and that he can do something with them. Once he is able to do that, he will be able to engage in a more concrete discussion about how to become more popular or, more importantly, how to feel good about himself in general.

Since this is a case in progress, the clinician can never be sure what the outcome will be or to what extent he may need to work with other family members or even school personnel. In addition, although it appears that Peter's compulsion to take and wear his brother's clothes is a function of his own horrible self concept and insecurity, there may be other, more specific factors that come to light over time. It is interesting to observe that the cheating, which was the presenting concern, has not really been addressed—yet. On the surface it appears to be a symptom of his sense of futility and perhaps lack of motivation in general. The behavior certainly got him noticed and got him into therapy. I do not believe it is the primary issue but rather a manifest symptom of something much more latent and troubling in his life.

BASIS OF PRACTICE

The knowledge base that demonstrates the importance and necessity of a strong, empathic therapeutic relationship incorporates all four levels mentioned earlier: intuition, practice wisdom, theoretical knowledge, and validated knowledge. Carl Rogers was probably one of the first practitioners and theorists to empirically demonstrate the validity and clinical significance of the use of empathy in his studies at the University of Chicago in the mid-twentieth century. His work was monumental in the demonstration that empathy could be curative. His work and therapeutic principles related to empathy and listening skills are used throughout the world to help train human service professionals from all disciplines (Rogers, 1957, 1961, 1965).

From a theoretical standpoint, attachment and object relations theories have postulated the crucial importance of attunement as a necessary condition of normal human development. Recent neuroscience studies have helped to validate those theories (Bowlby, 1969; Cozolino, 2002; Siegel, 1999; Greenspan & Shankar, 2006). The consensus of research in the clinical and theoretical literature is that the therapeutic relationship is the key factor to successful therapeutic work (Prochaska & Norcross, 2003). The ideas and models proposed in this chapter are strong versions of intuitive, practice wisdom, theoretical, and validated knowledge. The information gathered from examining these elements is both descriptive and prescriptive in its focus. We know it to be true and we know how we must implement it in order to engage with adolescent clients (Powers, Meenaghan, & Toomey, 1985).

SUMMARY

This chapter has discussed the nature of the therapeutic engagement process in work with an adolescent client. Although working with all types of clients demands strong listening skills, engaging with adolescents requires techniques based upon key developmental principles. Understanding the important areas of a teenager's life enables the astute clinician to develop a language and clinical style that are conducive not only to trust but also to ongoing diagnostic assessment and treatment modification. The case example used in this chapter demonstrated that process in action. Once engagement and meaningful assessment have occurred, it becomes the task of the clinician to determine what theoretical approaches are most useful and how to incorporate them into working with an adolescent. Research information clearly demonstrates the intuitive and validated sources of knowledge that dictate the development of a strong therapeutic relationship when working with adolescents.

RECOMMENDED RESOURCES
Readings

Jeffrey Applegate, "Transitional Object Reconsidered: Some Sociocultural Variations and Their Implications," *Child and Adolescent Social Work* 6, no. 1 (1989): 38–51. New York: Human Services Press.

E. T. Gendlin, *Focusing* (New York: Everest House, 1978).

Stanley I. Greenspan & Stuart G. Shankar, "A Developmental Framework for Depth Psychology and a Definition of Healthy Emotional Functioning," in *Psychodynamic Diagnostic Manual (PDM)*, pp. 431–482 (Silver Springs, MD: Alliance of Psychoanalytic Organizations, 2006).

A. S. Gurman, "The Patient's Perception of the Therapeutic Relationship," in Gurman & A. M. Razin, eds., *Effective Psychotherapy: A Handbook of Research* (New York: Oxford University Press, 1977).

Donald F. Krill, *Practice Wisdom: A Guide for the Helping Professionals* (Newbury Park, CA: Sage, 1990).

Carl R. Rogers, *Client-Centered Therapy.* (Boston: Houghton-Mifflin Company, 1965).

Lawrence Shulman, *The Skills of Helping Individuals, Families, Groups, and Communities* (Pacific Grove, CA: Thomson-Brooks/Cole, 2006).

Film/Television/Media

Ordinary People (1980) and *Good Will Hunting* (1997). Both of these films are excellent portrayals of therapeutic work with adolescents.

Internet

http://www.focusing.org/ This site provides comprehensive information on E. T. Gendlin's work.

4

Application of Theoretical Underpinnings: A Differential Approach to Practice with Adolescents

The previous three chapters have introduced the practitioner to the fundamental theories necessary in order to have a comprehensive understanding of the adolescent client and her family, as well as to the formulation assessment and engagement principles that can help him establish a therapeutic relationship with her. This chapter will discuss the major theories that are utilized in working with most clients. It will also enable the clinician to determine, based upon the nature of the case, which approach is most likely to be successful. This is a daunting task for any clinician, but a necessary one if he is to help the teenager.

There is no universal approach that fits all clinical situations. Some are more appropriate than others to a particular case. Very few highly experienced practitioners use a particular theoretical approach exclusively. Most clinicians practice what might be called *informed eclecticism*. As the clinician develops his theoretical and applied template for practice, he incorporates a variety of theoretical approaches and techniques (Beutler, 1999; Franklin & Jordan, 2003; Roth & Fonagy, 1996). The choice of clinical style depends upon what has worked. This is a pragmatic choice, based upon years of trial and error. There are many theories and approaches to clinical practice (Hubble, Duncan, & Miller, 1999). The following discussion is a basic review of the five basic approaches along with clinical case examples to illustrate them.

COGNITIVE BEHAVIORAL THERAPY (CBT)

Cognitive behavioral theory/therapy (CBT) is a theoretical approach to practice that includes cognitive and behavior theory in a relatively short-term, structured format. Each of these theories can stand on its own merits and has been used by clinicians in working with a variety of clients including adolescents for many years. They have recently been combined into what might be described as a problem-solving or task-centered approach. CBT has become the buzzword for this type of clinical work. Cognitive theory is an approach to practice that emphasizes thinking as the primary factor in a client's behavior and emotions. Some of the early contributors to this theory included Alfred Adler, one of Sigmund Freud's disciples; Albert Ellis, who developed rational emotive therapy in the 1950s and 1960s; and Aron Beck.

Cognitive theory and therapy holds that people are influenced in their actions by their inherent beliefs about the world and themselves. Some of these beliefs may be conscious, but many are not. Human problems come from operating on faulty or irrational beliefs. The role of CBT is to recognize and challenge those irrational beliefs, thereby changing negative or destructive behavior.

At the core of cognitive theory is the notion that all thought, including values and assumptions about the world, is layered in the mind in what are referred to as *schemas*. Schemas are developed throughout life but most especially in childhood and adolescence. The hierarchy of schemas runs from the most fundamental values and beliefs about life (unconscious in nature) to simple, everyday notions about all human actions, for example, it is wrong to run a stop sign, or it is bad to lie. Assumptions about life and the subsequent behaviors that result from them direct all of our actions. Problems result when we have irrational beliefs, ideas, and values that contribute to troublesome behaviors in life. It is the goal of the clinician in cognitive therapy to help the client identify the thoughts and beliefs that are getting in the way of healthy living and direct new thinking that will lead to a change in behavior and a happier life (Adler, 1963; Beck, 1976; Dobson, 2000; Ellis, 1973; Kendall, 2000).

Behavior theory posits that all human actions are the result of what we have learned or been conditioned to do. Some of its major theorists are Ivan Pavlov, B. F. Skinner, and Albert Bandura. When our actions are reinforced by either reward or punishment in a repetitive and consistent manner, those behaviors become the basis of our functioning in life. Bandura's social learning theory is a good example of these ideas. According to Bandura and other behaviorists, a child is conditioned to behave in certain ways through rewards, punishments, and observation of significant others in the world. Dysfunction, according to behavior theory, comes from learned behaviors. Domestic violence can be explained from a social learning perspective as the development and ongoing use of dysfunctional learned behaviors in intimate relationships with others. The child learns and is conditioned to use violent behavior throughout life. When he becomes involved in an intimate relationship with a partner, violence is one of the learned and conditioned behaviors that is used to handle conflict or anxiety (Bandura, 1977; Pavlov, 1927; Skinner, 1953). The focus of treatment from a behavioral therapy standpoint is to identify the dysfunctional behaviors and help the client to learn new, more adaptive and healthy approaches to the same situation. There are a variety of techniques that behavior therapists use in working with their clients. The main thrust, however, is to eliminate negative or destructive behaviors by substituting new behaviors that are reinforced inside and outside the therapy. This can be accomplished, for example, through role plays in the counseling sessions and homework between sessions.

CBT is a therapeutic approach that combines the elements of both cognitive and behavior theory. Recognizing that thoughts and behaviors are intimately connected, CBT addresses both in a highly structured therapeutic model. There are many varieties of CBT. Albert Ellis's rational emotive behavior therapy (REBT) is one of the most recognized CBT approaches. Ellis utilizes the A B C D E approach to CBT. *A* stands for activating events or adversities, in other words, the presenting problems. *B* is for irrational beliefs, the distorted thoughts and ideas that have contributed to *A* and help to sustain them. *C* represents the consequences of both *A* and *B*. *D* involves the process of exploring and disputing the faulty or self-destructive beliefs. *E* stands for the effective new emotions, behaviors, and philosophies that help alter *C*. REBT and CBT are highly structured approaches that carefully identify, track, and modify the thoughts and behaviors of the client. The focus is on the here and now. There is very little exploration of underlying feelings or history except that which relates directly to the presenting problem. CBT has been a highly effective therapeutic approach for many types of problems and is strongly encouraged by managed care companies because of its relatively short duration and quick problem resolution (Ellis, 1973).

CASE EXAMPLE

How would a clinician utilize CBT in working with an adolescent client? The following is a good case example. Kitty is a fifteen-year-old girl who was brought to therapy because of her mother's concerns about her depression. Kitty comes from an intact nuclear family (mother, father, and brother). They live in a middle-class suburban community. From the onset of therapy Kitty has been cooperative in sessions. Although she was not self-referred, Kitty is agreeable to therapy. She was in therapy once before but had a bad experience. According to Kitty, her therapist was overly paternalistic, condescending, and violated her confidentiality by telling her parents what she talked about in sessions. I assured Kitty that I would do my best to respect and honor her privacy within the bounds of ethical requirements. Everything she discussed in therapy with the exception of self-destructive behaviors would remain confidential. I realized that Kitty's parents would want to know the general progress of therapy, but Kitty and I would discuss what specific information I would share with her parents. Kitty agreed that she was somewhat depressed but was not exactly sure why or what to do about it. She was a somewhat withdrawn, shy girl, irrespective of any depression she might be experiencing. Kitty could be described as an introvert. She had friends and was somewhat social, but spent much of her time alone reading science fiction/fantasy novels and working on computer graphic art. Shortly after she began to see me, Kitty decided that she wanted to work on losing weight. She believed that much of her sadness was related to her size, and that losing weight might help remedy the situation. From my standpoint Kitty was somewhat overweight but resembled her mother in stature. I believed that Kitty's weight was related to her eating habits and possible depression but also part of her inherited constitution. I did, however, agree to help Kitty work on this self-identified weight problem.

In addition to spending all therapy sessions discussing Kitty's week, we also began to focus directly on her weight loss program. We began to explore together Kitty's beliefs and ideas about weight, exercise, and the extent to which she wanted to incorporate a weight loss philosophy into her value system. These ideas were not presented or discussed in these words but in a language that had developed between the two of us over a period of time and that Kitty was comfortable with. Another very important part of this plan was to help Kitty decide how she would like to approach losing weight. Kitty decided that she would like to use running as her exercise and weight loss program. Every week Kitty and I would review her weekly running schedule as well as her weight loss. Kitty was anxious about using the scale, believing that the incremental weight loss she might experience week to week would be a deterrent to her overall goal. Instead, Kitty measured her weight loss by how her clothes fit. This was a useful and nonthreatening way for her to stay committed to the goal. In addition to this structured weight loss regimen, Kitty and I continued to discuss other key emotional and relationship factors in her therapy. The CBT-like structure served as part of the foundation of Kitty's overall approach to her life problems.

This case example helps to illustrate the use of a form of CBT with a client who is struggling not only with her weight but also with her self-esteem and perhaps a mild form of depression. Utilizing the modified CBT approach, Kitty is able to work on a specific identified problem area while still engaging in other therapeutic discussion that can also be useful. A more rigid CBT approach with Kitty might have been alienating and perhaps seemed too stilted. Given her earlier bad therapeutic encounter with another therapist, it seemed important to establish a strong, trusting, nonjudgmental therapeutic relationship in order to form the basis for effective work. My flexibility in utilizing a modified form of CBT allowed Kitty to engage in it without feeling uncomfortable. In fact she truly owned it.

FAMILY SYSTEMS THEORY

Human beings are social animals and need other people in order to survive emotionally. All people have grown up in some sort of family structure. Living in a family helps to shape one's values, ideas, and behavior throughout

life. Family systems theory as well as family therapy models are other important clinical avenues for working with adolescents. Some teenagers can benefit from family therapy much more than individual work. In addition, much
of the work done with adolescents in general is often a combination of individual and family work. The unique and delicate combination of these two
approaches is crucial to successful work with adolescents of all ages.

Family therapy models and approaches developed in the late 1950s and
early 1960s utilizing basic systems theory. The unique contribution of family
therapy was the emphasis on examining the entire family system and its
impact on the individual. In general, family systems approaches focus on the
here and now. The concepts and techniques of family therapy aim toward an
understanding of the entire system: its functions, structure, content, and
process, and how to successfully intervene in order to alleviate identified
problems within the family. Problems from a family systems standpoint are a
function and symptom of systemic issues, not individual dynamics. This
approach is an important and useful lens through which to understand the
adolescent.

In order to understand family therapy it is useful to discuss some of the
major concepts of the approach. A *system* is a group of interrelated people
who function together in common purpose. There are many types of systems in life, including the classroom, the workplace, the peer group, and
especially the family. All systems have *boundaries*. Boundaries are the artificial and subjective barriers that dictate structure and function within the system, in this case the family. Boundaries range from completely open or
chaotic to completely closed or enmeshed. Both extremes are usually considered to be dysfunctional. All families should be understood *contextually*.
In other words, each family has its own unique culture that has developed
over time. What is functional for one family may be dysfunctional for
another. The concept of boundaries can help the clinician understand communication, discipline, roles, rules, and values, as well as how interactive the
family is within the community. An example of an extremely open or chaotic
family might be one in which adolescents have no curfew. They can come
home whenever they want, even if they have school the next day. Parents in
this example may believe that teenagers should define their own structure.
Of course this type of chaos is probably not good for the adolescent struggling to find her own limits and identity. Ultimately either the police or state
child welfare system would probably intervene with this family to help create greater structure and security for the teen. An extremely closed family
system could be one in which the adolescent is home schooled and not
allowed to interact in any way with the outside world, even to watch television. The parents' intention might be to insulate and protect their child from
what they perceive as a dangerous society, but such restriction does not
allow the teenager to negotiate the necessary skills to interact and succeed
in life outside the family. Both of these examples demonstrate the dangers of
extremity in the ongoing development of a family system's boundaries.

Within all family systems there are also *subsystems*. Subsystems are smaller systems within the family that carry out important functions for the entire family system. Subsystems have implicit rules and roles that dictate their function. In an intact nuclear family, for example, the parents are actually two subsystems. The first is the parental subsystem, which manages the parenting function for the children within the family. The other subsystem is the marital subsystem. The parents are also a subsystem that provides emotional, intellectual, and sexual gratification to its members through their own intimacy. The natural boundary of this subsystem seems self-explanatory. Some topics and activities should be contained within the parental subsystem and not shared with children. Sexual activity between parents is a good and probably universal example of a parental subsystem taboo or boundary. Four- or five-year-old children should not be allowed to hear their parents discussing their sexual relationship, let alone witness them having sex. This is an example of a clear breach in family boundaries.

Communication is also a key concept in family therapy. The way a family and its subsystems communicate is a diagnostic indicator for how the family as a whole functions. Once again, there are explicit and implicit rules regarding not only what can be discussed in a family but also the way it can be discussed. Sex is a good example of this. An extremely open family system may have no clear limits about how graphically sex is discussed. This could be a serious problem for young children as well as adolescents. An extremely closed family system may have the implicit rule that sex is never discussed, not even by the parental subsystem in the privacy of the bedroom. This too can cause problems. How do children learn about sex, values, behavior, and so on if they are not addressed in some way within the family? The communicative style of each family system can shed important light on the diagnostic picture of the adolescent client within it.

The manner in which the family members interact with each other is also an important feature of family therapy. Individual family members may engage in *coalitions* with other family members in an attempt to deal with family stress and conflict. These coalitions can cause problems when they jeopardize family functioning or interfere with the healthy and optimal functioning within family subsystems. A mother and son who form a coalition against an alcoholic father are an example of this. If a mother talks only with her son about the father's drinking, it circumvents the possibility for future work within the marital subsystem regarding this problem. It also develops an unnatural alliance which could interfere in the parental subsystem. Mom may be much more likely to favor the son in arguments with the father about discipline, rules, and privileges. Careful assessment of family dynamics and structure is a very important element of the diagnostic and ongoing work with the teenager.

Circular causality is another key concept in family therapy. A change in one part of a system can affect the entire family. Nowhere is there a better example of this than when a child becomes an adolescent. Rules, roles, communication, subsystems, and so on are all affected by this one shift in the family.

Family systems theory also examines the family's functioning in terms of the *family life cycle*. For those families that decide to have and raise children, the family life cycle is a helpful paradigm in understanding family functioning within specific stages or times periods of family life. From the beginnings of family formation through coupling, to the initial stages of raising infants, and the final adjustment to an empty nest, the family is pushed through a number of unique challenges and life tasks. Adolescence is considered one of the major family life stages. Particularly in adolescence, the family structure and function change in order to adapt to the dramatic shift in the adolescent's personality and behavior. The once compliant and cooperative little boy now becomes the defiant and oppositional teenager. Communication may become very different. Rules and roles that were not of much concern in childhood now become extremely important to family survival. Even the way the adolescent relates to his parents may dramatically shift, necessitating an adjustment in the parental and marital subsystem. In fact, many families begin to experience problems in the marital/couple subsystem as a result of a child's entering adolescence and the subsequent shift in family dynamics.

Of course there are many different types of families, from many diverse backgrounds and situations. The next chapter is devoted to this topic. Divorce, single parenting, blended families, stepfamilies, racial, cultural, and spiritual factors as well as numerous other situations affect the development and functioning of all families.

There are many different types of family therapy approaches. Bowenian family therapy, structural and strategic models, contextual family therapy, narrative/solution-focused approaches, and even object relations models are excellent vehicles for successful work with adolescents and their families. Each of these approaches has its own unique set of concepts and techniques, but all of them operate on the same fundamental systemic principles discussed above (McGoldrick, Giordano, & Garcia-Preto, 2006; Nichols & Schwartz, 2006).

CASE EXAMPLE

A case example will help to demonstrate the application of family therapy principles in working with adolescents. Bill and Brian are fourteen-year-old identical twins who were referred to therapy as a result of being caught breaking into their high school computer system. These two very intelligent and perhaps gifted boys are what one might consider computer geeks. They saw a challenge in attempting to break into the high school computer system and did not really think or feel that their actions were serious in nature.

The high school suspended the boys from school and future use of any type of computers on school grounds for the remainder of the year. The twins were also restricted from computer use at their mother's home.

Bill and Brian come from a divorced family. Their parents have been divorced for several years. The boys live with their mother but spend their weekends with their biological father. Mom and Dad both agree that the boys could benefit from therapy, but they are not very consistent in their parenting approaches to the twins. Dad appears to be a bit looser in his expectations of the boys. As an example, Mom has restricted the twins' use of computers at home, whether for schoolwork or recreation, but Dad allows them to use the computers when they stay with him. The boys have not shared this fact with their mother, however, and neither has their father. The onset of adolescence for Bill and Brian, combined with the recent divorce, has obviously contributed to their problem.

Bill and Brian are both vehemently opposed to therapy. Bill is a bit more open to trying it, but Brian does not see the point. Brian has said, "We admitted we did something wrong. That should be the end of it. Why do we have to talk about it?" Both Mom and Dad feel that their boys could benefit from therapy that would help them express their emotions to a greater extent, as well as be more respectful and cooperative with adults. The twins appear to be very oppositional, arrogant, and even a bit entitled in their personal styles. Much of this takes the form of their superior air regarding their intellectual ability and computer expertise. Needless to say, both of the boys are a challenge to engage in therapy. I decided to work with each of them individually, as well as do some family work because of the nature of Mom's and Dad's concerns regarding authority issues with the boys. In other words, there are major problems not only at school but also home and in the community in general.

My individual work with the twins was from a psychodynamic perspective, which will be discussed later in this chapter. Family work, however, was crucial to addressing the problems with these boys as well. In addition to weekly individual sessions with each of the twins, Mom and her two boys would meet with me for family therapy once a month. These sessions focused on helping Mom develop firm and consistent limits and structure with the twins, as well as improving family communication. The content of most family sessions initially addressed the twins' concerns about having their computer privileges revoked. Both Brian and Bill complained continuously that the punishment was not fair, as well as asking when they would get to use their computers again. Although Bill was a bit more respectful in his tone with Mom, Brian continued to insult her and raise his voice, as well as threaten to and actually leave the room. Brian's behavior seemed reminiscent of a three-year-old's temper tantrums. The twins were really a handful to deal with in session.

Through careful and patient discussions with Mom and her twins in family work, the boys began to see that Mom was in charge, not them. The family sessions were used to clarify and restate Mom's concerns about her boys and exactly what kind of behavior and communication was acceptable in the family. Communication had completely broken down, and in many ways the twins were out of control. Their offense at school might have been considered symptomatic of their inability to control their impulses as well as a sense of entitlement. Family sessions focused on confronting the twins' inappropriate language and behavior as well as giving them some clear and concrete examples and expectations for their behavior. Initially this family work was extremely tedious. Virtually every minute of the sessions was filled with complaining, crying, and challenging of Mom. It became my role to help empower Mom to be firm, clear, and consistent in not only communicating with her boys but also not allowing them to talk to her in an abusive manner. Over time, Bill and Brian began to see that they could no longer manipulate their mother as they had previously, and that in order for them to have any type of privileges in their lives, they would have to begin to be more respectful and cooperative in their language and behavior. This type of family intervention was a useful way to firm up the boundaries of the family as well as help Mom reestablish her role as an authority figure. It also was a necessary adjunctive piece to the ongoing individual work with both twins. Individual work alone with the boys could not have been successful if some type of family work was not done in conjunction with it. This case example illustrates that many types of adolescent problems are not only individual but also family oriented in nature. Successful work entails the unique and carefully constructed combination of both family and individual theory and technique.

PSYCHODYNAMIC/ATTACHMENT/RELATIONAL THEORIES

A number of psychodynamic, attachment, and relational theories were addressed in chapter 1. They will be revisited now as viable and necessary therapeutic approaches with many types of adolescents. Object relations theory, self psychology, and relational approaches are especially salient forms of intrapsychic intervention because of their focus on the inner emotional development of the self of the adolescent, the adolescent's ability to achieve object constancy, and the inevitable mutual interactions in the clinical relationship. Object relations theory posits that the infant/toddler gradually internalizes a consistent and reliable emotional image of the primary caretaker(s) that can then be utilized in times of stress, anxiety, and tension to self-soothe. Peter Blos, who was also mentioned earlier, theorized that adolescents revisit the separation/individuation task in a different manner. Whereas the task in childhood is to separate self from other, the task in adolescence is to separate self from family. The process has essentially the same intensity and the same result, emotional independence. It is not surprising, then, that although adolescents are more than ten years older than the toddler challenged with initial separation tasks, their behavior is often remarkably similar to the toddler's. For example, many teens alternate intensely and unpredictably between states of dependence and independence in many relationships, but particularly with their primary caretaker(s). This ambivalence is similar to the way in which a toddler demands to have her needs for dependency and independence responded to immediately. Combined with this need in adolescence, however, are the teen's budding self-esteem, identity formation, and sophisticated cognitive approach to the world. This complex behavior can be purposeful, oppositional, and defiant at times but more often is unconscious and troubling to the adolescent. It becomes the therapist's task to help adolescents struggling with these issues to be comfortable with their identity, build their self-esteem, and modulate their emotions.

Object relations theory would suggest that it is the task of the clinician working with a teenager to first develop a *holding environment,* a physical and emotional space within the therapeutic relationship in which the adolescent can feel safe enough to be herself and spontaneously express her thoughts and emotions. Only then can the teenager recognize herself as a separate individual in much the same way the toddler achieves a degree of emotional separation through the consistent and reliable way in which the primary caretaker(s) allows him to be both dependent and independent according to his needs. In therapy with the adolescent, this is achieved through conversation. Of course, this process is quite variable depending on the teenager, her presenting concern, her earlier success at separation/individuation, and a myriad of other factors. But for some adolescents, some form of object relations or relationship therapy is essential to the successful completion of this task.

Self psychology, another form of psychodynamic treatment, can also be an invaluable approach to working with teens. As mentioned earlier, self psychology examines the inner emotional development of the self through the incorporation of what Kohut called self-objects. All human beings have an intrinsic emotional need for the three types of self-objects: mirroring, idealizing/merging, and twinship. These are the emotional equivalent of the need for food and oxygen. The need is much greater for a child but continues regardless of age.

In adolescence, the teenager has ideally been able to establish a relatively cohesive self, as self psychology would call it. That means that in early childhood the teenager was able to get enough of her self-object needs for mirroring and idealizing/merging met so as to develop the ability to meet her own emotional needs. Through repetitive and consistent mirroring or validation of her talents and abilities, and through idealizing and emotionally merging with important emotional caretakers in life, the small child was also able to gain a sense of security about herself. The development of these self-objects is very rudimentary in childhood, however. They must continue to be nourished in adolescence, in the same way that teenagers need more physical nourishment than adults. The adolescent who has not had his self-object needs met sufficiently in childhood will be emotionally hungry for them. This deficit may be expressed through a variety of dysfunctional behaviors including social isolation, depression, acting out, and drug use. It becomes the task of the therapist to provide a therapeutic milieu in which such a teenager's self-object needs can be met.

The third self-object need, twinship, is especially important during adolescence. Teenagers need to have others in their lives who are similar to themselves. They are striving to become emotionally independent from their primary caretaker(s) and family, and yet they still have dependency needs. This is a paradoxical dilemma that can be helped through the use of twinship self-objects. If the teenager struggling with insecurity, anxiety, depression, and isolation can connect with another who shares her concerns, she does not feel so alone. Adolescents' need for the peer group is a twinship self-object need. The peer group enables the teenager to be separate from family while still meeting his emotional needs for mirroring, merging/idealizing, and twinship. The peer group is not the only way in which self-object needs are met, however. Older people, especially trustworthy adults, can also serve that purpose. The therapist working with an adolescent with self-object deficits can be instrumental in helping her overcome her problems.

Mitchell's relational concepts help integrate and expand some of the contributions from object relations and self psychology theories. The ongoing and inevitable mutual contributions from the personalities of both the clinician and the adolescent are influential in the therapeutic process. The therapist's ongoing awareness and use of his own professional self enhances the adolescent's ability to understand and grow in the context of such a relationship. Appropriate identification and use of self can be a key factor in helping the adolescent (Mitchell, 1988; Stolorow, 1992).

CASE EXAMPLE

The following case example illustrates the use of self psychology in working with adolescents. Bill and Brian, the twins who were mentioned earlier in regard to family systems theory, are also a good example of teenagers who can be helped through the use of a psychodynamic clinical approach. Bill's and Brian's obnoxious and entitled behavior could be interpreted as a reaction to their underlying insecurity as well as emotional immaturity. It is certainly true that both Bill and Brian, like most adolescents, are struggling with their own narcissism as they develop their identities. A certain degree of self-centeredness is absolutely normal for most adolescents. However, the twins' extreme arrogance, entitlement, and rudeness reek of narcissistic insecurity. Most people who have been diagnosed with so-called narcissistic personality disorder or even traits of this diagnostic category are easy to spot and remarkably easy to understand once you recognize that their obnoxious behavior is a result of their underlying insecurity. I am always fascinated by any person who feels the need to brag about her accomplishments and put on superior airs with her peers. If that person were truly comfortable with her sense of self and identity, why would she feel so compelled to convince everyone else of her greatness? Usually humility comes with confidence, because one's sense of identity is secure within oneself. The extent to which such people signal to the world their knowledge, skills, and accomplishments can be a diagnostic indicator of how empty and insecure they really are inside. Such is the case with Bill and Brian.

I decided, and their parents agreed, that the best approach would be a combination of family therapy and separate individual work for each twin. In order to help Bill and especially Brian modify their obnoxious and in some ways self-destructive interactions with others, I decided to use self psychology to bolster their self-esteem and fill their self-object deficits. Both Bill and Brian were initially hesitant to allow me to form any type of relationship with them. The first few individual meetings with both of them felt very awkward as I tried to engage with them and develop a common language and ground in which to work. Bill was fairly civil to me in sessions, answering questions in a perfunctory fashion but not providing much detail or elaboration about anything. Brian was outright rude and indignant that *he* had to come to therapy. I decided to go with this issue as a starting point for both of them. We would work on trying to help each of them individually become more of what their parents would like them to be. This topic did not hold their attention for very long, and we soon had to move on to other conversation in order to help them progress. I discovered quite innocently in conversation with each of them that they both would open up if we talked about computers, the Internet, programming, and so on . . . DUH! Why didn't I recognize earlier that this vehicle would be most conducive to safe conversation? I learned quickly that the best way to encourage both Bill and Brian to communicate in sessions was for them to be regarded as the experts and me as the student. If I made any statements that could be construed as flaunting my own knowledge of computers (remember, I love computer games), the twins would respond with their usual arrogance and entitlement. The focus of interaction must be entirely on them. Anything else might be interpreted as a threat or as an unempathic response. I implicitly and explicitly understood that my responses to their conversations regarding these areas needed to mirror them. I was genuinely positive about their comprehensive knowledge and computer expertise. I praised their enthusiasm, creativity, and specialness in a genuine and sincere manner. Bill responded to this approach by discussing at length the Web sites he was creating and his plan to develop a new form of online telephone communication. These ideas were actually very creative and compelling, and I had no difficulty mirroring Bill's accomplishments. When I mentioned to Bill that he could probably make a fortune once he developed his new communication system, he emphatically stated, "No, I would distribute the program for free online!" Bill went on to talk about how unethical (my word) he thought it would be to selfishly make money on something the whole world should get for free. Over time this personal ideal served as an obvious transition to helping Bill recognize the disparity between his own values and the incident at school when he and his brother broke into the security system. Bill came to recognize through careful and consistent mirroring from his therapist that he truly was special, which helped him have sincere regret for his actions at school.

Brian was a different story. From the onset of therapy, Brian insisted that he was very different from his brother and did not want to be compared to him in any way. This is often the case with twins. Developing a separate identity in adolescence can be a more complex process when there is another who not only looks like you but possesses your genetics in virtually every way. It appeared that Brian's self-object needs, especially for mirroring, were much greater than his brother's. This was why Brian was more obnoxious, entitled, and rude with just about everyone, especially authority figures. I had to develop a different approach to help Brian meet his self-object needs. With Brian, I resorted to discussing my gaming computer. I learned very quickly that if I sounded too knowledgeable, Brian would respond with his usual condescending discussion aimed at letting me know how much he knew and I didn't. I decided to engage Brian in a discussion about what type of computer would be the best. What kind of hard drive should one purchase, video card, sound card, DVD drive, and so on. I related and responded to Brian as my expert computer consultant. Brian initially seemed to balk at this approach, even though it was sincere. Over time, however, he began to enjoy coming to therapy because it made him feel good. He too was being mirrored. The intensity of the mirroring in sessions was much greater than any relationship in his life and served to repair his self-object deficits from a self psychology viewpoint. Brian gradually began to be more pleasant, first in sessions, but eventually with his parents, teachers, and peers.

This case vignette is a good example of how a clinician can utilize psychodynamic theory in working with adolescents. Some teenagers need this type of approach because of their difficulties in developing a secure inner life. CBT or more surface-oriented approaches are not as helpful with this kind of issue. Psychodynamic theories and techniques specifically address these more underlying dynamics.

NARRATIVE AND SOLUTION-FOCUSED APPROACHES

It may seem odd to discuss narrative and solution-focused therapy in the same section, but both approaches have a great deal in common. Narrative and solution-focused models developed in the 1980s and are steeped in postmodern and constructivist philosophy. Simply put, both of these therapeutic models espouse the notion that reality is not absolute or objective but is created by all human beings (De Shazer & Berg, 1997; Monk et al., 1997;

White & Epston, 1990). Life and experience are contextual. Even two children of similar ages raised in the same family (the twins mentioned above) could have entirely different views of their world based upon how they internalized their experience. Narrative and solution-focused approaches help clients attend primarily to the present. While narrative therapy helps the client tell his story in-depth, it also aims at helping him deconstruct and reconstruct a new narrative that helps him function better in life. Solution-focused approaches as well promote the philosophy that clients (or *consumers,* as they are often referred to in solution-focused work) are their own best experts in solving their problems. The therapeutic work enables the consumer to develop her own solutions to her problems in a relatively short-term cognitive approach. Each of these clinical models has specific techniques that help the client examine her present problem and develop new ways to approach or understand it without delving into the past or gaining insight into early life experiences. Both approaches externalize the problem. The problem is the problem, not the client.

Central to the success of solution-focused therapy is the use of the "miracle question." Early on in therapy the client is asked to imagine that when he goes to sleep that night a miracle will happen and his problem will be solved. What would that look like? How would things be different? The client is engaged in a problem-solving venture that helps them create his own solutions to life's problems. From that intervention, the therapist (sometimes referred to as *facilitator* or *guide*) works together with the client to construct concrete and specific ways in which he can change his life.

Narrative approaches are a bit more abstract and obscure in technique, but the philosophy is the same. Help the client to tell her story, deconstruct her narrative to help externalize the problem, and reconstruct a new narrative that is more positive, empowering, and constructive for the client's present situation. Again the client is the expert, and the therapist's role is to help her find and construct a new narrative through gaining a different perspective on her situation. This approach as well is very cognitive in nature. Narrative therapists will often ask their clients to journal about their thoughts and situations. This very practical and pragmatic approach can serve as a basis for further examination and reconstruction later in therapy.

What is useful about both of these postmodern approaches in working with adolescents? First, they do not place great emphasis on delving into the past or on extensive insight in that area. Adolescents tend to avoid lengthy discussion or exploration of their past. That is because they are moving toward autonomy and emotional independence from their primary caretakers. Discussion of these issues serves only to stir up dependency feelings or memories, or even conflicts. Fortunately, many teenagers seem to conveniently forget these things, probably a form of repression that serves to foster their growth toward autonomy. Postmodern approaches such as narrative and solution-focused models do not require the teenager to go much beneath the surface. In addition, these models treat the adolescent as the expert. These approaches are also typically short in duration, which makes them attractive to school counselors and social workers as well as short-term community-based settings.

CASE EXAMPLE

The following is a case example utilizing a narrative approach in working with adolescents. Clyde and Carol were another set of twins who came to see me for therapy several years ago. They were outstanding high school students, who ended up being numbers 1 and 2, respectively, in their high school class. Their parents referred them to me because they felt that Clyde and Carol needed to develop better social skills in order to be more successful in their future college careers. Both Clyde and Carol were extremely compliant in therapy, doing their best to honor their parents' wishes. They were each very enjoyable to see in therapy but seemed like miniature adults in their interactions. They also came across as very intellectualized in their conversations. Clyde was the most extreme in this regard, and even though I knew he was only seventeen when I started to see him, he acted like a thirty-year-old. I saw Clyde and Carol throughout their junior and senior years of high school and right up until they left for college in the fall. They both made good progress in learning to express their emotions, and we worked a great deal on helping them prepare for college life. I did not see either of them during their freshman academic year but received a call from the parents early the next summer. Clyde was experiencing tremendous anxiety and depression and wanted to resume therapy with me to help him with these concerns.

As Clyde began his second round of therapy with me, I realized that he certainly had grown emotionally. He had gotten all As in his freshman year and had also received awards for his academic prowess. Naturally these accomplishments were not the problem. Clyde was troubled by racing and intrusive thoughts about life in general and his future. He had taken a summer job in the human resources department of a company that was in the process of severe downsizing. Clyde had become troubled by watching his fellow employees (most of whom were already out of college) struggle with an uncertain future. His racing and intrusive thoughts were about the uncertainty of life. What was he really doing? What would his future be? What was he working toward? Was any of this worth it? These and many more questions intruded into Clyde's mind continuously. Clyde was in an existential crisis. Considering his age, now nineteen, this was in fact a fairly normal part of young adult identity formation. For Clyde, however, a wonderfully talented young man, this was new territory. All his life, the future had been certain. Everything he did was planned by his parents and aimed toward giving him a successful life. But Clyde now felt that things were amiss. Something didn't fit anymore. He wasn't so sure that he would be safe or even that he knew who or what he wanted to be. He knew that he would be all right academically and that he most likely would get a very prestigious professional position. Clyde didn't mean to be arrogant, like the other twins mentioned above; he was just comfortable with the facts about his potential future. What Clyde did worry about was everything else. As he went through his freshman year getting straight As, he was initially happy but eventually felt a sense of emptiness about himself. He realized that his academic accomplishments were only a part of life. He also realized that his ideals (or even life narrative?) were changing, and he didn't know what he believed anymore. This became the thrust of our work together.

Utilizing a narrative approach, I helped Clyde discuss in depth his recollection of his past view of himself and how that view no longer seemed tenable for him. Therapy sessions throughout the summer focused on helping Clyde see that the anxiety, depression, and uncertain feelings he was experiencing were a problem outside of himself and not (as he imagined) a flaw in himself. He began to recognize that his developing identity included this process of uncertainty and that he was in fact the master of it. As he was able to normalize the thoughts and feelings that persecuted him initially, Clyde became able to relax and approach his life with a new story or narrative about himself. This new Clyde narrative was much more complex and abstract than the one of a few short years ago, but reconstruction of it helped him own it and feel much more comfortable with his life as he approached his sophomore year at college.

This case example, although admittedly focusing on an older adolescent, is a remarkable example of how a postmodernistic or constructivist approach to practice can be a very helpful model with many teens. If adolescents are able to externalize many of their troublesome problems and brainstorm about them with an objective, supportive, and nonjudgmental therapist, they may be able to solve them. Narrative and solution-focused models can be a refreshing, creative, and expedient approach to problem solving for many teenagers.

NEUROSCIENCE

The theory of neuroscience, mentioned in the first chapter, is a cutting-edge adjunctive aspect of the therapeutic process of all the theories already discussed in this chapter. Neuroscience is the study of the brain and how it functions. Central to the discussion of clinical work with adolescents are the ways in which neural pathways develop in the brain and help the young teenager manage her thoughts, feelings, and behavior. The infant's and young child's brain develops through repetitive experiences of the cognitive, emotional, and experiential variety. The more functional, repetitive, and adaptive early life experiences are, the more solidified they become in the network of the brain. This network is somewhat analogous to hard wiring. The more stable and secure the neural pathway has become, the more it might symbolically resemble a very strong, secure, and physically solid electrical wire. If the experience is repetitive, adaptive, but primarily cognitive in nature, the wiring may be strong but not very large. The more complex the early experiences—that is, cognitive, emotional, experiential, and so on—the larger and more secure the pathway. For example, an infant begins to develop the ability to self-soothe through the internalization of experiences it has with its primary caretaker(s). This internalization can be represented physically and chemically in the brain by the concept of neural pathways. If the infant is fed reliably and consistently but without any emotional qualities to it (loving look by the caretaker, stroking the infant's head), the neural pathway related to initial self-soothing may be limited to physical properties only. If that experience is rich in emotion, verbal interaction (cognitive), and experience, the wiring will be not only strong but complex and solidified. On the other hand, if that initial feeding experience is neglectful or even physically abusive, the infant internalizes an entirely different type of pathway that if repeated could contribute to self-destructive types of self-soothing. Whatever the young infant has experienced early on can have dramatic implications throughout life because it is internalized in the neural pathways of the brain.

There are three very important concepts from neuroscience that are worth addressing here. One is *neural plasticity*. Although neural pathways in the brain are solidified very early in life, modification or rerouting of the neural pathways is always a possibility. The person who has suffered a stroke often must learn how to walk and talk all over again. This process of developing new pathways is what neural plasticity helps to explain. It is a rerouting of existing pathways through new experience.

Neurogenesis is another crucial concept. Until recently, it was thought in many neuroscience circles that human beings develop a finite number of neurons in their brain. Neurons are the cells that are used to transmit chemical and electrical signals that tell us how to think, feel, and so on. It was assumed that the individual acquired his or her total number of neurons by the early twenties. Recent studies have demonstrated, however, that in some circumstances, human beings may be able to grow new neurons even later in life. This is an exciting discovery because of its implications for neuroscience and clinical work.

The final concept to be discussed is the notion of critical or *sensitive periods* of brain development. There appears to be a timetable in the development of the brain. Certain growth needs to happen by a certain time or it may not happen at all or be severely hampered. For example, if an infant is severely sexually abused it may become so traumatized that brain development is inhibited and its ability to manage emotions in life is severely compromised. Sensitive periods are a relative concept, varying somewhat depending on the individual's neurological makeup, but they are important for diagnosis, assessment, and intervention planning with adolescents (Cozolino, 2002; Siegel, 1999).

The implications of these concepts are crucial to clinical work with not only teenagers but people of all ages. The field of neuroscience helps clinicians understand that when they are providing therapeutic services to adolescents, they are affecting their brains. Ongoing repetitive clinical work is a concentrated therapeutic laboratory in which new pathways can be developed that lead to healthier functioning in life. Even short-term types of therapies can bring about this type of change in the brain. This is a remarkable discovery. For many years clinical work has been considered more of an art than a pure science. Neuroscience helps to explain the physical changes that can result from a well-informed clinical approach. What is interesting about this process is that is does not seem to matter which type of therapy approach is used. What matters is that it is the right approach for the right situation. Cognitive, behavioral, psychodynamic, family, narrative, solution-focused, client-centered, Gestalt, and many other forms of treatment can modify the neural networks of the brain according to neuroscience.

CASE APPLICATIONS

A brief application of this knowledge to several of the cases above helps to demonstrate this point. The CBT-like approach utilized with Kitty focused on the repetitive discussion and behavioral activity of exercise to help her lose weight. This focused and structured process helped Kitty develop new neural pathways that influenced not only her daily physical routine but also her thoughts and emotions. Without realizing it, Kitty was reprogramming her brain to think, feel, and act differently. Brian was helped to feel better about himself through the use of self psychology. The mirroring that Brian experienced over time became internalized as a new or modified neural pathway to help him develop greater self-esteem. My decision to focus exclusively on his low self-concept and attempt to modify it using mirroring self-object techniques can be understood much more fully utilizing the concepts articulated by neuroscience. Clyde's existential dilemma was treated from a narrative perspective. Narrative therapy is primarily cognitive in nature, but it also influences the client's emotions and feelings about his story. As Clyde was able to deconstruct and externalize the problem and reconstruct a new narrative, he was also altering the neural structure of his brain. The repetitive rewriting process, done in an empathic, nonjudgmental laboratory, enabled Clyde to modify the neural networks in his brain and add a more sophisticated cognitive/emotional aspect to his thinking.

These brief vignettes help to illustrate the ways in which neuroscience would explain brain growth through clinical intervention. Medication can sometimes accomplish the same thing. This information is an important and useful lens for the clinician working with adolescents. If the therapist understands what areas of the client's brain functioning may need modification, she can carefully construct therapeutic interventions that will be most successful.

INFORMED ECLECTICISM OR INTEGRATIVE PRACTICE

Now that many different types of theories for working with adolescents have been addressed, how does one know which one to use and in what ways? It is rare that a clinician uses only one theory or approach with any type of client. In fact many therapists would say that they operate under the concept of *informed eclecticism.* This means that they use a variety of theoretical ideas and techniques to help them think about and intervene with their clients. The clinical practice template mentioned above houses the clinician's repertoire of theory, empirical knowledge/experience, and technique. It operates automatically in the mind of the experienced clinician. But what does this actually look like in real life?

Even though I discussed my clinical work above as discrete types of theory and intervention, I was lying! In fact, I always utilize informed eclecticism in my clinical approach. I can't help it; it is now an automatic part of my clinical self. The cases discussed above all lend themselves to multiple theoretical understanding and intervention. They all can benefit from a mixture of technique, as long as it is informed and not random. Kitty is a good example. Had I insisted on a purely traditional CBT approach with her, Kitty probably would have felt controlled. Kitty is a teenager, she needs her autonomy in order to develop a sense of self, and she had just experienced a mistrustful relationship with a previous therapist. The CBT-like aspects of the case enabled Kitty and me to construct a reasonable plan that would help her lose weight at her own pace, but in addition our sessions focused on her emotional life and contained elements of narrative, and even family systems theory as we discussed her relationships with her father and mother. When working with the twins, Brian and Bill, I consciously utilized family systems theory to help strengthen the loose parental boundaries, but my family interventions were always influenced or tainted by a psychodynamic understanding of the boys' low self-esteem. Conversely, as I worked with Brian and Bill individually, I also kept in mind their family dynamics and how my interventions would also address problems in the family in addition to helping the boys feel better about themselves. I used primarily narrative therapy with Clyde, but I could have easily attempted to view him through a psychodynamic or even CBT lens. Although our discussions were very abstract and the sessions clearly had a client-centered, nondirective feel, there were many times I encouraged Clyde to try different approaches to his daily tasks. So my approach was not purely narrative but directive and reminiscent of CBT. To remain in a rigid and inflexible approach when the client clearly needs something else is not helpful. It is incumbent upon the clinician working with teenagers especially to develop a flexible and eclectically informed approach to practice.

BASIS OF PRACTICE

All of the practice approaches mentioned above developed from an intuitive knowledge base. Clinicians had a commonsense notion that they could be helpful in both understanding and working with clients. These same models entered into the realm of practice wisdom as clinicians began to validate their professional experiences of clients through their ongoing successes in therapeutic practice. Theoretical knowledge helped to further enhance the intuitive and practice wisdom of many of these approaches by formulating theoretical hypotheses that helped predict what would happen with clients and guide the therapeutic process (Krill, 1990).

The debate has been raging for years on which approach to practice is most successful as evidenced by the studies that have been performed. The evidence seems clearly to indicate that the therapeutic relationship is one common and necessary factor for successful treatment regardless of the approach (Prochaska & Norcross, 2003). However, there seems to be varying degrees of agreement regarding the success of specific clinical theories and methods.

This controversy is highly political and would take the length of this text to address. There are some therapeutic approaches that lend themselves better to research because the concepts within them are easier to operationalize and measure (Heineman, 1981). For example, it is much easier to measure a stimulus-response form of treatment, like behavioral therapy, than it is to measure narrative, psychodynamic, or even family therapy models. The more complex the method, the more difficult to accurately operationalize the concepts for measurement; one is never quite sure that what is being measured has been adequately defined to be measured. Thus, research on therapeutic models is controversial and can be quite complicated.

James O. Prochaska and John C. Norcross's text *Systems of Psychotherapy* (2003) does a tremendous job in exploring a wide range of clinical approaches, including the ones mentioned in this chapter. According to their comprehensive examination, there are varying degrees of success and validated knowledge for most of them. Thomas O'Hare's recent book *Evidenced-Based Practices for Social Workers* (2005) is a good reference guide to the systematic study of some of the recent literature on research with practice interventions. Evidenced-based research tends to focus primarily on the validity of intervention and is not strongly tied to theoretical knowledge (but see Roseborough, 2006).

Research into clinical practice will continue to be a rich source of validated knowledge for the practitioner working with adolescents. I encourage the reader to balance this type of validated knowledge with his own intuition, practice wisdom, and theoretical training.

SUMMARY

This chapter has presented the clinician with a variety of fundamental theories that are essential to working with adolescents. CBT, family systems theory, psychodynamic approaches, and narrative/solution-focused models are key to enhancing the development of the clinician's theoretical template. Neuroscience dramatically enriches the practitioner's understanding of the effectiveness of all of these approaches. The case examples helped to demonstrate not only the utility of each theory but also the need to practice from a stance of informed eclecticism. Research in the area of practice models tends generally to acknowledge the relative validity of a variety of clinical approaches. The difficulty with such models is to determine the extent to which they capture the phenomena being studied. The reader is encouraged to continue to pursue his search for intuitive knowledge, practice wisdom, theoretical knowledge, and validated clinical studies. All are important sources for the seasoned clinician working with adolescents.

RECOMMENDED RESOURCES

Readings

Judith S. Beck, *Cognitive Therapy* (New York: Guilford Press, 1995). This book is a user-friendly source for CBT concepts and techniques.

Louis Cozolino, *The Neuroscience of Psychotherapy* (New York: W. W. Norton, 2002). This is an excellent source for understanding neuroscience concepts and their relationship to and utility for practice.

Miriam Elson, *Self Psychology in Clinical Social Work* (New York: Norton, 1986). Miriam Elson worked extensively with Heinz Kohut, who developed self psychology. Her book presents his concepts with clarity and compassion.

Eda G. Goldstein, *Object Relations Theory and Self Psychology in Social Work Practice* (New York: Free Press, 2001). This classic work comprehensively covers object relations and self psychology with depth, clarity and utility.

Stephen A. Mitchell, *Relational Concepts in Psychoanalysis: An Integration* (Cambridge MA: Harvard University Press, 1988). This classic book on relational theory does a solid job of presenting the inherent complexity of the concepts.

Gerald Monk, John Winslade, Kathie Crocket, & David Epston, eds., *Narrative Therapy in Practice: The Archaeology of Hope* (San Francisco: Jossey-Bass, 1997). This is a good review of narrative therapy.

Thomas O'Hare, *Evidence-Based Practices for Social Workers* (Chicago: Lyceum Books, 2005). This text is a thorough review of the evidence-based literature.

Internet

http://www.integrativetherapy.com/index.php This Web site provides good information on the process of theoretical integration in psychotherapy.

5

The Essential Interplay of Family in Adolescent Practice: Implications across the Family Life Cycle

The importance of family systems theory as a model for both diagnostic assessment and treatment intervention has been addressed several times already in this text. Although adolescents are indeed moving toward physical and emotional autonomy in their lives, they are really still children. Parents and caretakers of adolescents usually have a strong investment in their children's lives and future. Most adolescents who come to therapy are referred by other concerned people in their lives, whether parent(s) or caretakers, the courts, the child welfare system, the school, and so on. In order to work effectively with a teenager, the clinician must involve these parties in the process to some extent. Future chapters will deal with the important issues of working with collaterals, the community, the courts, the schools, and other key figures in the adolescent's life. This chapter will focus exclusively on working with families.

THE FAMILY LIFE CYCLE

Family systems theory discusses the stages of emotional development that every child-rearing family passes through as the children grow and develop (McGoldrick, Giordano, & Garcia-Preto, 2006; Nichols & Schwartz, 2006). Each of these relative stages of development contains within it specific tasks that when accomplished lead to a strong and emotionally healthy family. Of course, these stages and tasks are all contextually constructed based upon the unique culture of the family.

The first family life cycle stage is that of *leaving home*. It is in this stage that young adults begin to emotionally differentiate from their family, develop intimate peer relationships, and become financially self-sufficient. It is the time when young adults begin to accept emotional and financial responsibility for themselves.

The *marital stage* is the second step in the family life cycle process. During this stage individuals begin the formation of a new family system through coupling and/or marriage. Implicit to this stage is the integration of several existing family systems into a new family. Along with this integration comes the addition of extended family, new family cultures, and the challenging task of blending these unique family structures.

The *child-rearing stage* is third in the family life cycle. The decision to bear and/or raise children brings forth a change not only in the number of members within the family but also in its relationship dynamics. Adjusting to the new role of parent is a challenging task for the marital subsystem. This new role as parents creates an entirely new subsystem in the family, the *parental subsystem*. For many couples this is a difficult time. They begin to realize that the addition of a child to the family drastically alters their lifestyle, intimacy, in fact every area of their lives. The involvement of extended family in this stage also can have a dramatic impact on family life. Different family systems often have different expectations with regard to child-rearing practices. Throughout childhood, the family continues to be pushed forward in its development. When children enter school, there is a new set of tasks and challenges. For the first time, children are being evaluated by societal systems outside the family. This process can have a profound effect on the way the family views itself.

The *adolescent stage* is the fourth in the family life cycle. As mentioned earlier, this can be a difficult time for many parents and caretakers as they adjust to a new role with their adolescent son or daughter. The extent to which they can allow their child to move through this process in a healthy manner can powerfully affect the family system. Far too often, parents/caretakers are unaware of how their own emotions are stirred up by the onset of their child's adolescence. This lack of awareness can result in emotional distance, extreme criticism, controlling behavior, avoidance, and excessive permissiveness. Much of the work with adolescents is highly influenced by the family dynamics of this family life cycle stage.

The fifth family life cycle stage is the *launching stage*. The most obvious part of this process is helping the adolescent/young adult to separate from the family and move into her own first family life cycle stage of leaving home. But the parents of this teen are also faced with the challenge of readjusting their roles as parents as well as their own marital/coupling situation. Far too often, parents struggle to reestablish intimacy in their relationship when an adolescent leaves home. The role that the teenager served in that family is now gone, and that dynamic has left a void in the family system. Recognizing and adjusting to that void is a challenging process.

The final family life cycle stage deals with adjusting to life without children. Parents need to find personal meaning in family and individual life after children have left home. Most families continue to stay involved with their children on some level, but the adjustment is still a challenge (Nichols & Schwartz, 2006).

From reviewing the family life cycle the adolescent practitioner can appreciate the profound ways in which rearing children can affect the family dynamics as well as parental roles, functions, and personalities in general. Parents are invested in their children's lives. The process of child rearing heavily influences the development of the parent's self. When parents decide to bring their adolescent to therapy, they have a strong personal investment in that process. After all, they have raised that child. They recognize on some level that they are responsible for what that teenager has become. In many ways the adolescent can be seen as a reflection of themselves. That is why it is so crucial to involve parents and caretakers in the therapy. How then should the clinician working with teenagers appropriately involve parents and caretakers in this process?

PARENTAL AND CARETAKER INVOLVEMENT IN WORKING WITH ADOLESCENTS

Adolescents usually come to treatment because they are somewhat off the track in their developmental process. Whatever the presenting symptom or problem, most teenagers are struggling with some type of transitional adjustment, life crisis, loss, family emergency, or physical or emotional problem. They are having trouble coping with the issue and need help getting back on track. The therapy process helps to identify the precursors to these issues and intervenes accordingly. Therapy for adolescents should not be prolonged any further than is necessary to help that teenager get back to a so-called normal path of development. Working with parents in that process is crucial.

From the onset of work with adolescents, it is imperative that the clinician have a discussion with the parent(s)/caretakers to coordinate a clear and consistent therapeutic approach. There are a variety of ways to approach this task. Usually, the initial phone call for treatment comes from the parent. The clinician should make every effort to engage that parent on the phone. That means to begin to establish an empathic, concerned, and professional relationship that will help that parent feel comfortable confiding in the therapist about the child. Of course, any information that is acquired from any source is always subjective and tainted by the unique perspective of that individual. Parents do not usually give false information to their teenager's prospective therapist, but the information they do give is their opinion. It may not be shared by their teenager or even other family members. However, it does give the therapist a good sense of exactly what it is that this particular parent thinks and feels is the problem. Understanding the parent's agenda is crucial to all further work with that adolescent. The parent(s) will want to know that their concerns are being addressed in therapy even if those concerns are not the same as the adolescent's. Forming an alliance with the parent(s) is as important as forming one with the teenager. Sometimes it is even more difficult to achieve.

A very important reminder to the clinician is not to blame the parent. Sometimes, particularly with young beginning practitioners, there can be a tendency to overidentify with the adolescent. Remember that each party has his or her own perspective, and in order to truly help an adolescent and her family, both perspectives must be empathically understood.

Depending on the nature of the case, it may not be a good idea to have the parent(s) sit in on the first session with the adolescent. However, some form of discussion surrounding parental concerns and identifying information is absolutely essential before seeing the teenager. The notion of informed consent is important here as well. Parents need to know what is in store for their adolescent in therapy and what the process will and will not entail. Such matters as the fee, limits of confidentiality, length of sessions, type of therapy, and so on are all an important part of this process. For example, it may be helpful for parents to be warned that it is not unlikely that their teenager will come home from a session and say, "Dr. McKenzie thinks you guys are nuts and that I'm right." No, Dr. McKenzie did not say that in session, but he was very empathic to the teenager's concerns and frustrations regarding her parent's discipline. His empathic responses such as "That's got to be really hard for you when they won't let you go out with your friends" can be interpreted as agreement with the teenager and opposition to the parents. Letting parents know that this type of feeling and behavior may develop as therapy progresses does not mean that you support or encourage the teenager's opposition to her parents. It is simply part of the development of trust that will ultimately lead to helping the teenager feel better about herself and function better in the family and life.

There are many times when it is advantageous to work with parents and adolescents separately and concurrently in therapy. Many parents have a difficult time understanding their adolescent child's developmental process. They may not remember what it was like to be a teenager. They also may have difficulty understanding that their adolescent son or daughter's developmental journey is a narcissistic one and that their children are really not able to be sympathetic to their concerns or needs. Some parents may even personalize the way in which their teenager is now behaving in life. Individual therapy or even couples therapy with parents struggling with these types of issues can be extremely helpful, not only to them but also to the adolescent and the family as a whole. Therapy of this type is usually a combination of support and education. The focus is to help the parents understand the nature of the adolescent journey better and provide ongoing therapeutic support for them as they come to terms with appropriate ways to help their child through the difficulties that have brought him to treatment.

As the parents are getting help through their own therapy, the clinician may also be seeing the teenager for individual treatment. The decision to provide service to parents and the adolescent should be based upon the clinician's assessment of the therapeutic alliance with the teenager as well as the nature of the problems presented for treatment. In some situations it may be contraindicated for the same therapist to see the parents and the adolescent in separate therapy, for example, if doing so might prevent the adolescent from being able to truly trust the clinician. But although in some situations this type of approach can be disastrous, in others it is absolutely crucial to the success of treatment. It has been my experience that this type of dual concurrent approach is effective when the teenager's problems are also integrally related to the family dynamics.

Working with teenagers from alcoholic or drug-dependent families is a good example of this type of situation. The teenager may be playing the scapegoat role in the family through their acting-out behavior, but this difficulty is integrally symptomatic of the family's emotional health. Working with the teenager alone would be helpful, but would not effectively address the entire scope of the problem. Combined work with parents, family, and adolescent is a more appropriate approach to this situation. Working with the parents and perhaps the family as a whole to help them understand the scapegoat role in drug-dependent families will enable the teenager to work more freely in his own therapy. Freeing the adolescent from the scapegoat role in individual therapy will also enable him to get back on the developmental track in his own life.

Individual work with parents can be quite an undertaking in and of itself. As mentioned above, the adolescent stage in the family life cycle can be a challenging one for many parents. Not only is their son or daughter moving away from them emotionally, but this process can also stir up memories and emotions from their own adolescent journey. It is very interesting and ironic that most adolescents do not seem to remember the earlier dependency feelings they had toward their parents in childhood. Parents as well often find it difficult to recall their own emotional struggles from adolescence. This type of repression I believe serves a very important function for both parents and teens. It insulates them from painful or anxiety-producing memories and feelings. For adolescents, it is much easier to move toward independence from parents and family if they are not as aware of their own infantile dependency feelings from childhood. Unfortunately for many parents, however, this selective recall can keep them from having much empathy regarding the emotional journey of their adolescent. Therapy for parents, whether it is in the form of couples work or individual counseling, can be a valuable resource in helping them negotiate the adolescent stage of the family life cycle.

I have seen many parents in individual therapy while I was seeing their adolescent son or daughter in practice. Many of these parents utilized their own therapy to work through their own unresolved issues of adolescence. By spending some time exploring and discussing these issues, parents are able to be better parents, able to identify and separate their own emotional issues from those of their adolescent. Such therapy can give them the degree of objectivity necessary in order to be more effective parents. The following case example helps to illustrate this process.

CASE EXAMPLE

George, a thirty-five-year-old male, brought his thirteen-year-old son Tom to therapy because of his concerns regarding Tom's defiant behavior at home. I began to see Tom in individual weekly therapy to work on these issues. Tom was a very assertive teenager but seemed to be very cooperative and appropriate in his sessions with me. I did at times have to set some firm limits regarding the use of the computer during our nontraditional therapy sessions, but Tom did not appear to have trouble with this limit. I met periodically with George and his wife (Tom's stepmother) to discuss Tom's progress in therapy as well as overall functioning in middle school and with his friends. It was during these meetings that it became clear that George was having the most difficulty with Tom. George began to realize that his struggles with Tom were reminiscent of his own emotional struggles with his father during childhood and adolescence. George decided that it would be helpful to spend some individual sessions exploring his past in order to help him achieve a greater degree of objectivity in parenting his son Tom. George came to understand that he tended to be more lenient with Tom because of how strict his father had been with him. George did not want Tom to feel the way he had as a child. George had felt abused, humiliated, and misunderstood for the greater part of his childhood and youth. He compensated for the guilt he felt when he was strict with Tom by being too lenient. Through individual therapy, George gained insight into his past, and this insight enabled him to set more reasonable and consistent limits with Tom without feeling guilty. Tom's behavior at home gradually improved as he initially tested his dad a bit but eventually settled into very age-appropriate functioning. This case example dramatically emphasizes the crucial importance of adjunctive parental work when it is diagnostically indicated. For many adolescent cases parental work of this nature is not necessary. However, it is incumbent upon the practitioner to be able to effectively assess the adolescent and his family structure and circumstances in order to determine if adjunctive concurrent work should be a part of the overall treatment.

In some cases, family therapy alone or in combination with individual work is the most effective approach in working with adolescents. When there do not appear to be clear rules, boundaries, or even communication in the adolescent's family, individual work alone will not help that adolescent. The clinician working with families of adolescents can serve the function of helping the entire family adjust to the adolescent stage and the unique challenges that it entails. The family of George and Tom above can be used again as an example of this type of work.

As George became more aware of his limitations and difficulties in parenting Tom, we began to discuss them with his wife, Lisa, in couples sessions. Once the three of us were clear about the nature of those issues, as well as how Lisa's past might figure into the picture, we decided to do some family work with Tom. Those sessions involved discussing decisions that needed to be made regarding Tom's autonomy and involvement in the family. Initially Tom was very defiant and insisted on having everything his way. He wanted to be able to play video games until midnight, he didn't think he should be forced to do any homework, he wanted to choose what he was going to eat for all meals and eat them whenever he wanted them, and so on. Tom was really out of control at home. Ironically, however, Tom did not demonstrate this same type of behavior in school. He was in fact a model student and very cooperative. It became my role as family therapist to help all family members work together to establish reasonable rules and communication. I helped Lisa and George set firm limits with Tom and consistently follow through on them. Tom initially pushed the limits on these new structures but backed off when he realized that both Lisa and his father would not budge. My individual work with Tom shifted to more discussion about his frustration with his parents and other age-appropriate issues such as peer relationships, school, and so on. Although Tom did not like this new structure, he eventually accepted it, and his behavior problems disappeared. George continued to deal with his guilt about taking a firm stand with his son but felt better as he saw Tom's behavior subside and realized that Tom knew he loved him even though he did not give him everything he wanted. Through ongoing couples work, Lisa and George were also able to be happier and more consistent in their parenting roles.

FAMILY, INDIVIDUAL, AND/OR COUPLES WORK

There are many situations in which family, individual, or couples work is a necessary and helpful adjunctive part of the adolescent's therapy. The decision should be based upon a careful and comprehensive diagnostic assessment like the one discussed in this book. Remember, however, that assessment is an ongoing process. The nature and type of parental work may vary over the course of the therapy. The main point to remember is that some parental involvement is necessary in all clinical work with adolescents. The failure to adequately involve the parents can have disastrous results.

CASE EXAMPLES

The following two case examples help to illustrate some of the positive and negative features of involving or not involving parents in the therapeutic process with adolescents. Many years ago, in the very beginnings of my private practice work, I made the mistake of inadequately involving the parents in an adolescent case. Julie was a seventeen-year-old girl who actually asked her parents to bring her to therapy to work on her depression. I spoke to both of her parents in the initial phone call. They informed me that Julie wanted to come to individual therapy because she was depressed. I gathered some information from them about their daughter, informing them about the process of treatment, confidentiality, fees, and so on. The parents insisted that this was Julie's therapy and that they did not want to intrude in any way. I took them at their word and proceeded to work with Julie on an individual basis. Julie was a wonderful client to see. She was verbal, intelligent, insightful, and very interested in working on her depression. Julie was not suicidal, and I saw no need to contact her parents, especially since they were so insistent on maintaining her privacy in therapy. I had seen Julie for about six sessions when I received a phone call from her parents. They informed me that they were taking Julie out of therapy with me because I had not stayed in touch with them about her treatment. When I mentioned that it was my understanding that they wanted me to maintain Julie's privacy, they both insisted that they did not mean I should have no further contact with them. This was their only daughter and they needed to know how she was doing. Needless to say, I learned an important lesson that day. Adolescents are part of a family. If you are going to work with them, even individually, you must have some type of continued involvement with the parent(s).

My work with the twins, Brian and Bill, as well as with their parents is a good example of a positive use of family in the therapeutic process. Although I met primarily with Brian and Bill in individual therapy utilizing a modified version of self psychology, I also worked with their mother and father in family therapy. The twins' sense of entitlement, arrogance, rudeness, and overall opposition were a major problem not only in the family but with their peers, school personnel, and many other people in the community. I decided quite early that therapy with this case had to be at least a two-pronged approach. In my individual work with the boys, I tried to develop a consistent, reliable, and empathic milieu in which both Brian and Bill might begin to repair some of their self-object deficits, particularly their need for mirroring and validation. With the family, however, I consistently served the function of a facilitator. My role with all family members was to help them develop and maintain clear and consistent structure, boundaries, and communication. Brian and Bill were extremely rude and oppositional with both of their parents. I helped the parents to consistently communicate to their twins the inappropriateness of their communication as well as what the consequences would be if that type of interaction continued. Because the parents were divorced, it was much more challenging to try to insure that there was consistency in both family systems. Meeting with the twins and both parents insured that the rules, roles, and consequences in both settings were consistent. The boys were given clear messages from both parents over time that they were to respect them and follow the family rules in both homes.

The boys began to realize that they would get more of what they wanted if they followed the rules of not only their family but society at large. Any problems that occurred outside the family were also dealt with in the family. The twins came to realize that they could not manipulate the firm structures of their world. This approach was combined with intensive individual therapy aimed at improving self-esteem. As the twins learned to feel better about themselves through their respective individual work, they felt less need to manipulate their environment in order to get what they wanted. They learned discipline and self-control as their self-esteem improved and their family structure remained consistent and reliable. This combined approach was absolutely necessary in order to help the twins function individually, in their family, and in the environment.

BASIS OF PRACTICE

One of the distinct advantages of using family therapy with an adolescent client is that it inherently broadens the assessment feature of clinical practice. On the levels of intuitive, practice wisdom, and theoretical knowledge, family systems assessment is by its very nature multidimensional and functional (O'Hare, 2005): exploring family dynamics and incorporating input from all family members, sometimes even including extended family, can help the practitioner working with adolescents to achieve a more contextual picture of the adolescent's world. This becomes even more important for families from diverse racial and/or cultural backgrounds, including gay, lesbian, bisexual, or transgendered adolescent children, or the heterosexual teens of gay and lesbian couples (Fairchild & Hayward, 1998; McGoldrick, Giordano, & Garcia-Preto, 2006).

From a validated knowledge standpoint, there are many who believe that family therapy models do not lend themselves to conventional research methodology because they are by nature nonlinear in their dynamics and do not fit well with conventional operationalization and measurement (Prochaska & Norcross, 2003). However, Prochaska and Norcross have examined a good deal of the conventional research on family therapy and concluded that (1) such therapy is at least as effective as if not more effective than individual therapy for a variety of problems; (2) for certain problems, many of which are central to working with adolescents (anorexia, juvenile delinquency), these models are the treatment of choice; (3) therapist relationship skills are an important factor in treatment outcome.

SUMMARY

This chapter has emphasized the crucial importance of combining family and individual work in adolescent therapy. Adolescents are part of a family system. That family system is moving through the family life stage of adolescence. This stage brings with it unique challenges not only for the teenager but also for her parents and family members. It is imperative that clinicians working with adolescents involve the parent(s) and caretaker(s) of those teens from the onset of therapy. Establishing solid ground rules and a working relationship with parent(s) is a fundamental part of successful adolescent treatment. In many cases, this process will entail not only family therapy, but also couples work and even individual therapy for parents. In order to help the adolescent negotiate her developmental journey of autonomy from the family, the clinician must understand and carefully assess the extent to which family systems work. Key in this work is a careful understanding of the unique issues of diversity within each family (Kurtines & Szapocznik, 1996). Family therapy models may not lend themselves to conventional research owing to their nonlinear dynamics, but studies have shown that they are indeed quite effective with many of the problems of adolescents.

RECOMMENDED RESOURCES
Readings

E. P. Congress, "The Use of Culturagrams to Assess and Empower Culturally Diverse Families," *Families in Society* 75 (1994): 531–540.

Robert Constable & Daniel B. Lee, *Social Work with Families: Content and Process* (Chicago: Lyceum Books, 2004).

M. McGoldrick, J. Giordano, & N. Garcia-Preto, eds., *Ethnicity and Family Therapy,* 3rd ed. (New York: Guilford Press, 2006).

Michael P. Nichols & Richard C. Schwartz, *Family Therapy: Concepts and Methods,* 7th ed. (New York: Allyn & Bacon/Pearson, 2006).

Elaine B. Pinderhughes, "Empowering Diverse Populations: Family Practice in the Twenty-first Century," *Families in Society* 76, no. 3 (1995): 131–140.

James O. Prochaska & John C. Norcross, *Systems of Psychotherapy: A Transtheoretical Analysis,* 5th ed. (Pacific Grove, CA: Thomson-Brooks/Cole, 2003).

K. B. Rodgers & H. A. Rose, "Risk and Resilience Factors among Adolescents Who Experience Marital Transitions," *Journal of Marriage and Family* 64 (2002): 1024–1037.

Film/Television/Media

Ordinary People (1980), *Boyz in the Hood* (1991), *The Joy Luck Club* (1993), *My Family (Mi Familia)* (1995), *Life as a House* (2001), *The Family Stone* (2005), *June Bug* (2005). These films depict the wide range of dynamics in family functioning.

Everwood (2002–2006), *Six Feet Under* (2000–2005), *The Sopranos* (2000–2007). These excellent TV series capture the complexity of family dynamics.

6

Use of Self and the Ethical Approach to Practice with Adolescents

The astute clinician recognizes that the use of self in the clinical relationship with adolescents is very important for the success of treatment. Use of self, of course, is not just self-disclosure. It consists of a wide range of subtle, overt, conscious and unconscious responses and interactions with the adolescent client. How and what one discusses with an adolescent client is an important decision that must be handled ethically. This chapter will examine the theoretical underpinnings of the so-called use of self in clinical work as well as examine and critique the different types of issues that may necessitate self-disclosure.

HISTORY AND ORIGINS OF COUNTERTRANSFERENCE THEORY AND USE OF SELF IN ADOLESCENT PRACTICE

Many years ago in my doctoral dissertation I wanted to examine the nature of the clinical relationship. I was especially intrigued by the fact that most if not all clinicians experience a wide range of emotions with their clients, and the way in which they understand and decipher the origins and meaning of those feelings can have a profound impact on all areas of treatment, especially on the use of the therapeutic relationship. The emotional reactions of both client and therapist contribute to the success or failure of the therapeutic relationship. The careful management of that relational process is at the heart of therapeutic work (Hubble, Duncan, & Miller, 1999; McNamee & Gergen, 2002; Mitchell, 1988; Stolorow, 1992). This is what one might call the use of self in clinical work (McKenzie, 1995). In contemporary clinical nomenclature this complex concept might be referred to as the intersubjective or relational area of the clinical relationship (McNamee & Gergen, 2002; Mitchell, 1988; Stolorow, 1992). A basic review of the transference and countertransference concepts, including the notions of intersubjectivity and relational therapy, will help set the stage for the discussion of this important aspect of the clinical relationship with adolescents.

Freud discovered and developed the concept of *transference* in his work with analytic patients in the late 1800s and early 1900s. In psychoanalysis, the patient free-associates and says whatever comes to his mind. The analyst must be a blank screen, that is, not pollute or gratify the patient in any way that may interfere in his ability to free-associate. One of Freud's most famous patients, Anna O., reached a point in her analysis where she found it difficult or even refused to continue to free-associate. Freud recognized this to be a resistance to the treatment and redoubled his efforts and encouragement that she continue to free-associate. Over time Anna O. did resume the free association, but with a new twist in content and emotion. She now free-associated almost exclusively about Freud himself. Freud initially was baffled and overwhelmed by this dilemma. This was a difficult resistance indeed. He must get her to resume discussing her issues, not her relationship with or fantasies about him, he thought. Anna O., however, refused to do much else but focus on her relationship with Freud. She discussed her feelings, wishes, hopes, and dreams about him. Freud eventually began to understand that this was an important issue for her. What did it mean? Freud hypothesized that perhaps Anna O. was in fact discussing issues in her own life history—important relationships, emotions, fears, wishes—and was disguising them unconsciously as symbolic issues with her analyst. In other words, she did not really feel this way about Freud (whom she presumably did not know much about) but was actually *transferring* onto him her own life issues. As Freud was able to decipher this symbolism and interpret it to Anna O., she was able to have insight not only into her relationship with Freud but into the meanings of those same interactions in her past and present life. Anna O.'s improvement in analysis was the proof that Freud had stumbled upon a remarkable discovery not only about analysis but about human nature in general (Freud, 1938).

This rudimentary discovery has important implications for all types of clinical work as well as for understanding an equally important element of human interactions. Most of us at some point in our lives distort or misunderstand our interactions with significant others owing to our past relationships. That is human nature, Freud would say. The important thing is to be aware of that distortion so that it does not interfere with one's life. Far too often, especially in intimate relationships, problems occur through misunderstandings, distortions, and projection. That is why the therapist's and client's self-awareness are an integral element of successful therapeutic work.

Along with the concept of transference, Freud also developed the notion of *countertransference* or, simply put, the therapist's transference. It was Freud's recommendation that therapists go through their own analysis in order to become aware of their own neurotic life issues so that these would not interfere in their analytic work with patients. This approach to handling countertransference became known as the *classical position*. The management of countertransference, however, has gone through a tremendous evolution over the past hundred years.

By the 1950s with the development of object relations theory, most experienced clinicians recognized that countertransference was a ubiquitous phenomenon. The countertransference of the therapist could not be eliminated through successful analysis or psychotherapy, as Freud once thought, but was ongoing. Each client brings with her her own transference issues based upon past and present circumstances, and those issues influence the therapist depending on that therapist's life history. This shift in countertransference theory and management became known as the *totalist position*. The South American analyst Heinrich Racker is probably most notable for developing a systematic way to recognize and manage countertransference issues in the treatment relationship (Racker, 1968; Tansey & Burke, 1989).

In recent years there have been even further modifications and evolution of the concept and management of countertransference. Recognizing that the development of the therapeutic relationship contains elements and contributions from both the client and the therapist, the *specialist position,* more recently referred to as the *intersubjective* or *relational position,* recommends that the clinician base his interventions upon the mutual development of an intersubjective relationship that is unique to the two parties involved and based upon each member's personal culture (Mitchell, 1988; Saari, 1986; Searles, 1979; Stolorow, 1992).

How does all of the complex theory and history presented above help us understand basic clinical work with teenagers? Recognizing that transference and countertransference can be important elements of clinical work with all populations is a useful part of any clinician's knowledge base. Knowing that the therapeutic work is relational and that there are potentially meaningful constructive and destructive elements involved helps the practitioner better serve the adolescent in practice.

Adolescents typically present and utilize transference in a much different manner than do adult clients. Many clinicians and theorists believe that it is not a good idea to encourage a traditional transference relationship with an adolescent. Adolescents are moving away from their infantile dependency, and too much exploration or revisiting of this time period can be overwhelming and even dangerous. However, it has been my experience that all adolescents present some form of transference elements in treatment and that the way in which the clinician responds out of her own countertransference can be extremely helpful and even pivotal in the successful treatment of adolescents. A review of another psychodynamic theory will shed some important light on this issue.

The theory of self psychology has been discussed in previous chapters. Kohut believed that all people have an emotional need throughout life for the three types of self-objects: mirroring, idealizing/merging, and twinship. That need is greater in infancy and childhood and becomes less as we reach adult emotional maturity. Adolescents are still growing and maturing physically and emotionally and also have a greater need for self-objects than do most adults. As adolescents begin their second individuation process, as Blos might say, they tend to invest less of their time and energy in the family and their emotional relationships with primary caretakers. But they still need emotional connections with important others in order to help them develop an autonomous and emotionally mature sense of self. Most teens turn to their peer group or other idealized figures for this type of emotional sustenance. Sharing common values, interests, ideas, and philosophies with a group helps to give the adolescent a sense of purpose, security, and self-esteem. They are not yet capable of knowing or trusting their own sense of these things. Belonging to the group provides the emotional security necessary to help them make the ultimate transition to a more adult sense of self.

Although all three self-object needs are certainly a part of the adolescent's move toward an emotionally secure identity, I believe that *twinship* has the greatest prominence during this time period. So much of the adolescent's life and sense of purpose during this time period is wrapped up in how he is or is not like his peer group. Whether or not many adolescents accept peers into their world often is a result of how well they fit into a peer group's perspective. When an adolescent moves from one group to another, the move usually has something to do with an internal shift in her sense of self. The goals, values, and ideals of her existing peer group no longer fit her, and she may then turn to another.

For example, in my own adolescence, my alcoholic father pushed me (figuratively and literally) to play high school football. Erikson might say that my decision to join the freshman team was a move toward foreclosure of a part of my budding identity more than my own choice. Be that as it may, I joined the high school football team and along with it became a part of that social clique. Each social clique that an adolescent may join or identify with is relevant to that teenager's identity search. The jock/athlete clique may be appealing or disgusting to a particular adolescent because of how it is understood by him and the meaning it holds for him. This is true for all social groups, even in adulthood. In hindsight, my reason for joining the football team and clique associated with it probably had more to do with complying with or even pleasing my father than with wanting to be in it.

Over time I found myself feeling alienated as I tried to join in the social activities associated with the jock clique. It felt unnatural to me, and I did not feel comfortable or even feel like myself when I was around many of the members of that peer group. To me they felt phony. As a result, over time I left that group and moved to one that I perceived as the antithesis of it . . . the greasers or what might be called gang bangers today. This group appealed to me on a conscious level because they were all disgusted with jocks and saw them as the enemy. This was just perfect for me. I could now find purpose in being opposed to another group's ideology. Of course I now recognize that this move was also a move against my father and in many ways represented the symbolic expression of my anger toward him. Did I have any awareness of these possible explanations at the time? No. However, I do believe that many teenagers are drawn to certain peer groups and interests for similar reasons.

Twinship with others during adolescence enables the teenager to develop confidence and self-esteem. Adolescents are continually searching to know how they are similar to or different from others in their world. When an adolescent enters into therapy, even if it is forced upon her, those twin-ship needs often come into play in the form of requests for self-disclosure from the therapist. When adolescents demand self-disclosure from their therapists, usually they are demonstrating their crucial need for twinship. This does not mean that the clinician must disclose every single detail of his life to the adolescent client. The practitioner should be sensitive to the rea-sons for those requests and bear in mind how a careful use of self-disclosure may help to solidify the therapy relationship.

If an adolescent is able to recognize that her therapist shares some of her own interests, ideas, values, and ideology, it helps to foster a much more secure therapeutic bond. It also serves the greater purpose of creating a con-text in which the dyad can now begin to discuss and explore many areas of the teenager's life. It is not necessary that the clinician share everything about himself or answer all questions that the adolescent asks about him. What is important is that the practitioner recognize the reason for this request and the possible benefits developmentally in responding carefully to them.

Mark A. Hubble, Barry L. Duncan, and Scott D. Miller's book *The Heart and Soul of Change: What Works in Psychotherapy* (1999) emphasizes the fact that there are a variety of different interventions and approaches that work in treatment. Key to success is the clinician's careful use of self, because of the adolescent's need for twinship in the identity formation process.

Another important reason to tend to the adolescent's need for twinship through the appropriate use of self is that it helps to solidify trust in the ther-apeutic relationship. From a self psychology standpoint, it helps to ensure the development of mirroring and idealizing/merging self-objects. Even if the practitioner is using a purely CBT approach with a teenager, the use of self and twinship needs can increase the likelihood of developing greater trust in an intervention plan. The relationship with an adolescent client is the crucial element in any successful treatment effort.

THE CLINICAL VALIDATION METHOD AND USE OF SELF WITH ADOLESCENTS

Most if not all clinicians experience extreme emotions or discomfort in their clinical work with clients from time to time. The intensity of these experi-ences can interfere with or derail the clinical work. Usually they take the form of uncomfortable or even overwhelming thoughts and emotions that may interfere with the clinician's objectivity, empathy, or even his ability to formulate and carry through on interventions. In the most traditional sense this can be understood as countertransference. However, countertransference as discussed above is essentially an intersubjective and relational process. That means that the feelings and emotions of the clinician derive from the therapeutic relationship as well as from the practitioner's own life. When a therapist working with an adolescent experiences overwhelming thoughts and emotions that interfere in the process, how does he understand and work through them?

The *clinical validation method* addresses the phenomenon discussed above. It is a simple process in many ways, with profound implications for clinical work. It goes something like this: Let's say a clinician working with an adolescent experiences extreme emotional anxiety in the session. Let's also say that this emotional anxiety is so overwhelming that the clinician has difficulty listening to the client. What can she do in the session to help her understand this process and get back on track?

The clinical validation method suggests that the practitioner explore her working models of self and other. A *working model* is the mental and emotional construct that any clinician has developed in her own mind about herself and her client. The method would suggest that the clinician first explore her own working model of self as it relates to the extreme emotions experienced in the session. This means allowing herself to become introspective and explore the ways in which these thoughts and/or emotions may be part of her own life experiences. Using the example mentioned above, a clinician might wonder, "Why am I feeling this intense emotion right now? Is there something the adolescent is discussing that in some way relates to my own life or my own emotional issues or vulnerability? Is there something about me that is being triggered by what is happening between us right now?" These and many other avenues of exploration are very helpful in trying to pinpoint whether or not the difficulty in therapy is tied to the clinician's experience, her working model of self. If upon some fairly comprehensive scrutiny, the clinician is not able to identify any issues associated with her own working model of self, she can then begin to explore her working model of the client.

The client's working model is based upon the clinician's ongoing development of a sense of the client's history, emotions, development, relationships, and so on. The clinician may ask herself: "Is there something about what the adolescent is discussing that may be filled with anxiety? Am I feeling something that the client is unaware of or working through in his life? Am I responding to some nonverbal cues from the client that could generate extreme anxiety in me?" These questions and many more will help the clinician explore her working model of the adolescent in order to identify the source of the difficulty.

One might ask, "Am I supposed to be doing all this while I'm actually sitting with the adolescent?" The answer is yes. We all listen on many different levels simultaneously in every clinical session. We have many different ears working all the time in session. We listen to the manifest content—the exact words the client is saying and the issues and events that are being discussed. We listen to the diagnostic part of the session, the clinical meaning of the material. We also listen to our own feelings about all of the things the client is discussing. We can't help but experience how this material makes us feel. We may also (dare I say it) be thinking about our own lives and when the session will be over and what other things we want to do that day. We listen on many different levels *simultaneously*. This is part of the professional role of the practitioner. It is part of the development of our professional self. It takes years to develop confidence in this ability, and it is also an ongoing process that is deeply layered. But we all listen on many levels all the time.

The clinical validation method would suggest that if the clinician is able to identify the source of the intense distraction, she is able to experience a sense of relief, and with that relief gain the ability to reengage with the client. The insight into the source of emotional distraction allows the clinician to be less troubled by it. She can now come back to the session and the client with a greater degree of understanding about self and other. She can attend more directly to the client and the client's issues.

This may sound like a rather linear progression: explore your own issues, explore the client's issues, find the source. Ah ha, insight! Everything is now okay. The problem is that most of the explanation for these types of difficulties lies in an intersubjective/relational realm of experience in which both the client and the clinician participate. It is probably never just the client's issues or the therapist's issues that are the source of the clinician's anxiety; it is more likely to be the result of an interactive process that combines elements from both worlds. However, that does not mean that the process of clinical validation is useless. The sense of relief and ability to reengage in the therapeutic process demonstrate the validation of the search. The following example may help to demonstrate this technique.

CASE EXAMPLE

When Judy came to see me for therapy she was a junior in high school. Her parents brought her in for treatment because they were concerned about her physical and emotional withdrawal from the family. They came in without Judy for the first session and expressed many of these concerns in person. In addition, Judy's father gave me a novel that Judy was apparently reading that gave him and his wife concern. The novel was very dark, depressing, and sexual in content. Judy's parents were worried that their daughter was withdrawing into herself and becoming obsessed with evil and the pessimistic parts of life. They told me that when they spoke with Judy about coming to therapy she was very open to the idea. I worked with Judy on an almost exclusively individual basis, with occasional family meetings to review how therapy was going. Judy's parents understood that my work with their daughter was confidential, but they also were informed that if I felt that Judy was in danger of hurting herself, I would certainly inform and involve them immediately.

I wasn't quite sure what to expect when Judy came in alone for the first session. She appeared somewhat odd in both her physical appearance and her approach to conversation and interaction. One might characterize Judy as being goth in her appearance. She initially dressed primarily all in black, with heavy black eye makeup, lipstick, and fingernail polish. Sometimes her hair would be jet black, sometimes black and pink, sometimes all blue, and so on. She seemed not only shy in her demeanor but also a bit disorganized in her ability to communicate her thoughts and feelings. Her ideas were not delusional or odd in any way, but her ability to accurately *express* those ideas seemed compromised. It was as if Judy were thinking and feeling a great deal about herself and life but unable to verbally express her thoughts and feelings as clearly as she wanted. This was how I first encountered her.

Despite the awkward nature of our initial interactions, it certainly appeared that Judy wanted to be there. She seemed pleasant and interested in discussing whatever was on her mind at the time. The problem for me was that there seemed to be a terrible disconnect between what Judy openly expressed in session and my ability to respond to it with words that fit for Judy. I wondered as I saw her initially if she was suffering from the beginnings of some sort of psychotic disorder. I had seen many teenagers and young adults who were in the early period of developing schizophrenia, but Judy was different. She seemed to be highly intelligent, sensitive, and introspective. Her trouble appeared to have more to do with a sense of isolation, a sense that no one was able to understand her unique inner world or validate it for her.

I genuinely liked Judy. As I got to know her, I realized that her initial goth appearance was but one of many that Judy possessed. Judy, as I soon found out, was an artist. She expressed this artistic ability in virtually every area of her life. Some weeks Judy came in with her hair up, skin-tight jeans, a rock group T-shirt, and sandals. The next session she might have her hair straightened and wear a severe minishirt with fishnet stockings and high heels. The next week, she might be dressed as a spinster librarian in a frumpy floor-length skirt, an antique blouse, and more traditional hairstyle. Although her physical look changed with the wind, her personal style of interaction was always consistent and reliable.

Judy was also into a variety of artistic endeavors in her life. She painted in a wide range of mediums—oils, pastels, watercolors, and so on. She also sculpted and did a great deal of work with photography. Judy enjoyed taking pictures of animals, landscapes, human interactions. She also wrote very symbolic and intensely emotional poetry about human relationships. I came to know this awkward Judy as someone who possessed great depth and yet felt misunderstood and isolated in life.

The awkwardness that I continued to experience with Judy was extremely troubling. I truly cared about Judy, enjoyed seeing her, and wanted desperately to help her feel better about her life. While I saw her I continually searched my own working model of self in order to ascertain how my own issues were contributing and/or interfering with Judy's therapy. I recognized almost immediately that the emotional identity struggle that she was obviously going through was in some ways similar to my own. Many sensitive adolescents (myself included) feel a sense of isolation and loneliness in their search for self. I too had very deep thoughts about people, relationships, life, sex, spirituality, and so on. The difference was in my ability to stay a bit more connected to people through mainstream activities and conversation. I did not suffer from the same type of emotional and verbal awkwardness as Judy did. Judy seemed so obviously handcuffed by her verbal ability. And yet it wasn't that she did not have a very wide vocabulary or social sense. Judy's difficulty seemed to lie in her inability to put her complete complex emotional ideas into the correct words for her. It was almost as if language as she knew it was not sufficient to capture the full meaning of her experience. I realized that my task was to help her find a way to do just that.

There were many different ways in which I tried (and eventually succeeded) in helping Judy feel better about herself. One of the ways was to share some of my own experiences with emotional confusion in response to the confusion that Judy seemed to be expressing in her conversations in session. When Judy seemed to stumble in her ability to express a complete sense of her experience about something in her life, I would help her piece it together. I might share how that particular incident seemed reminiscent of something I had gone through in high school with friends, parents, or teachers. I would attempt to convey the complexities of emotion that I had experienced back then and how troublesome they had been for me. I would also share how isolated and alone that type of thinking could make one feel. I was attempting to form a *twinship* experience with Judy. I wanted her to realize that although she might not feel able to communicate her exact emotions regarding a particular experience, I could relate to it. I perhaps had had a similar experience.

CASE DISCUSSION

This use of self eventually helped Judy not only to feel a greater sense of connectedness with another (me) but also to develop the ability to communicate it to others. One might say that it was a form of attunement or, from a neuroscience standpoint, that Judy was developing new neural networks that enabled her to transmit her thoughts and feelings in clearer language. Language, after all, comes from successful completion of early attachment with primary caretakers. Even though our conversations were always focused on day-to-day events, relationships, artistic endeavors, and so on, we were building a new relationship in which Judy could better define herself and feel more competent in life. The intensely relational and intersubjective nature of our therapeutic relationship is what was so helpful to Judy in the end.

There were many more elements and aspects to this interesting and multifaceted case. I saw Judy for several years. She graduated from high school and went on to major in photography at a nearby liberal arts university. She has become much more confident in herself and knows that her perceptions of the world and others are a true strength in life. She has also been able to find happiness in a series of romantic relationships at college. I still see Judy from time to time. Our sessions focus on some of the same issues that she brought the first time we met. The difference is that Judy now has found those elements to be a welcome part of her identity. Our work together enabled her to recognize that unique strength.

BASIS OF PRACTICE

The use of self that stems from transference/countertransference theory incorporates elements from all four of the areas of research knowledge discussed in this text; intuitive knowledge, practice wisdom, theoretical knowledge, and validated knowledge. All clinicians should now know through the advances in attachment research and neuroscience that intuitive notions about the importance of the therapeutic relationship are valid (Cozolino, 2002; *PDM,* 2006). The specific elements of the transference/countertransference process within the therapeutic relationship have been studied for decades (Luborsky et al., 1988). The use of self has also been one of my primary interests throughout my professional career, including my own dissertation work (McKenzie, 1995, 1999). However, the concepts remain elusive owing to the difficulty of operationalizing them for valid and accurate measurement. For example, most of the clinician's countertransference is by definition unconscious, which means she cannot validate it until at least sometime after the process has occurred. This makes the validation process complex. The clinical validation method discussed above comes very close to remedying that difficulty, however, because it incorporates all four elements of research knowledge in a very practical manner in the here and now.

SUMMARY

This case although complex and certainly not typical demonstrates the ways in which the clinician can use himself in not only understanding but intervening with teenagers. The therapy relationship is truly intersubjective. In order to help many adolescents search for their identity, the skilled clinician must draw upon his own inner experiences and empathically identify with them. This technique will be different with each client that one sees in practice. Some work will be much more concrete and goal directed. Other work will be much more emotional and inner directed, like the work with Judy mentioned above. What is important to remember is that adolescents are searching for their own sense of self and identity. That process is different for each teenager. The astute clinician's ability to allow himself to vicariously identify with the adolescent's inner and outer experiences is the key to the development of a successful therapeutic relationship. In addition, the carefully timed and selected use of self can be of tremendous help in forming a twinship relationship that fosters the healthy development of identity (Racker, 1968; Tansey & Burke, 1989).

RECOMMENDED RESOURCES

Readings

Mark A. Hubble, Barry L. Duncan, & Scott D. Miller, *The Heart and Soul of Change: What Works in Psychotherapy* (Washington, DC: American Psychological Association, 1999). This book does an excellent job of comprehensively examining the literature related to the success of the therapeutic relationship.

Fred R. McKenzie, "The Clinical Validation Method: Use of Self in the Therapeutic Relationship," paper and conference publication presented at the International Conference for the Advancement of Private Practice of Clinical Social Work, Charleston, SC, June 1999. This paper, published in the proceedings, examines the history of the countertransference literature, as well as highlights Heinrich Racker's technique in light of contemporary practice.

Sheila McNamee & Kenneth Gergen, eds., *Therapy as Social Construction* (Newbury Park, CA: Sage, 2002). This book examines the therapeutic relationship from a postmodern perspective.

Carl R. Rogers, *On Becoming a Person* (Boston: Houghton Mifflin, 1961). This classic work examines the therapeutic relationship and the importance of empathy as part of the curative process.

Harold F. Searles, *Countertransference* (New York: International Universities Press, 1979). This is a collection of works by Searles, who is known for his clinical and developmental insight as well as the candid and powerful ways in which he is able to share this knowledge with the reader.

R. D. Stolorow, "Subjectivity and Self Psychology: A Personal Odyssey," in A. Goldberg, ed., *New Therapeutic Visions: Progress in Self Psychology,* vol. 8, pp. 241–250 (Hillsdale, NJ: Analytic Press, 1992). This is an important article on the subjective aspects of self psychology in clinical practice.

Michael J. Tansey & Walter F. Burke, *Understanding Countertransference: From Projective Identification to Empathy* (Hillsdale, NJ: Analytic Press, 1989). This is a comprehensive text on the countertransference phenomenon.

Film/Television/Media

Good Will Hunting (1997). A wonderful depiction of the complexity and mutual contribution to the therapeutic relationship.

7

Nontraditional Approaches to Working with Adolescents

Until now this text has discussed clinical work with adolescents from a relatively traditional perspective; in other words, formalized fifty-minute-hour psychotherapy. In actuality, a large portion of practitioners who see adolescents utilize a variety of forms of what might be characterized as nontraditional practice. This type of work may take the form of physical activity outside of the consulting room such as playing basketball, going for a walk, driving to McDonald's for a burger, or visiting the mall. These types of activities not only can be a wonderful addition to so-called traditional psychotherapeutic work with teenagers but in some circumstances hold greater promise and provide more emotional healing than sitting in an office and trying to discuss the adolescent's life. This chapter will address the theoretical underpinnings of what has always been an intuitive inclination for many practitioners working with adolescents in a variety of settings. There has been virtually nothing in the clinical literature to help explain the intuitive draw toward utilizing nontraditional methods with adolescents. Yet it has been an integral part of much of the highly successful work with teenagers. This chapter especially has been long overdue in the clinical and theoretical literature on practice with adolescents.

CLINICAL RATIONALE FOR NONTRADITIONAL WORK WITH ADOLESCENTS

What is the rationale for modifying one's clinical approach in working with any population, modality, or theoretical orientation? Because it isn't working. Many of the greatest clinicians and theorists developed their ideas out of the tremendous frustration they encountered in trying to fit their clients into a prescribed type of approach. Heinz Kohut, Salvador Minuchin, Steven de Shazer, and even Sigmund Freud himself made severe modifications in their approaches based upon the clinical roadblocks that they encountered with their various clients. When something consistently isn't working, one must change one's approach. This is also true for work with adolescents (Hubble, Duncan, & Miller, 1999; Krill, 1990).

The nontraditional approach to working with teenagers seems to have had its origins in the youth work movement of the 1960s. As mentioned earlier, most adolescents who come for therapy are not self-referred. As a result, many of them are extremely difficult to engage in a trusting therapeutic relationship. Forcing a teenager to sit in a consulting room and talk about his thoughts and feelings is a daunting task. Many adolescents aren't quite sure what to talk about or even know what they are feeling. Resistance is frequently a part of many adolescents' approach to counseling. Creative practitioners learned very quickly that engaging teenagers in discussions and activities that were emotionally nonthreatening yielded much greater results than forcing them to talk about things they either didn't want to discuss or didn't know how to discuss. These practitioners learned that when they used what might be understood as play and recreational activities, the so-called resistant or stuck adolescents were able not only to open up in practice but actually to get better.

This has always been a very exciting and interesting part of my work with adolescents. Long before I became an academic, I did extensive nontraditional work with teenagers in a variety of contexts. In the 1970s I was hired as an outreach worker in the northwest suburbs of Chicago. It was my job to form relationships with teenagers in informal settings so that they could become aware of the services of our agency. It was also my job to form therapeutic relationships with these teenagers to help them discuss problems and issues in their lives. Of course it was also my responsibility to make appropriate referrals to my agency's counselors should the situation warrant it. The problem, we at the agency soon realized, was that the adolescents seen in an outreach setting did not feel comfortable making the transition to seeing a counselor in the office. They much preferred to share their concerns in an environment of trust and safety on their own turf. This type of clinical work is certainly nontraditional, but it is also certainly as viable as any that might be done in a traditional counseling office. Fortunately, my agency at the time was very open-minded and accepting of this type of nontraditional approach and intuitively recognized the therapeutic value of it.

CASE EXAMPLE

Let me give an example of how I approached relationship building as an outreach worker in the mid-1970s. At the time I had extremely long hair that went well past my shoulders. I dressed in wide bellbottom pants and usually wore colorful gauze shirts. I would hang out in the local parks in the summertime. I drove our brightly decorated agency van to these locations and attempted to initiate conversations with teenagers through a variety of direct and indirect means. Teenagers knew I was from the agency because the van was marked with the agency logo and services. Many times I would get out of the van, sit at a nearby picnic bench, take out my tarot cards, and begin to do my own reading. I was really not an expert on tarot, but I knew enough about it to recognize that it was a wonderful vehicle to help anyone project his own thoughts and feelings. Teenagers would often times approach me and ask who I was and what I was doing. I always told them I was an outreach worker (informed consent) and explained that I was playing with tarot cards. They usually became fascinated with the game and wanted me to do readings for them. These readings invariably led to discussions about family, friends, school, and so on. In the process, these teenagers also learned about the agency, its services, and me. This turned out to be a highly successful way to engage adolescents.

It's important to remember the historical context in which I was working. Back in the 1970s, there were smoking areas in community high schools. Students with parental permission were allowed to go to these areas and smoke cigarettes freely on school grounds. Such smoking areas were a great place to meet and build relationships with teenagers. I would probably be arrested if I attempted anything like that today. However, back in the mid-1970s this was perfectly normal. What is important to recognize is the informal manner in which conversation, trust, and clinical process can develop in a nontraditional setting.

As I have grown in my professional education and experience, I have never forgotten or given up the important aspects of nontraditional work with teenagers. Although I no longer use tarot cards in my clinical work with adolescents, I might play Yu-Gi-Oh cards with them. I certainly would never smoke a cigarette with any teenager. I am obviously bound by present-day laws and ethical mandates in any type of therapeutic work with adolescents. The particular game, activity, or medium is not as important as the way in which it helps the clinician engage, build trust, and enable the teenager to communicate his concerns.

THEORIES OF NONTRADITIONAL WORK WITH ADOLESCENTS: PLAY AND EXPERIENTIAL LEARNING

Play in infancy and childhood has long been recognized as a pivotal part of emotional development. Perhaps the most influential theorist in this area was D. W. Winnicott. Winnicott came from what is now known as the British object relations school along with several other key figures including Melanie Klein, Ronald Fairbairn, Harry Guntrip, and others. Object relations theory's monumental contribution was in detailing how the internalization of aspects of the other in infancy helps to form the basis of the self. The end result of this emotional process is *object constancy:* the young child's ability to self-soothe and feel relatively safe and secure when alone. In his article "Transitional Objects and Transitional Phenomena" (1953), Winnicott details how the ability to play in a safe and secure good-enough holding environment enables the infant to create a transitional object that serves the purpose of temporarily soothing it in times of stress and anxiety. A transitional object can be anything (teddy bear, blanket, pacifier, toy) that is created or found by the infant to serve the purpose of stress reduction and soothing when a caretaker is unavailable. Play becomes the process through which all children can create transitional objects and gain emotional mastery over their world.

In childhood and even adolescence, human beings are learning how to manage their emotions, understand themselves, and find a way in which to communicate the thoughts and feelings surrounding the developmental process to others. Young children are not as able as adults to understand their cognitive and emotional issues and communicate them verbally. Language acquisition is a developmental process. It begins with early attuned attachment and develops through a complex cognitive, emotional, and experiential process inherent in the child's secure relationships with others (Greenspan & Shankar, 2006). The young child learns how to manage his emotional, cognitive, and experiential selves through play. Play becomes the essential vehicle through which children gain a sense of mastery in their world, even before they acquire language. It is this process that is utilized in play therapy with children and nontraditional work with many adolescents (Applegate, 1984).

When children play, they are acting out different types of roles or scenarios in life in order to experience the thoughts, emotions, and activity essential to master them. Children's play is often an unconscious metaphor of real-life challenges or conflicts. A small child may not be able to articulate the anger she feels about her parents' divorce, but she certainly can demonstrate it symbolically through play. An eight-year-old girl might not be able to verbally discuss the frustration, anger, and confusion she feels when mommy and daddy leave her home, but she can certainly play that conflict out symbolically in her use of a dollhouse. The small child may have no clue that she is symbolically enacting her family's conflict through play, but the intensity of emotion she demonstrates in her play not only is diagnostically important but serves the purpose of helping her release some of the emotions she is struggling to manage in her world. The play therapist in this scenario does not have to interpret the meaning of this play to the child; she feels better just being able to act it out experientially. This process is also the essence of nontraditional work with adolescents.

DAVID KOLB'S THEORY OF EXPERIENTIAL LEARNING

David Kolb (1984) proposed a four-stage theory of experiential learning that is also an important element in understanding nontraditional work with adolescents. (1) The experiential learner has a specific experience. (2) This experience gives the learner the opportunity for reflection. (3) The insight that comes from those reflections forms the basis for further action (4) and examination. Experiential learning is an essential part of the learning process and takes place not only in childhood play but also in any form of recreational activity.

Although adolescents in general do not play the way young children play, they still use experiential activities to work out many of the cognitive and emotional challenges of life. The hobbies, sports, and academic and recreational activities that teenagers choose to become involved in reflect their emotional and cognitive makeup. Engaging in some of those activities with adolescents will allow us to learn more about them, just as young children let us know about them through their symbolic play. When adolescent clients are either unwilling or unable to verbalize their thoughts and emotions in a traditional clinical process, engaging in activities with them can be an important alternative or even adjunctive part of the therapeutic endeavor. Practitioners from many disciplines and professional settings are drawn to these types of interventions with adolescents because they intuitively recognize their therapeutic value and symbolic importance—just like play therapy with children.

COMPREHENSIVE CASE EXAMPLE

A case example will help to illuminate this discussion. Many years ago in my agency work experience I encountered a trying young man named Bill. Bill was about thirteen years old when I first met him. At the time, I was trying to develop an activity group for junior high school students through my agency. The purpose of the group was to help junior high students who were having emotional difficulty in school. The group was to serve as a non-threatening environment in which to meet and discuss thoughts and feelings about their lives in a safe recreational setting. I interviewed all prospective candidates individually in order to make sure they would be appropriate for the group. Bill was referred by his school counselor, but he was very interested in the group. He seemed pleasant enough in my screening interview and I decided to accept him as a member. I soon learned to regret that decision.

Our colorful van picked up the six group members (boys and girls) at their homes after school and brought them to the youth agency, where they met in our agency drop-in activity room for group sessions. The group usually met for about an hour and spent the time playing games such as pool, foosball, and video games and discussing general issues in the group members' lives. All of the members seemed to benefit from the group except Bill. Virtually every week Bill caused some type of problem in the group. If it wasn't teasing the female members of the group on our drive to the agency, it was harassing group members as they tried to play games in the center. Bill seemed obsessed with interfering in the group members' lives. He also seemed to be unable to keep himself from doing so. After many attempts to work with Bill both in and outside the group, my co-leader and I decided to remove Bill from the group. Bill could not function in the group without causing continual conflict.

I did not see Bill for several months after kicking him out of the activity group. However, he eventually contacted me once again for services. Bill had been arrested for vandalism of community property (blowing up a lamp-post) and was mandated to come for weekly individual therapy. Bill wanted to see me for counseling since he knew me, and I decided hesitantly to take him on as a counseling case. Bill lived some distance from our agency, and both of his parents worked, so I agreed to pick him up at his home for our weekly counseling sessions.

Bill was what one might call a resistant client. He had a difficult time ver-balizing his thoughts and feelings in sessions and beyond that didn't quite seem to know what to talk about. I tried in vain to help him verbalize these things in session, but Bill squirmed awkwardly in the counseling room and clearly had tremendous difficulty communicating in any sort of traditional manner. Out of desperation and my own frustration, I decided to try a dif-ferent approach with him.

I knew that Bill enjoyed video games. I also knew that there was a video arcade just a few short miles from his home. I decided that we would spend our weekly time at the arcade. Bill was obviously much more comfortable playing video games during our sessions, but an interesting thing happened as we entered into this new arrangement. On our way to and from the video arcade each week, Bill began to open up in his discussions about many dif-ferent aspects of his life. He would talk about school, family, peers, hobbies and interests, and so on. As long as we didn't have to face each other one on one in a counseling office, Bill was open and forthcoming in talking about many different areas of his life. Even though the majority of our weekly ses-sion time was spent in the video arcade playing games, the real work seemed to happen in the fifteen or twenty minutes that we traveled to and from the arcade.

As I got to know Bill's world through our weekly travels, I learned a great deal about him and his background. When I would pick Bill up at his home, he would often invite me in for a soda. I got a chance to see his home environment and get a sense of the emotional feel of it. Every time I entered Bill's home, no one was home, and all of the shades were drawn. His house seemed very disorganized, dirty, and depressing. When we did talk about his family, Bill didn't seem to have much of a relationship with either of his par-ents. He was the youngest child in the family, and his two older sibs had long since moved out of the home. Bill was truly alone and isolated. I began to realize that he was a child who truly needed to feel connected to others and appreciated by them. I wondered whether his delinquent behavior was per-haps a reaching out for some type of structure or concern from someone in his life.

Because Bill was mandated to come for counseling, he was a captive audience for me in our nontraditional counseling arrangement. As time progressed, Bill began to use our relationship to introduce difficult dilemmas for my advice or consideration. It seemed almost every week Bill would casually mention some type of crime he was contemplating. These crimes would range from minor theft to vandalism or major robbery. At first I was alarmed that Bill would soon be arrested again and perhaps be sent to detention. I soon discovered, however, that Bill was testing me with his plans.

Each week that Bill would mention a potential crime he had planned, I would explore the nature of the plan, why he wanted to do it, who was involved, and what he wanted to get out if it. Bill would always reassure me that his crime was foolproof and that there was no way he would be caught. Silently I was very nervous for Bill, but outwardly I didn't show it. Instead, I intuitively responded by encouraging him to really think about the consequences of his actions and what might happen if he did get caught or arrested. In addition, I also told him that I really cared about him and did not want to see him go to jail. Bill's response to my concerns was always to minimize the risks and assure me that he would be fine.

Between the sessions I would wait anxiously to see if Bill had been arrested. I initially anticipated that I would get a phone call from either his probation officer or his family informing me that Bill indeed was now in jail. Interestingly, that never happened. When I would pick Bill up each week and casually ask him about his plans from the week before, Bill would inform me that something had fallen through and he decided not to rob, steal, or vandalize. I began to realize that Bill was using our sessions to test my concern for him. Did I care about his safety, his life, his future? Of course I genuinely did, and Bill used our time together to continually test and validate that fact.

Another piece of important information about this case was crucial to its outcome. Bill of course knew about our agency's drop-in center, "The Room" (my creative title). The Room was open several nights a week to any junior high or high school student. The drop-in center contained a pool table, foosball table, video games, and a TV, as well as a stereo music system. It was staffed by professionals and trained volunteers. Adolescents coming to The Room could do pretty much whatever they wanted as long as they didn't break the main rules of the center. Teenagers could not smoke in The Room; they had to go outside. They needed to sign up for activities, and they also had to use respectful language with staff and others. There was also no violence allowed. Bill really took a liking to The Room.

He came to the drop-in center almost every night it was open. He really enjoyed the opportunities to play all of the games in the center. Unfortunately, he was a major troublemaker. Bill continually broke all of the rules and was constantly being kicked out of The Room. When a teenager was kicked out of the drop-in center, he had to meet with professional staff to talk about what happened and what needed to be different in order to be allowed back in the center. Bill was always having these types of talks. It seemed as if both staff and teenagers really didn't like Bill very much. That didn't stop him from coming to the center, however. He seemed to thrive on the constant attention from staff and enjoyed being so important.

Our agency also provided many teenagers with recreational activities that focused on outdoor experiences. These usually consisted of camping trips or wilderness activities in upper Michigan or Wisconsin. Professional staff was trained in what were called outdoor adventure experiences. The purpose was to expose adolescents to experiential activities that would challenge them to grow emotionally through therapeutic recreational means. Groups of teenagers supervised by trained therapists would test their ability to face unfamiliar surroundings and work together as a group in order to learn self-discipline and cooperation. These groups were highly successful and of course very nontraditional from a clinical standpoint. These types of experiences were also designed for adolescents who were having difficult times in their lives. Bill signed up for almost every one of these activities, much to the dismay of the professional staff leading them.

Virtually every camping trip or outdoor experience that Bill went on became a crisis for the entire group. Bill was uncooperative, teased people, talked back to staff, and so on. This was a difficult issue to manage in the middle of nowhere with a group of eight to ten adolescents. Bill often spent the majority of time on these trips confined to his tent for some type of major rules violation. For example, one night around the campfire Bill pulled out a small pocket knife (obviously not allowed) and asked staff, "What are you going to do about it?" Staff continually wondered why Bill wanted to come on these trips if he was going to cause so much trouble. He certainly didn't appear to be getting anything out of them. Besides, the other teenagers seemed to hate him.

A wonderful part of this agency was the fact that all staff—traditional clinical counselors, drop-in center workers, as well as outdoor adventure staff—always consulted together about the teenagers involved in the agency. Weekly staff meetings were partially organized around the therapeutic staffing of many of our problem kids. Bill was discussed continuously. From those discussions came the realization that Bill was working through something in his behavior on all levels—with me in therapy, with the drop-in staff, and on the outdoor trips. We worked as a staff to provide Bill with a comprehensive nontraditional approach geared toward providing structure, building his self-esteem, managing his impulses, and helping him feel a sense of purpose and identity. This took quite a long time, probably several frustrating years, but Bill did improve.

Gradually, Bill began to become civil not only to staff, but also to the other adolescents whom he interacted with in many different settings. As he adopted more positive behaviors, he was rewarded with positive accolades and privileges from staff. Bill actually became somewhat of a model drop-in kid over time. In therapy with me, he learned that I really cared about him and was worried about his future. He began to abandon his weekly plans of crime and instead started developing and talking about other, more constructive interests in life. These initially came from his outdoor experiences at the agency. Over time and after going on many trips in which he had to be reprimanded over and over again, Bill became one of the strongest youth leaders in the outdoor adventure program. He learned to develop a more positive self-image by working through his conflictual relationships with professional staff and fellow adolescents on all levels in the agency. His improvement was a collaborative agency effort. It wasn't just his therapy with me, or his time in the drop-in center, or his involvement in outdoor adventure programming; Bill needed all of those pieces in order to help him work through his anger and sense of isolation to ultimate acceptance by others. This type of case is an excellent example of the advantages of nontraditional therapeutic work with adolescents.

What is Bill doing now? That's a very interesting part of his story. Bill graduated from high school after I left the agency. I had taken a position as executive director at a nearby suburban youth and family agency very similar to the one I had just left. This agency was much smaller than the one I had come from, and my role as director included doing clinical work, supervision, fund-raising, and community work, as well as shoveling the driveway in the winter and many other odds and ends. Bill had joined the Navy and came back to my old agency to visit me. When he heard I no longer worked there, he traveled some distance to pay me a visit at my new place of employment.

I was trying to fix a broken screen door when Bill drove up in his car. He watched me struggle with the repairs for a while and finally offered to help. I told him I could handle it, but Bill insisted on doing the work. As we talked (again over an activity), Bill told me how well his life was going. He loved the Navy and had done quite well in his time there. Bill informed me he had become a Navy Seal. Bill's specialty was demolitions. He was now being paid by the government to destroy things. Bill loved this new work. He had sublimated his previously destructive behavior into a reputable career. Sublimation is considered one of the highest and most mature forms of emotional functioning one can attain. After all of his difficulties in adolescence, Bill had finally found purpose and comfort in life.

CASE DISCUSSION

Although this complex case example dates back some years, the basic principles are still highly relevant in present-day therapeutic work with adolescents. Contemporary practice settings such as schools, mental health settings, residential and group facilities, and even private practice environments may not allow for open-ended and unstructured approaches to nontraditional therapeutic work with adolescents. Fear of litigation and other contemporary legal concerns may have restricted the freedom practitioners used to have in implementing more creative recreational approaches with adolescents. However, even within the bounds of most contemporary ethical and legal constraints, most creative practitioners can still utilize a variety of forms of "nontraditional" interventions and activities. For instance, although it may be against agency/school policy to transport a teenager in your car to a fast-food restaurant for more nonthreatening conversation, one might still be able to engage with an adolescent around a game of Uno in session. If a clinician has access to a computer, she may be able to play computer games that challenge the teenager to problem-solve or examine the meaning of a conflict. Appropriate use of the Internet to surf the Web with a teenager can be a useful educational tool as well as enable the practitioner to enter into the teenager's world and learn about his friends and interests. Listening to music can be a valuable addition and adjunctive piece of the therapeutic relationship with teenagers. There are countless other examples of these less controversial therapeutic techniques. The reader is encouraged to seek them out through the bibliography of this text (Schaefer & Cangelosi, 1993).

BASIS OF PRACTICE

The basis for nontraditional approaches to working with adolescents has remained primarily at the theoretical level (Bratton & Ray, 2000; Kolb & Fry, 1975). Practitioners working with adolescent clients, whether individually or in groups, continue to utilize many of the approaches and techniques discussed in this chapter. The case study approach presented in this chapter demonstrates the intuitive, practice wisdom, and theoretical rationale for incorporating recreational, play, and other nontraditional interventions with adolescent clients like Bill. Although admittedly this case is anecdotal, the method involved was thoughtful, rigorous, and based upon theory, practice wisdom, and intuitive knowledge of the situation. The outcome was obviously successful. Further research in the area of play therapy techniques and recreational approaches to adolescents may yield promising results at the validated knowledge stage.

SUMMARY

This chapter has discussed the importance of nontraditional work with adolescent clients. The theoretical underpinnings of play therapy and experiential learning help the practitioner understand the necessity of utilizing a variety of creative approaches in forming trusting therapeutic relationships with those teenagers who are not able to benefit from more traditional psychotherapeutic approaches to practice. Activity, metaphor, and symbolism combined with carefully devised experiential exercises help to form the basis for a strong therapeutic approach to adolescent practice. The case of Bill helps to illustrate the essential interplay of these crucial elements in comprehensive collaborative clinical treatment. This type of creative and intuitive therapeutic work with adolescents is one of the most essential and effective tools of any clinician working with this population.

RECOMMENDED RESOURCES
Readings

Jeffrey Applegate, "Transitional Phenomena in Adolescence: Tools for Negotiating the Second Individuation," *Clinical Social Work Journal* 12, no. 3 (1984): 233–243. This is a wonderful article emphasizing the way adolescents revisit the transitional object phenomena from childhood in adolescence.

S. Bratton & D. Ray, "What Research Shows about Play Therapy," *International Journal of Play Therapy* 9, no. 1 (2000): 47–88. This is a good empirical article on the value of play therapy.

Monit Cheung, *Therapeutic Games and Guided Imagery* (Chicago: Lyceum Books, 2006). This book covers some of the techniques of play and games that can be used from a therapeutic perspective.

D. A. Kolb & R. Fry, "Toward an Applied Theory of Experiential Learning," in C. Cooper, ed., *Theories of Group Process* (London: John Wiley, 1975). This is a good source on the theory of experiential learning.

Charles E. Schaefer & Donna M. Cangelosi, *Play Therapy Techniques* (Northvale, NJ: Jason Aronson, 1993). This book is a solid reference for play therapy techniques that can be applied to work with adolescents.

D. W. Winnicott, *Playing and Reality* (New York: Routledge, 1971). This is a classic collection of Winnicott's essays on the importance of play as a developmental accomplishment.

Film/Television/Media

The Karate Kid (1984). This film demonstrates the power of sublimation and nontraditional approaches to healing.

Internet

http://www.infed.org/biblio/b-explrn.htm This is a good site for content on experiential learning.

8

Culturally Competent Practice with Adolescents and Families

Adolescent clients come from a variety of racial and ethnic backgrounds. It is incumbent upon the clinician not only to be aware of different cultures but also to be able to work with them in what is now called a culturally competent manner. Cultural competence is a professional characteristic that is necessary for all practitioners, regardless of professional discipline. Social workers, psychologists, and other mental health professionals must be aware of their own cultural biases as well as those of the clients with whom they work in order to provide effective clinical services to them. But what exactly is cultural competence, and how does the clinician work toward attaining and utilizing it in his practice with adolescents?

CULTURALLY COMPETENT PRACTICE WITHIN THE CONTEXT OF IDENTITY FORMATION

At the present time there is no consensus on the definition of cultural competence (Weaver, 2005). There seems to be general agreement that it consists of an awareness both of one's own cultural biases and of the need to make an honest attempt to understand the client's world from her perspective. These sound like obvious principles inherent in all clinical work. The problem is the subtle and indirect ways both clinicians and clients misunderstand or misinterpret each other's culture. The movie *Crash* puts forth the message that we are all capable of prejudice and distortion. What is important in dealing with that issue is to recognize that each human being is unique, regardless of cultural heritage.

There may be some very general cultural traits or qualities that a certain racial or ethnic group may possess, but even within any particular group, there is tremendous variation based upon a variety of factors including socioeconomic status, spirituality, gender, education, and—probably the most significant one—life experience (McGoldrick, Giordano, & Garcia-Preto, 2006). Cultural competence requires that the practitioner continuously work toward an understanding of self and other in the clinical setting. This particular issue presents some highly challenging features for those

96

clinicians working with teenagers from diverse backgrounds (Stampley & Slaght, 2004).

One of the key issues in adolescence is the search for identity. Teenagers from minority cultures have at least a twofold challenge in that regard. They must come to terms with their own racial or ethnic identity while at the same time struggling to figure out who they are within the society at large. Some have argued that coming to terms with one's own racial/ethnic identity is perhaps the most crucial factor in feeling a sense of satisfaction with self and the world (Muuss, 1996; Phinney, 1991). Only once that has happened can the adolescent move toward the later challenges in life. True intimacy with another, for example, can occur only when one has embraced a sense of one's own racial and ethnic minority status. Of course identity formation is occurring from the moment of birth and social interaction, but true identity formation can happen only when one is capable of abstract thought. That process happens in adolescence.

In working with minority youth, the culturally competent clinician must remember that her teenage client is coming to grips with who he is in a majority culture. The racial and ethnic background of the clinician can be both a help and a hindrance in working with minority youth (Boyle & Springer, 2001; Chung & Bemak, 2002). A Caucasian therapist certainly cannot know what it is like to grow up as a minority youth, but neither can a clinician from that same minority group. A minority counselor's own racial or ethnic experiences may actually cloud her judgment or empathy when working with minority youth from the same background. Culturally competent practice requires that all clinicians regardless of their own diverse backgrounds and experiences remain open and continually aware of their potential blind spots in working with all clients.

Perhaps the most important element in identity formation for minority persons, however, is understanding the inherent societal oppression and discrimination that most likely will be experienced throughout their lives. This profound power differential is a key force in identity formation that individuals from the majority culture are not aware of in their life development (Zayas, 2001). An astute, culturally competent clinician must be aware of these contemporary and historical issues as well as utilize exquisite timing and judgment in deciding if, how, and when these very real and powerful issues can be dealt with in treatment.

One chapter on cultural competence cannot possible capture the entire range of information or technique necessary to work with diverse adolescents. The reader is encouraged to explore the recommended readings and Web sites at the end of this chapter for more comprehensive information. Monica McGoldrick, Joe Giordano, and Nydia Garcia-Preto's classic book *Ethnicity and Family Therapy* (2006) is an excellent resource in this area.

The following case involving a middle-class suburban African American adolescent touches on some of the complex issues of identity formation when influenced by racial, ethnic, and socioeconomic factors. It is also an excellent example of the challenges faced by clinicians who may not have a great deal of experience working with clients from racial and ethnic backgrounds different from their own.

CASE EXAMPLE

Karl was a thirteen-year-old African American boy referred to me for therapy by his school social worker. The presenting concern centered on Karl's difficulties in seventh grade. Karl was performing poorly in school and seemed to his teachers and school personnel to be withdrawn socially from his peers, both in and outside class. The school social worker suggested to Karl's mother that he might benefit from some individual counseling.

Karl was the youngest in a family of four. He and his three siblings were all originally foster children with the parents who eventually adopted them. None of the children were biologically related. Only Karl was African American. His two older brothers and older sister were Caucasian. He and his siblings came from physically abusive families. Karl experienced severe emotional and physical neglect during his first few years of life. He also witnessed a good deal of physical violence and drug-using behavior on the part of his biological mother. I learned about this history from Karl's adoptive mother. She explained to me that she did not think Karl had any memory of it because he was so young, probably between the ages of birth to three. She also explained that Karl originally was placed with her around the age of three but was temporarily returned to his biological mother's care at age four and promptly removed again within the year because of further neglect.

According to Karl's adoptive mother, Karl was extremely delayed when he came to live with her. Although he was three years of age he did not speak and was hesitant to engage with anyone in the family. As Karl spent more time with his adoptive family, he began to attach more to his parents and siblings. However, his adoptive mother remembers him always being a little cautious in his social interactions.

Karl's adoptive parents, Pat and Pete, were in the process of divorce when I first met them. Pat was particularly concerned about how the divorce was going to affect the children, since they had suffered so much disruption in their early lives. The two oldest children had already moved out of the family home. Only Karl and his older brother Adam, sixteen, still lived at home. Pat was worried about how to help both of her sons deal with the pending separation and divorce.

In order to give a complete picture of Karl's situation, I will discuss his case using the practice formulation presented in chapter 2.

1. *Is there any evidence of "constitutional" factors that may have contributed to the present situation? If so, how have they affected the adoles-*

cent? It appears as if Karl may have suffered tremendous trauma and neglect in his early life. From a neurological standpoint, it is likely that he may have been unable to achieve the consistent and adequate attachment relationship necessary to help him form healthy and stable neural networks in the areas of emotional and cognitive development. This may have resulted in his inability to relate to others in a more emotionally healthy manner. As a result, Karl is emotionally stunted in his social development. This is evidenced by his adoptive mother's account of Karl's language and social difficulties when he first came to her. It may also account for some of the problems Karl was having in school, both socially and educationally, at the time of the referral.

2. *What level of psychosocial development do you believe the adolescent has achieved? Do you believe the adolescent is fixated or regressed at all? What factors lead you to believe this may be the case?* From a chronological standpoint, Karl is in Erikson's stage of identity vs. role confusion. However, from the history presented by his adoptive mother one can surmise that he may have had difficulty in all previous stages. By the time he was placed with Pat, Karl had already suffered severe trauma. All of his early developmental tasks would have been compromised by this abuse. For instance, from a trust vs. mistrust standpoint, Karl had learned that his world was not reliable or safe. This may have resulted in a heavy reliance on the primitive fight-or-flight response inherent in the amygdala part of the brain. Karl's limbic system was not able to develop sufficiently owing to the fact that there were no reliable caretakers to interact with in his environment. He may not have been able to develop the initial capacities to self-soothe that most normal infants acquire in their relationships with primary caretakers.

From an autonomy vs. shame and doubt and initiative vs. guilt standpoint, Karl again may have been compromised or limited owing to the emotional neglect he had experienced. He did not come to live with Pat until the age of three, and by that time he probably had already suffered a great deal of neglect that severely inhibited his neurological development. From a practical viewpoint this could help to explain Karl's socially withdrawn manner in his new adoptive family. He did not learn how to become independent because he did not have consistent adults to interact with who could encourage that part of him. These time periods are also when language acquisition occurs. Attuned mirroring from primary caretakers is the precursor to the development of language. Karl's inconsistent, neglectful, and absent early caretaking probably accounts for his difficulty in school later in life.

Erikson's industry vs. inferiority stage emphasizes not only the development of skills and talents but perhaps more importantly the ability to manage emotions in a more mature manner, as well as to relate to peers. Clearly because of his earlier deficits, Karl was unable to develop these social abilities. This was evident in the presenting information from both the school social worker and Karl's mother Pat.

Thus, Karl's emotional difficulties and deficits in all previous stages of development left him extremely vulnerable as he approached his chronological stage of identity vs. role confusion.

3. *What type of attachment did the adolescent have with his primary caretakers, and how did these early developmental periods affect his present relationships with family, peers, and significant others?* Based upon the limited amount of information we have from Pat, one might suspect that Karl developed an avoidant attachment or perhaps an anxious/avoidant attachment with his biological mother. She seems not to have been available to Karl in any consistent way, which may have led Karl to fend for himself. Karl may have learned to withdraw as a means of emotional survival. This early attachment style seems to have evidenced itself in Karl's first experiences with his adoptive family as well as his difficulties in school.

4. *Why is the adolescent in need of service right now? Is he self-referred, or does someone else believe he needs help?* This question has already been addressed.

5. *Does the adolescent see himself as being conflicted or in need of help, despite the fact that he may not be self-referred? To what extent can he see his part in the situation? Does the adolescent have the capacity to be introspective and/or to view himself objectively? What is the extent of his observing ego?* When I first began to see Karl, I would have to say that he did not have much, if any, observing ego. He also did not really see the need for therapy. Karl described school as boring and did not appear to be concerned about his lack of peer relationships. He was pleasant in therapy but not very talkative. As a result most of our initial work was nontraditional, consisting of computer games and general nonintrusive discussions about family, peers, and school. As time went on however, Karl became much more verbal and did begin to demonstrate the capacity for an observing ego. Part of this ability was the result of his entering into puberty and Piaget's formal operations thought, and part was a result of the therapeutic relationship.

6. *Is the adolescent's defensive structure adaptive or maladaptive?* Karl's defenses and his use of them progressed in much the same way that his capacity for an observing ego developed. Initially he utilized some rather primitive ego defenses. Karl tended to deny his part in any difficulties and projected blame on others rather than taking any responsibility for his own thoughts, emotions, or actions. As he matured, however, and the therapy progressed, Karl became able to utilize defenses such as intellectualization, rationalization, and even some early forms of sublimation in his interactions with significant others.

7. *How would you assess the adolescent's family system, and how does it affect his present situation?* Karl's biological family system was probably

extremely enmeshed, with little if any emotional or physical boundaries. Communication was also probably nonexistent or abusive in nature. In short, during his very formative years, Karl learned not to talk or at least to stay out of the way.

Karl's adoptive family was a different story. When he was first adopted his parents were still married, although I suspect there was probably a good deal of tension in the marital relationship and, as a result, in the family in general. From my conversations with Pat, it appears as if she was actively involved with her adopted children, but her husband was more removed from the family. Pat seems to have been able to provide an emotionally stable family environment in which Karl could begin to feel secure and progress in his development. In my meetings with Karl and his mother, it is apparent that they both love and care a great deal for each other. Pat, however, is somewhat loose and hesitant to set firm limits with any of her children. This has resulted in some serious motivation problems for several of her male children. Pat's failure to help her children know the expectations of the real world through the provision of reasonable limits and expectations in the family seems to have resulted in a type of dependent functioning and lack of initiative in Karl. Given the horrible early lives her adopted children experienced and the estranged marriage Pat is in, emotional enmeshment and excessive permissiveness with her children are easy to understand. These family dynamics have affected Karl's ability to approach adolescent life with a sense of purpose and initiative.

8. *Are the adolescent's parents/caretakers invested and willing to recognize there might be a problem and help work on it?* Despite any ambivalence on Pat's part about taking a firmer stance with her children, she is extremely devoted to them and a very willing participant in the therapy process. Pat meets with me occasionally to discuss her interactions with Karl and the rest of the family. We brainstorm together about Karl, his schoolwork, his peer relationships, his family interactions, and even issues related to his racial identity. Karl's father is not interested in being involved in the treatment, although he consistently pays the fee without question. I have no sense of whether or not he is supportive of the therapy.

Pat is a highly intelligent woman in her early sixties. She has put tremendous energy into raising her children and is prepared to do whatever it takes to help Karl succeed in life. She also recognizes the important ways in which Karl's early experiences have shaped his later development. She can admit to her own lack of structure with Karl, which may have exacerbated his difficulties. In short, Pat is the ideal parent to work with in therapy.

9. *Are there particular issues of diversity that heavily influence the adolescent's situation?* Despite all the physical and emotional challenges Karl has faced in life, I believe that the development of his racial identity is

the pivotal part of treatment at the present time. Karl is a sixteen-year-old African American male living in a predominantly white upper-middle-class suburban community. He is one of only three black teenagers in his high school. Karl is well known but does not have a core group of people from his own race with which to identify. This factor can cause difficulties for him. On the one hand, Karl's identity has been shaped by the white community in which he grew up. His sense of self is that of a member of the white community. On the other hand, Karl is African American, complete with a family history that he is not aware of and perhaps is not even interested in knowing about. Finally, Karl is black. He looks different from his high school peers, except the two other black students. His physical appearance is a constant reminder to him and others that he has a different racial heritage. Karl resembles the actor Jamie Foxx, which certainly helps him in his social interactions in school, but he also is struggling with a sense of social isolation in regard to his unresolved racial identity.

10. *What environmental factors are relevant to this situation?* Karl lives in a fairly enriched environment. His adoptive family, although financially burdened by a recent divorce, is still able to provide Karl with virtually any type of resources he needs. Pat has set Karl up with a tutor and pays for his involvement in the school choir and sports activities. The community in which Karl lives has tremendous resources. Karl has ample opportunity to utilize many resources within it. On the other hand, Karl is African American. He stands out in this community. It is unclear how Karl is perceived by others and how his obvious difference in appearance may affect the way in which opportunities are available for him. How this important factor plays itself out in Karl's life remains to be seen.

11. *What resources are available to the adolescent in dealing with this situation? What are the adolescent's strengths?* Resources are plentiful, as discussed in question 10. Karl is a very charming, engaging, and attractive young man. I have seen him for several years now and have seen him move from an awkward early teenager into a handsome young man. He resembles both Denzel Washington and Jamie Foxx in his appearance. This is a real asset for Karl, and combined with his capacity to be charming and engaging, is a solid strength. Karl is a talented singer. He is involved in both his church and high school choir. Karl is a good athlete. Unfortunately, he is not able to consistently maintain a high enough grade point average to qualify for high school sports. Karl is active in informal sports with his peers. Karl is also resilient. He has weathered a tremendous amount of childhood neglect and abuse and is poised to move into young adult life.

12. *Based upon all of the factors above, what is your intervention plan, and what do you think the outcome might be?* Karl, his mother Pat, the high school, and I are working toward helping him get through school.

His major difficulties are in the areas of academic achievement and social interactions. Karl is also slowly becoming aware of his need to understand his racial identity. Therapy is focused overtly on helping him perform better in school and manage his behavior with peers, and more subtly on beginning to explore his racial identity.

CASE DISCUSSION

My work with Karl seems to have unfolded in two parts. When Pat first brought Karl to see me, he was socially withdrawn and struggling in school. He was also thirteen years old, in seventh grade, and just beginning adolescence. Through a prolonged and collaborative effort with the school, his family, and outside resources, Karl was able to ultimately perform well enough in school to graduate from junior high. Karl had extensive "outside" testing done to identify his learning difficulties, spent about half a school year being home-schooled by his mother Pat, returned to eighth grade, and was able to do well enough academically to graduate. (This situation will be discussed further in chapter 9.)

As Karl entered high school, a whole new set of issues presented themselves. Karl had grown about six inches in the year and a half since I first met him. When I first saw Karl, he had a little-boy look about him. He was short, stocky, and awkward in his mannerisms. Entering high school, Karl was almost taller than me (I'm five feet ten), had developed a solid muscular build, and was also beginning to interact much more with his peers.

He joined the high school football team and did quite well until he was forced to quit owing to a low grade point average. Karl became involved in the high school choir, since he had always loved music and had sung for years in his church choir. He also seemed to have no difficulty making friends. I soon found out, however, that much of Karl's new confidence was directly related to his drug use. This new development in Karl's life made it easier to interact with peers, but it also led to some difficult issues with them and with adult authorities.

Karl was a very withdrawn child and struggled with that issue throughout most of his elementary and junior high years. This developmental difficulty originated from early and chronic neglect and his abusive infancy. Karl did not develop the neurological capacities to self-soothe or negotiate successful social engagement with others. He improved somewhat through his life with his adoptive mother Pat but always struggled with that aspect of his personality.

Karl found drugs, especially alcohol and marijuana, helpful in buffering his social awkwardness and anxiety. From a neurological standpoint, these drugs performed the functions that he could not naturally do for himself because of his severe early deprivation. He quickly began to use drugs chronically, even during school hours, to help bolster his self-confidence and social interactions. This it did, but unfortunately this type of drug use also impaired his intellectual abilities. Karl began to have difficulty in all his high school classes. Eventually he got caught using.

Another negative aspect of Karl's drug usage was a lack of impulse control. Karl began having difficulty controlling his temper and also began to develop a reputation for himself as a fighter. He was proud of this newfound skill. Peers both feared and respected him. This was the beginning of a new identity for Karl. He struggled academically, was not allowed on the football team, felt awkward in social situations, and lived with a sense of social isolation. These new behaviors and the resulting identity that they brought with them were fueled by his drug use.

One might also suspect that Karl carried a great deal of rage within himself owing to the severe and chronic early abuse that he suffered. His new physical prowess, fueled by chronic drug abuse, affected Karl's impulse control. He was now able to direct his anger outward in his environment, rather than withdraw as he had done most of his life. Karl was finally beginning to feel some sense of control in his life, as well as an identity that others seemed to fear and respect.

Karl managed to stay out of trouble with the legal system through all of this activity. All of his disciplinary interactions were with school personnel. Fortunately as well, Karl also had several advocates in his life, the high school social worker, his former football coach, a high school dean, his mother, and me. Most of us recognized that Karl's behavior was a function of his past difficulties. As a result, everyone worked with Karl to help him manage these difficulties.

What I began to realize, however, was that there was also an implicit identity factor in all of Karl's problems. Karl was struggling with "identity vs. role confusion." Karl had no real-life African American role models to utilize in this search for identity. Karl had only stereotypical African American role models: sports figures and entertainers. I began to realize that Karl's heavy drug use also served as a buffer for his mounting confusion regarding his identity as a young African American male. He was using his physical prowess as both a defense and a skill to develop his identity. Using drugs and alcohol gave Karl a false sense of social confidence with which he could face anxiety-provoking social situations. He recounted countless parties in which he would get so drunk that he blacked out. His friends told him later that during these times he went around the room "making out" with all the white girls.

Karl's problem behaviors eventually came to the attention of the school authorities. He was put on an in-school drug abuse program in which he did mandatory weekly drug drops. In addition to his counseling with me, Karl also met weekly with a school drug counselor. His behavior and activity were now closely monitored. Karl responded well to this imposed structure. Although he faked his drug drops and continued to use, his drug use did decrease. It seems that these limits were in some ways reassuring for him. They served to do what his mother was unable to do—set firm and clear limits for him.

With these limits in place, and my new awareness that Karl's drug use and behavior were also related to his racial identity development, the therapy progressed. Karl and I began to talk more about his blackness. He was proud of the fact that girls found him attractive. He even said, "White girls like attractive black guys, and they ask you out!" Obviously this was a one-dimensional aspect of his black identity, but it served as a focus for discussion. For the first time, Karl could and wanted to talk about his racial identity with me. He shared with me how he could imitate white girls, and he did hysterical impersonations of his peers in session. Karl was truly beginning to come to grips with aspects of his diversity. He, of course, knew he was not white and that his peers saw him and related to him in at least some ways as a black male. Karl began to spend time sorting these issues out with me in therapy.

Although I had no idea what it must be like to grow up black like Karl in a virtually all-white suburban community, I had a history with him. We had shared many experiences in his life, and I had helped him develop more effective ways of getting along with others. Our history together enabled each of us to break through any racial barriers that might have inhibited progress in therapy. This is what culturally competent practice is about. It comes from an ability to suspend judgment and work with a client from his own perspective (Chung & Bemak, 2002).

Karl still struggles in his life. He still uses substances occasionally to bolster his self-esteem. However, he does not rely on them to function. As a result, his fighting has stopped. He has better impulse control. He also recognizes how using can impair his judgment. But most importantly, he is beginning to examine his racial identity in a white culture.

There is much more work to be done if Karl is going to come to grips with his identity as an African American. But that journey has to happen at Karl's pace. He may want to reconnect with his birth family. He may want to seek out other black peers with similar circumstances. These are issues that I am well aware of but will work on only as Karl needs to work on them.

BASIS OF PRACTICE

The concept of cultural competence is a relatively recent one and has been most researched in the social work literature, owing in part to that profession's emphasis on diversity education and practice. Intuitive, practice wisdom, and theoretical knowledge all point to the importance of self-awareness and real-life experiences with diverse others as the key to culturally competent clinical practice. Recent studies seem to emphasize this important fact (Stampley & Slaght, 2004).

SUMMARY

This chapter has examined cultural competence in the therapeutic relationships with adolescents. A skilled clinician must be aware of his biases as well as be open to understanding the unique ways in which all clients from diverse backgrounds shape their identity. Karl's case example is a special one. Karl is black but lives in a white community. His history is shaped by extensive trauma and abuse. That history inhibited his development in childhood and strongly influenced the ways in which he approached his search for identity in adolescence. Drugs and alcohol along with intense rage nearly destroyed Karl. Yet these behaviors ironically and temporarily buffered him in his search for identity. A careful and sensitive understanding and handling of the functions of these behaviors from the standpoint of racial identity formation were crucial for Karl's development. Culturally competent practice requires this kind of scrutiny and insight in order to truly understand and help clients from diverse backgrounds deal with their search for identity.

This case is but one example of the multitude of ways in which racial and ethnic identity is a focus of treatment with adolescents. It would have been easy for me to ignore the very real factor of Karl's racial and ethnic status in favor of focusing on the development of his adolescent identity in general. Karl is struggling with a number of issues that go beyond his sense of identity as an African American male. However, that piece of his identity is clearly missing. If Karl is going to come to grips with his identity, then he will have to sort out the extent to which being "black" is a part of it. For Karl, this may be a lonely journey, but he will not be truly alone in his search as long as I can be with him as he pursues it.

Many adolescents from racial and ethnic minorities struggle with identity formation in ways different from Karl's. Some live in neighborhoods where their own group predominates. For them, the issues will be different. They may have to decide the extent to which they want to incorporate a racial/ethnic identity that is similar to that of their peers or even their family. The struggle may also entail dealing with the very real yet often subtle racism and oppression that most young minority teens experience from the majority culture. Therapy for these adolescents will look quite different from Karl's therapy. Yet the search for identity is still at the core of the developmental task in adolescence.

This chapter has attempted to highlight the importance of cultural competence in therapeutic work with adolescents from diverse cultures. Racially and ethnically diverse teenagers have a dual task in their journey toward identity formation and emotional autonomy. They must come to grips not only with who they are but also with who they are as a racially or ethnically diverse youth in a predominantly white society. The culturally competent clinician must not only be adept at helping these diverse youth negotiate this process, but also keep keenly aware of the ways in which their own cultural biases may inhibit or interfere in an effective therapeutic outcome.

RECOMMENDED RESOURCES
Readings

D. P. Boyle & S. A. Springer, "Toward a Cultural Competence Measure for Social Work with Specific Populations," *Journal of Ethnic and Cultural Diversity in Social Work* 9 (2001): 53–71. This article proposes a model for measuring cultural competence in practice.

Ian A. Canino & Jeanne Spurlock, *Culturally Diverse Children and Adolescents: Assessment, Diagnosis and Treatment* (New York: Guilford Press, 1994). This text is a good reference for working with culturally diverse adolescents.

R. C.-Y. Chung & F. Bemak, "The Relationship of Culture and Empathy in Cross-cultural Counseling," *Journal of Counseling and Development* 80 (2002): 154–159. This article explores key therapeutic elements and their relationship to cross-cultural work.

Cheryl Stampley & Evelyn Slaght, *Cultural Competence as a Clinical Obstacle, Smith College Studies in Social Work* 74, no. 2 (2004). Smith studies always provide useful information for the therapeutic process.

D. W. Sue, A. E. Ivey, & P. B. Pedersen, *A Theory of Multicultural Counseling and Therapy* (Pacific Grove, CA: Brooks/Cole, 1996). This is a good source for multicultural work.

Hilary N. Weaver, *Explorations in Cultural Competence* (Belmont, CA: Thomson, 2005). This book helps to clarify the nature of cultural competence and its use in practice.

L. H. Zayas, "Incorporating Struggles with Racism and Ethnic Identity in Therapy with Adolescents," *Clinical Social Work Journal* 29 (2001): 361–373. This article examines how experiences with racism affect identity formation in adolescents.

Film/Television/Media

A Raisin in the Sun (1961), *A Patch of Blue* (1965), *Save the Last Dance* (2001), *Saved* (2004), *Crash* (2005). All these films present powerful pictures of significant aspects of the dynamics of diversity.

Internet

http://ns1.fga.com/aaaa/ This is the Web site for the American Association for Affirmative Action.

http://www.ksu.edu/ameth/naes/ This is the Web site for the National Association for Ethnic Studies

http://eric-web.tc.columbia.edu/families/other.html This Web site offers Internet resources for urban/minority families.

http://icg.stwing.upenn.edu/~konrad/iia.html This is the Web site of the International Interracial Association.

http://www.siu.edu/~jandris/HTMLDocuments/ANDRIS/diversity.html This Web site offers diversity resources.

http://www.naacp.org/ This is the Web site of the NAACP.

http://www.nul.org/ This is the Web site of the National Urban League.

http://www.rain.org/~kmw/aa.html This Web site offers information for African Americans.

http://www.bin.com This is the Web site for the Black Information Network.

http://web-dubois.fas.harvard.edu/ This is the Web site for the W. E. B. Du Bois Institute.

http://www.melanet.com/ This is the Web site for the National African Leadership Summit.

http://www.nclr.org This is the Web site for the National Council of La Raza.

http://www.latinolink.com/ This is the Web site for LatinoLink.

http://www.mit.edu:8001/afs/athena.mit.edu/ This Web site provides Asian American resources.

http://hanksville.phast.umass.edu/misc/NAresources.html This Web site is an index of Native American resources on the Net.

http://www.tucson.ihs.gov/ This is the Web site of the Indian Health Service.

9

Working with Adolescents in Schools: Academics, Behavior, and Social Networks as Diagnostic Indicators for Assessment and Intervention

The developmental importance of adolescents' involvement in schools has been discussed at length earlier in this text. The child's entry into the educational environment introduces her and her family to an entirely different arena of life. Children and their parents become scrutinized by educational professionals for the first time. The child and her entire family system experience the impact of societal pressures.

This situation affects not only the individual development of the child but also the family's development. The educational experience in childhood is different from that of the adolescent. As mentioned earlier in this book, adolescents go through a myriad of physical, cognitive, and emotional changes. These changes affect their ability to successfully negotiate their educational experiences. Understanding these factors in greater depth will help the clinician be more successful in working with teenagers and their families.

This chapter will examine the educational, relational, and experiential aspects of the school experience. School is a diagnostic microcosm for the clinician working with adolescents. Successes as well as difficulties in the areas mentioned above have profound effects on the development of the adolescent. We will explore the relevance of each of these areas to identity formation. The implications of difficulties in these areas will also be discussed. Traditional as well as nontraditional approaches to treatment in these areas will be addressed. Finally, the varied roles of professional practitioners in and outside of the school setting will be examined. Different roles require differential approaches with the adolescent in question. Successful work with adolescents in the schools demands a comprehensive under-standing of all of the above.

ACADEMICS

On a cognitive level, the move from elementary school to middle/junior high and high school is a dramatic shift on a number of levels. Most school set-tings in junior high and middle school require the young teenager to move from classroom to classroom throughout the school day. He is no longer in one classroom all day long, with the same teacher. He is now exposed to many teachers, many rooms, and a more structured and autonomous sched-ule. This is a major shift in life. I can remember when I first entered high school (I was in Catholic elementary school through eighth grade), the schedule was very stressful. Not only was I in a new physical environment with older adolescents, I also had to learn a new schedule and be on time to class, or else!

The work requirement in junior high and high school is quantitatively and qualitatively different from that in elementary school. Not only is there more work to do, but the work is more demanding and complex. Fortu-nately, most adolescents are or have moved into Piaget's formal operations stage of cognitive development by that time. This means that they are cognitively capable of understanding and working on more abstract and complex material. Unfortunately, those teenagers who are cognitively chal-lenged may begin to experience an even greater disparity between them-selves and their contemporaries. This can have both educational and social consequences.

The emotional changes that adolescents are experiencing as a result of puberty can dramatically affect the ways in which they react to the demands of the new academic rigor. The new interest in romantic relationships also has a tendency to draw them away from education. Social relationships often have an increased importance as well. It is a rare teenager who can excel at academics and social relationships. Usually one or the other suffers. This is important information for the clinician and the parents of teenagers. It is not an excuse but helpful information in deciding on a course of action in treatment.

Another very important factor in the adolescent's approach to sec-ondary education is the way in which her family reacts to it. Children are often viewed as extensions of their parents. As a result, parents may have an unusually strong investment in their adolescent's middle and high school education. Any success or failure has the danger of being interpreted (of course unconsciously) as the parent's success or failure. This may have the unfortunate effect of putting tremendous pressure on the teenager. It may even lead to what Erikson called "foreclosure" of identity (Marcia, 1966).

Identity foreclosure results when an adolescent feels "compelled" to develop an identity that is based on the expectations of his caretakers to the exclusion of his own ideology. This results in an "empty" sense of self in adult life because the adolescent has prematurely closed his identity development. This emptiness can lead to a delayed identity formation and in the extreme perhaps involve depression, addiction, and unhappiness. Most parents never consciously impose their own expectations on their children. They give them guidance and support and hope that they are successful. It is only when adolescents do not feel free to pursue or even struggle with the development of their own choices that identity foreclosure may take shape. Clyde, the client I discussed in chapter 4, is a good example of an adolescent who is struggling with identity foreclosure. It is not a matter of blaming his parents; for whatever reasons, Clyde has been leading the academic life that he felt he should lead, rather than finding his own life.

Parents and families may also assume the opposite position in regard to their adolescent's education. Although teenagers are moving toward a more autonomous approach in managing many areas of their life, they still need to feel that their caretakers are concerned and invested in their education. A number of theories can address this situation, but self psychology might argue that the teenager's need for mirroring and idealizing requires that his caretakers show interest in his secondary education. Most adolescents are not capable of going it totally alone throughout junior high and high school; they need to be supported by adults that care about them. If family caretakers are not able or willing to provide this type of support, the adolescent may experience a sense of loss and isolation that could lead to poor academic performance regardless of intellectual potential. Therapists and practitioners both in and outside of the school can serve this function in a variety of ways through both traditional and nontraditional approaches to treatment. Individual, family, and group interventions can be extremely helpful in getting the adolescent back on track.

Academics, then, from an adolescent development standpoint, constitute a wide range of important issues and factors. The astute practitioner working either in or outside of the school must be aware of how this important element of development can affect the teenager, her family, and the entire school environment. It is also crucial to be mindful of the multitude of mitigating factors that can influence the educational experience in both a positive and a negative manner.

PEERS/RELATIONSHIPS

There are several different theories that are helpful in understanding the adolescent's need for a different type of peer relationship in junior high and high school. Adolescent boys and girls are drawn to potential romantic partners owing to the physical changes in their bodies. I can remember quite clearly when I became interested in girls. It was as if I had never seen them before. Prior to adolescence, I thought of girls as almost an annoyance. Suddenly, I found myself feeling sexually attracted to them without understanding what that feeling was or why I was having it. I could do nothing about it. I was going to feel it whether I wanted to or not. This new experience is true for the adolescent that is gay, lesbian, bisexual, or heterosexual. It is a part of physical development that affects his or her entire worldview.

As the adolescent begins the process of what Erikson referred to as identity formation, the peer group takes center stage. In early childhood identity is shaped primarily from the primary caretakers and extended family. Many different theoretical perspectives help the clinician understand this phenomenon. With the onset of adolescence, however, there is a move toward relative autonomy from the primary familial structure and a greater emotional investment in relationships outside of the family. Both parents and clinicians have experienced the intense denial of family involvement and a greater interest in spending time with peers. Why would that be?

Peers represent at least two very important developmental factors for the typical adolescent. First, peers serve what Kohut and the self psychologists might call a twinship need. By spending time on and investing emotional energy in building relationships with others who are like them, adolescents not only feel more secure but also begin to identify with some of the characteristics of their peers. This identification may solidify into an aspect of their identity. Adolescents may belong to several peer groups over the course of their teenage development, and the very act of being involved in those peer groups or cliques shapes their emotional lives or identity. We choose who we are based upon a number of important factors, including constitution, family relationships, and culture. But the initial identification that comes from belonging to a peer group begins the process of adult identity formation.

Second, the peer group serves as an important emotional buffer in allowing the adolescent to separate from her family. Adolescents are not quite adults, but they are also not quite children anymore. As they move further away emotionally from their parents and family, teenagers still need a strong source of emotional support. The peer group serves that purpose. In a sense, it is a new family, complete with its own norms, values, philosophy, style of dress, and culture. Acceptance or rejection from a particular group holds great meaning for many adolescents. The social hierarchy in any middle or high school can have profound impact on the adolescent. Her perceived place in that hierarchy and the relative status, emotional security, or isolation inherent in that position can drastically affect the teenager's sense of self.

Thus, practitioners who work with adolescents must pay close attention to peer associations. Peer problems that adolescent clients bring to their high school counselor, school social worker, or outpatient therapist may seem superficial in nature. However, from a developmental standpoint, they are crucial aspects of budding identity formation. Each important encounter with a valued peer has profound implications for the adolescent's development of character and identity.

As adolescents become more emotionally and intellectually sophisticated, their peer interactions also become more complex. Teenagers in their middle and high school years struggle with issues related to friendship, alliances, boundaries, compromise, and control. If the clinician in or outside of the school recognizes that each of these seemingly simple problems can have a profound impact on identity formation and the ability to form successful interpersonal relationships in life, he will be able to approach them with the seriousness they deserve. Adolescents are learning how to develop the interpersonal skills that will guide them throughout their lives by interacting each day with their peers in and outside of the classroom setting.

BEHAVIORS

Sometimes adolescents have a difficult time managing and controlling their behavior in the school environment. The most extreme examples of this difficulty usually result in specialized behavioral placements within or outside the school setting. Most of the so-called BD (behavioral disordered) teenagers are worked with through a combination of behavioral and educational interventions. The etiology of these problems is complex, and there are a multitude of factors that contribute to their development and continuation.

Infants and children are not born with the ability to soothe themselves or manage their behavior in the same ways as adults. This ability is a developmental accomplishment and leads to the ability to handle stress and frustration throughout life. Each infant is born with a particular hereditary predisposition regarding the ability to manage emotions and frustrations, but the ability to develop it comes from an attuned "good-enough" environment. Winnicott (1992) suggests that behavioral acting out comes from an unmet need for love and structure.

When an adolescent steals, according to Winnicott (1992), it is not because he really wants the object but because he has emotional needs that have not been met in the environment. Many clinicians can certainly remember working with teenagers who expressed little interest in what they had stolen; it had more to do with the thrill or the sense of accomplishment in getting it. Ultimately, most of them found the experience of stealing empty because it was not really giving them what they needed—the ability to feel good inside through their own self-soothing. The delinquency serves as their best attempt to meet those emotional needs.

Infants and toddlers do not immediately understand that there are or will be limits to their behaviors. It is the caretaker's job to provide structure, to tell the small child no. How else do they learn what the limits of their world will be? For some parents and caretakers, saying no to their child is difficult. It is sometimes easier to give in or let things go. However, if the young child does not learn the boundaries in her own family, she will seek them out in the world outside. Her delinquent gestures are aimed at finding her limits. If taken to an extreme, or not responded to early enough in life, these types of behaviors may lead to criminal behaviors.

Winnicott's theory (1992) is certainly not the only explanation of behavioral difficulties in adolescence. According to Alfred Bandura's social learning theory (1977), children model their behaviors after the people in their lives who are important to them. This type of identification can include mimicking behaviors that are aggressive or destructive. If not modified by the family, children exposed to a cycle of excessive violence or aggression may have severe difficulties with their behavior in adolescence.

Infants and children may also have behavioral difficulties that come from their genetic predisposition or organic problems from neonatal development. When a clinician is working with an adolescent with behavioral problems, it is very important to rule out organic or hereditary etiology before deciding on a course of action in treatment. The school setting is ideal for assessing teenagers from a multidisciplinary standpoint. The physical, psychological, environmental, and social aspects of the adolescent's situation must be thoroughly examined in order to make the correct diagnosis regarding behavioral problems.

If it can be determined that the teenager's behavioral difficulties are primarily organic or hereditary in nature, medication or some other type of medical intervention may be the primary approach to help remedy it. This does not mean that counseling is unnecessary. More often than not, some type of counseling support is crucial as an adjunctive part of the overall approach to a more medically based behavioral problem. ADHD is a good example of this.

Once it has been determined that the teenager does qualify for an ADHD diagnosis and he has been put on the proper dosage of medication, the adolescent and family are going to need ongoing support to help them adjust to a new life free of the ADHD symptoms. This means therapy aimed at helping that child catch up developmentally. The teenager is going to need to develop the skills to function at a pace similar to that of their peers. This catch-up period can take many years depending on the severity and chronicity of the ADHD.

Behavioral difficulties are caused by a variety of physical, environmental, and emotional factors. Some of these problems begin to surface in adolescence owing to the complex developmental factors inherent in that time period. Other childhood behavior problems become exacerbated in adolescence because of its dramatically new and complex challenges. Practitioners working with teenagers must be knowledgeable about these factors in order to understand and appropriately address them with their adolescent clients and families.

SPORTS AND TRADITIONAL SCHOOL AND EXTRACURRICULAR ACTIVITIES

Many adolescent boys and girls participate in athletics. Many also participate in a variety of organized school clubs and activities such as drama, debate, and cheerleading. The successful involvement in these types of activities can help to shape a positive sense of self from a physical, social, psychological, and cognitive standpoint. They are not without their challenges and difficulties, however.

There are tremendous pressures to succeed in sports. If an adolescent is able to do that, he will reap significant benefits in the positive formation of his identity. If he has difficulty, however, the reverse may be true. Because extracurricular activities are so highly valued and carry with them a strong social aura, success or failure in them has a profound impact on the teenager in question. Remember that adolescents are shaping their identities throughout their teenage years. Even though they may be exceptionally bright or athletically gifted, they are still in the process of developing their identity. Care must be taken to give them the amount of emotional support they need whether they succeed or fail in their endeavors. These types of difficulties are often overlooked in a middle or high school that has its hands full with behavior problem teens.

Many teenagers become involved in alternative activities that serve the same developmental function as those sanctioned by the school. Some adolescents are in bands; some are involved in park district sports or activities such as judo, hockey, or dance. Other teenagers may be involved in serious online computer gaming with their peer group. Many teenagers today are also involved in the Internet as a means of continuous social contact through such activities as instant messaging and Web sites such as MySpace.

MySpace is an example of an Internet Web site in which teenagers can create a personal Web page about themselves. Often these sites have features that allow the teenager to permit or deny access to peers based upon their own preferences. This can be a potential source of tremendous social acceptance or rejection for an adolescent. It is an electronic extension of peer relations but also an activity that enriches identity development. The astute clinician can certainly utilize these types of activities in not only getting to know her teenage clients but helping them to further develop their sense of self and social interactions.

Probably the most extreme example of potentially destructive or pathological nontraditional activity is gang involvement. Gangs and gang activity including style of dress, music, and behavior are common in today's adolescent culture. For many teenagers, the identification with these symbols and culture serves as a bridge to help them separate from traditional family and mainstream culture. Although alarming to many adults, the activities of many of the adolescents who identify with the fringe gang culture never develop into dangerous or criminal behavior. This does not mean that the practitioner working with an adolescent who enjoys and identifies with rap music or hip-hop should not pay close attention to the meaning and purpose it holds for that client. The sometimes intense and angry themes inherent in gang-style culture are dangerous if internalized and taken to extremes by the adolescent. It becomes the role of the therapist to ascertain the meaning of these themes and the extent to which they may be modifying the adolescent's identity in a destructive or pathological manner. These themes may simply be a means to an end, which is the second separation-individuation process. However, they can also signal a move toward antisocial or even criminal behavior that the clinician must address in treatment and in the client's immediate world.

Although gang affiliation can serve as a source of emotional support for many socially and emotionally alienated adolescents, it ultimately will lead to crime and delinquency, which put the teenager on a path from which she may not be able to escape. Gang affiliation is both a personal and a community problem. Many teenagers see it as their only way out of an oppressive life. Association with the gang is in many ways their salvation. It provides emotional and physical resources that the adolescent does not perceive to be in her environment, or that may actually not exist. For many teenagers, it is their best choice to survive in an oppressive world.

The task for the therapist working with a gang member is extremely difficult. It requires helping the teenager to visualize hope and opportunities beyond what are supplied by the world of gang involvement. If there are few realistic options and resources, this work may be doomed to failure. The longer the adolescent is gang involved, the more entrenched he becomes in his identification with the gang culture. The key to successful therapeutic work with potential gang members is to be able to help them become aware of less destructive resources that can provide the same type of emotional and physical support that they receive from the gang. The therapist can serve as one of these examples, but if there are not additional sources of support in the community, the prospects for success are extremely limited.

INTERVENTIONS

The areas discussed above are just some of the key elements that many adolescents struggle with in their teenage years. There are many different types of traditional and nontraditional approaches to work with these key factors. Effective work depends on the nature of the clinical role as well as the setting in which one works. Intervention must be based upon a comprehensive understanding and ongoing differential assessment of the adolescent in his environment.

The clinician working with troubled adolescents whether in or outside of the school setting needs to understand the origins and meaning of their problems if they are going to be of any help in resolving them. Specific clinical roles may not lend themselves to resolving the adolescent's academic, emotional, or behavioral problems. School counselors and social workers usually have limited time to address the issues mentioned above. As a result, most school professionals work with teenagers on a relatively short-term basis and in groups. This does not mean that their understanding of the etiology of these problems should also be limited. A comprehensive differential assessment can help inform even short-term work with adolescents seen in schools.

Clinicians seeing adolescents on an outpatient basis usually do have the luxury of spending more time in the treatment process. They also have the opportunity to work with parents and families of their teenage clients. However, even in relatively long-term adolescent work, the same diagnostic principles apply. A few case examples will help to illustrate these approaches.

CASE EXAMPLE

Karl, the African American adolescent discussed in chapter 8, offers a good example of the ways in which an outpatient therapist can work cooperatively with the family and school in the helping process.

Karl was referred by the school social worker. She was concerned about Karl's poor academic performance in seventh grade. He was withdrawn, socially isolated, and not performing up to his academic and intellectual potential. The school social worker did not have time in her schedule to provide Karl with the type of therapy she felt he needed in order to succeed in school. She had tried to involve Karl in a social skills group composed of children with similar difficulties, but Karl was not responsive and seemed to withdraw even further. The school social worker felt that Karl needed more intensive long-term individual work to help him learn to engage more with both his peers and the academic environment.

This is not an atypical situation. The school environment is focused on academic performance. Adolescents' problems are considered only when they interfere in the educational process. As a result, there is usually not the opportunity or time to provide lengthy therapeutic work to those teenagers who need it. That is why collaboration between practitioners in and outside of the school setting is so crucial to the success of troubled teens. This very skilled and experienced school social worker recognized that Karl needed more intensive work than she could provide in the school setting.

Karl's mother was concerned that he might have some type of learning disability. His school performance, however, was not poor enough to qualify him for school-funded special testing. Every school district has criteria by which students are evaluated in order to decide whether they qualify for special educational services. Karl was above this standard, although he was failing most if not all of his classes.

Karl's mother brought him to see me because of his academic problems, which were the presenting concern and referral issue, but also because she realized he might be having difficulty adjusting socially. Therapy was aimed at helping Karl function better in both of these areas.

When I initially began to see Karl, he was still in school. I periodically kept in contact with school personnel in order to monitor how Karl was doing both socially and educationally. In addition, I usually split my session time between Karl and his mother.

On a practical level, Karl and I worked on helping him identify what his school difficulties were, both academically and socially. Our conversations vacillated between these two subjects. Karl, although relatively young, was verbal and cooperative in the counseling sessions. He knew that school was boring to him, a usual complaint from adolescents, but also that he had trouble staying focused on the educational tasks. He said he had no trouble remembering certain things but had a difficult time staying interested in his schoolwork. He had particular trouble feeling motivated enough to consistently do his homework. As a result, he continually got poor grades in this important part of his overall grade. His mother and I tried to develop a system for doing homework, complete with rewards for consistency and higher grades. Karl did not seem able to stay on task. Eventually I began to realize that perhaps Karl did have some type of processing problem such as ADHD. I decided to refer Karl and his mother for an assessment.

Since the school district did not believe that Karl had a profound enough educational problem to warrant testing, Karl's mother decided to pursue that testing on her own. I referred them to a local university that specialized in comprehensive psychological testing. I knew of this university because of my association with several of its professors in my agency consulting work over the years. The psychology department offered comprehensive psychological, emotional/developmental, and educational testing on a sliding scale to anyone regardless of geographical location. There was an initial assessment followed by several days of comprehensive testing to determine the nature and extent of Karl's overall functioning in the areas mentioned above. Karl was identified as having a discrepancy between his verbal and performance IQ, as well as a learning disability related to cognitive processing. It was recommended that he receive specialized tutoring targeted at this particular area of difficulty in order to help him improve his school performance.

The information from this testing was given to Karl's school. It helped the school personnel understand the nature of Karl's educational difficulties. What had been seen as not trying before was now understood to be a result of Karl's cognitive processing problem. In addition, the discrepancy between Karl's verbal and performance IQ scores showed that he had the ability to communicate through language despite his poor performance on homework and tests. This information was a major turning point in Karl's understanding of his educational difficulties. It also helped his mother advocate for him and get him the specialized tutoring services necessary to improve his academic performance.

Unfortunately, because Karl did not meet the deficiency standard which would enable him to qualify for special educational services, his mother was forced to seek outside help. She was referred to a private tutoring service. Through sharing the results of Karl's private testing, Mom was able to set up a comprehensive program aimed at improving his abilities to understand and process educational content. The school was kept informed of the progress of this service, and eventually Karl started to perform better in school.

This improvement did not happen right away. Karl continued to struggle with his grades and social interactions. He began to refuse to attend school. Eventually he had missed so much school that his mother, in consultation with me, the school social worker, and other key school personnel, decided that it would be best for him to be home schooled until the end of the academic year. Karl continued his tutoring, and he also continued his therapy with me. This two-pronged approach eventually resulted in his return to school in eighth grade.

My work with Karl became much more focused on helping him build his self-esteem in order to feel comfortable reaching out to peers for friendship. This was a difficult task because of Karl's inclination to isolate himself at home playing video games. I used this medium—computer and video games—to help establish a strong relationship with Karl. We usually spent time in our sessions talking about family, school/tutoring, video games, and peer relationships. Over time, Karl began to feel more confidence in himself. I believe that this was mainly due to the consistent mirroring that he received from me.

Self psychology suggests that all people have a lifelong need for mirroring. Karl's mirroring needs in early adolescence were amplified by his family situation, early developmental problems, educational deficiencies, and racial identity. In order for Karl to feel secure enough in himself to succeed both educationally and socially, he would need to develop a strong sense of self. I accomplished this by spending time with him aimed at helping him realize his accomplishments, first in video games, later in other educational and social pursuits. Over time, from a self psychology standpoint, Karl became confident enough to return to school and graduate eighth grade.

Karl's initial return to school was not easy. He had been home schooled for almost an entire year. Whatever social relationships he had were no longer as secure as when he was in school. Owing to the intensive and ongoing tutoring he had received, he didn't seem to suffer from the same type of educational difficulties he had previously encountered. As a result, Karl seemed better able to focus on developing some friendships both in and outside of school. Karl's time away from school also helped him appreciate the loss of this social connection, and he was more motivated to connect with others. We worked together to help him develop some friendships. He gradually began to open up more and initiate contact with peers, which led to some satisfying relationships.

CASE DISCUSSION

Karl's high school years and the challenging struggle to attain his racial identity have been covered in chapter 8. His ability to enter into that search was in large part due to the work he had done in middle school. Karl's early life and family situation had a profound impact on every stage of his development. From a neuroscience standpoint, his neural networks were dramatically influenced and solidified by the trauma, neglect, and stress he experienced consistently as a small child. These experiences probably affected his cognitive and emotional capabilities. Adolescence set the stage for a much more pronounced struggle with these difficulties. Enhanced cognitive challenges in middle school often bring forth or highlight educational problems that may not evidence themselves in elementary school. The onset of puberty, and the identity vs. role confusion life stage task of adolescence, usher in challenges in the social realm that cannot even be imagined in childhood. Karl met these challenges well with the comprehensive help of his mother, his therapist, school and university professionals, and outside tutoring services.

This complex and lengthy case example demonstrates a variety of ways in which the competent clinician needs to understand and work with the school in order to help an adolescent succeed in the educational setting. In this example the clinician was an outside therapist. She could easily have been a counselor in the school setting itself. School social workers, counselors, or guidance counselors can understand and provide the types of assessment and services evident in this case. Many school professionals are hampered by the policies and limitations of their particular schools or districts, but that does not mean that they are unable to help teenagers get the type of services they need in order to be able to succeed in school. More often than not it is necessary to work collaboratively with a number of outside sources in order to identify the student's strengths and problems. This case example serves to illustrate the complexity of school problems, as well as the necessity of creative intervention to help the adolescent succeed.

BASIS OF PRACTICE

There has been extensive research on the "best practices interventions" for working with children in the schools. Cynthia Franklin, Mary Beth Harris, and Paula Allen-Meares's 2006 text *The School Services Sourcebook* details this extensive research, covering such areas as mental health diagnoses, developmental disabilities, health and well-being, child abuse, dropouts, and violence. The reader is encouraged to review this key contemporary source of validated knowledge.

SUMMARY

This chapter has presented the myriad of complex developmental factors that contribute to an understanding of the way in which the school setting affects adolescents. It is imperative for all clinicians, regardless of setting or theoretical orientation, to comprehend these factors in order to assess and work with their adolescent clients and their families. Clinical work with adolescents cannot be successful in isolation from the rest of the adolescent's life. School is a pivotal part of the adolescent's world. The diagnostic implications of school involvement on all levels are an essential part of the assessment and treatment planning. Ongoing collaborative work where appropriate can be the deciding factor in a successful outcome.

RECOMMENDED RESOURCES
Readings

Cynthia Franklin, Mary Beth Harris, & Paula Allen-Meares, eds., *The School Services Sourcebook: A Guide for School-Based Professionals* (New York: Oxford University Press, 2006). This is an excellent handbook for social services.

X. Li, B. Stanton, R. Pack, C. Harris, L. Cottrell, & J. Burns, "Risk and Protective Factors Associated with Gang Involvement among Urban African American Adolescents," *Youth and Society* 34 (2002): 172–194. This is a good text on the implications of gang involvement for development.

Film/Television/Media

To Sir with Love (1967), *The Breakfast Club* (1985), *Dazed and Confused* (1993), *Mean Girls* (2004). All these films focus on adolescents in high school.

Internet

http://www.myspace.com/ This a good site to acquaint the reader with how contemporary teens utilize the Web as a source of social contact.

10

Adolescent Group Work: Theory and Technique

Adolescence is a unique time in the physical, cognitive, and emotional development of the teenager. The myriad of changes in virtually every area of life profoundly shape the adolescent's view of self and other and set the stage for multiple interactions with others throughout the remainder of the life cycle. Involvement in groups is one of the pivotal mechanisms by which teenagers continue to learn about self and other.

Prior to adolescence, most children's participation in group activity usually centers on sports and other social activities of a superficial nature. By superficial, I mean focused on the activity itself. Children are not as capable as adults of exploring the deeper meaning of life or the complex realms of the mind, self, and other. In fact, children can't even begin to comprehend what these discussions are about even if they hear them.

For example, I can remember my first experience with the notion of abstract thought and my peer group. I went to a Catholic K–8 school. I was probably in seventh grade when this incident happened. Our teacher, Sister Camille, had asked all of the students to prepare brief oral presentations for the class on any topic that was interesting to us. One of my classmates, Michael, presented on existentialism. He went on and on about this philosophical concept. I was totally lost and perplexed. I felt like an idiot. What was this existentialism, and why didn't I have a clue about it? I thought that Michael must be really smart, and also that I had to be extremely stupid because I clearly could not get what he was talking about.

Why didn't I understand Michael's philosophical discussion about existentialism? I didn't get it because I was not yet capable of abstract thought. Reality, as I knew it, was concrete, absolute, totally predictable, and certain. The possibility that there were relative realities, that human existence was unexplainable, unique, and multifaceted, was not a concept I was capable of comprehending. Michael could; Michael had already entered into Piaget's cognitive stage of formal operations. He could play with abstract ideas, see himself as an isolated individual in a sea of others searching for the meaning of life. Little Fred McKenzie wasn't there yet.

Why talk about this example, and what does it have to do with group work? In addition to experiencing a good bit of anxiety about myself as I listened to Michael's report, I also felt a sense of isolation from my peers. Did they get what he was talking about? Was I the only one who was so stupid? I needed to talk to my peers to understand myself better. I needed the support of my peer group. My search for identity could not happen in isolation; I needed to interact with others of my own age and circumstances in order to have a perspective on my own identity. The group was integral to this process.

DEVELOPMENTAL *I*MPLICATIONS OF THE *U*SE OF *G*ROUP *W*ORK *T*HEORY WITH *A*DOLESCENTS

As adolescents move into the stage of identity vs. role confusion, interaction with the peer group becomes perhaps the main mechanism by which identity is shaped. Adolescents no longer look to their families for emotional support. Parents, family, and primary caretakers continue to provide what Kohut called "self-object" functions. Teenagers continue to be "mirrored" (validated) by these key figures. Adolescents may even utilize their parental figures as idealized others for a sense of merger and identification. There may also be ways in which parents and family serve twinship needs for teenagers, by sharing in similar interests, ideas, and so on. But although teenagers certainly continue to be influenced throughout life by their families and primary caretakers, in adolescence there is a conscious effort to seek out relationships outside of that structure to help shape identity apart from the family. The peer group serves that important function.

In order to navigate through what Blos (1967) calls the "second individuation process," adolescents begin to see themselves as individuals outside of their family system (Applegate, 1984, 1989). The peer group becomes the vehicle through which an identity and cohesive self is formed. Peers now become the primary sources of self-objects. Peers mirror each other, idealize each other, and provide an essential twinship function.

Kohut's concept of twinship self-objects is one of the most helpful concepts with which to understand why adolescents are so drawn to groups. Teenagers are immature adults. They are in the process of shaping their identities, and identification with peers helps them to internalize and modify their own identities. Adolescents seek out others who are like them. Adolescents cling to peer groups in which there are similar ideologies. Cliques become stereotyped iconic support groups that identify teenagers through lifestyle, dress, music, spirituality, ethnicity, and philosophy. The essential features of the group dictate who the adolescent is. This sharing of identity through the group meets the adolescent's twinship self-object needs. He is now identified as belonging to a group of similar others. For now, this identification *is* his identity. The group meets the dependency needs that were previously provided by the family. It is the bridge through which adolescents negotiate the journey to adult identity formation.

If there is any truth to this premise, then it stands to reason that group work with adolescents can help them work through a variety of important issues in their lives. Professional group work, however, is different in at least one very important way from the adolescent peer group. It is facilitated by an adult, a professional group worker. Adult presence, leadership, and facilitation in the adolescent group become the linchpins for therapeutic success.

Developmentally, the adult group work facilitator can serve a quasi-parental role. Adolescents are moving away from family in their push toward autonomy and identity formation. The peer group is an important bridge in that process, but most, if not all, peers are also struggling with their own sense of confusion and uncertainty in their journey toward identity formation and emotional autonomy. The group work leader is an adult, but not a parental figure. Group work leaders can become key models for the adolescent peer group, satisfying both twinship and idealizing self-object needs. Their knowledge of the adolescent developmental process is invaluable in providing the therapeutic interventions needed for a particular type of adolescent group. The skilled group worker is able to utilize the strengths, emotions, struggles, and overall qualities of the adolescents within the group to facilitate change within all members of the group. That is the unique power of group work. Systems theory tells us that the whole is greater than the sum of the parts. It is this concept that helps explain the power of the group for adolescents struggling to find themselves. The professional group worker uses herself and all members of the adolescent group to bring about change (Yalom, 1985).

Group work with adolescents, like individual treatment, can be provided in both traditional and nontraditional formats. There are many different types of groups that are effective in working with teenagers. Most high schools, junior highs, and middle schools work with adolescents in groups. Family service agencies, mental health centers, psychiatric hospitals, criminal justice facilities, YMCAs and YWCAs, as well as private practitioners see adolescents in groups. The types of groups vary according to the population served, the nature of the organization, and the type of concern. Group work can range from traditional psychotherapy to nontraditional recreational activities. All types of group work can be therapeutic if understood from a developmental framework. All can bring about dramatic change in the adolescent through the group process if the group worker understands that process and recognizes how to utilize himself and the group members within it.

GROUP WORK THEORY: IRVIN D. YALOM

Although group therapy was introduced in the 1940s, group work services have been provided in this country since the early 1900s (Yalom, 1985). In social work, the settlement house movement emphasized group affiliation and peer support as a key factor in helping the immigrant populations adapt to life in the United States (Turner, 1996). The 1960s popularized encounter groups, T-groups, as well as the traditional psychotherapy group experiences. The managed care movement of the 1980s ushered in group treatment as a more cost-effective mechanism by which to treat such ailments as eating disorders, depression, schizophrenia, and drug addiction. The success of Alcoholics Anonymous and groups like it is based upon the power of group support.

Perhaps the best-known and most respected pioneer of group work theory is Irvin Yalom. His highly regarded and classic book *The Theory and Practice of Group Psychotherapy* (1985) has become the fundamental text for educating group workers from all disciplines. Yalom puts forth eleven primary therapeutic factors necessary for successful group psychotherapy. The group must (1) instill hope, (2) promote the recognition of universality, (3) impart information, (4) promote altruism, (5) correctively recapitulate the primary family group, (6) develop socializing techniques, (7) model imitative behavior, (8) facilitate interpersonal learning, (9) foster group cohesiveness, (10) create catharsis, and (11) include existential factors. These eleven factors encompass the therapeutic elements that are part of any type of professional group experience.

Several of these therapeutic factors are particularly relevant to the adolescent experience. By promoting the recognition of universality, the group helps its members to realize that they are not alone in their experiences. Nowhere is this more important than in the journey to identity in adolescence. Through the group work modality, the adolescent can come to recognize a shared experience with her peers. This emotional twinship gleaned from a group experience helps the adolescent discover her identity and begin to shape a true sense of self, similar and yet different from the other.

Altruism, group cohesiveness, and interpersonal learning are key to the adolescent group member's realization that dependency on others is a part of life. We all learn, grow, and develop through an affiliation with the primary support group. In adolescence, this affiliation is with the peer group, but the process of mutual interdependence does not stop.

There are many different types of adolescent groups: traditionally therapeutic, educational, and nontraditional or recreational. Yet all types utilize most if not all of Yalom's key therapeutic principles. In order to understand the essential properties and therapeutic value of group work with adolescents, clinicians must educate themselves in the key therapeutic principles mentioned above.

All groups progress through a series of stages. Yalom discusses the following formative group stages:

1. *Orientation, hesitant participation, search for meaning, dependency.* In this first group stage, members come to grips with the task of the group, as well as a beginning to have a sense of themselves in relationship to

the group members. For adolescents, this entails developing trust not only in the group leader(s) but in their peers. The greater the structure within the group, the less anxiety the adolescent member may experience. This is because adolescents in general do not have a strong sense of their own identity. Too little structure can be overwhelming. Too much structure, however, can be confining. Remember that adolescents are moving toward emotional autonomy and separation from their primary caretakers. The last thing they need is another parental figure dictating the structure of their world. On the other hand, certain types of groups warrant structure. The key here is to be sensitive to the developmental factors and create group structure that allows for safety and freedom of expression.

2. *Conflict, dominance, rebellion.* Once an initial atmosphere of safety and trust has been developed, the group begins to struggle with issues of autonomy, compliance, structure, and meaning. In much the same way that infants need a secure holding environment before they can discover their own spontaneity, group members must first experience a secure environment in which to then define themselves as individuals and as a group. This stage may include a struggle with the group leader as well as negotiation of roles among the group membership. As in childhood, group members test the leader to discover the limits of the group and each other. It becomes the role of the group leader to facilitate that process. There is a delicate balance between maintaining the structure of the group and still allowing group members to experience ownership of the process. Some form of relative autonomy and rebellion is part of the adolescent journey. A skilled adolescent group leader must be adept at negotiating this balance.

In addition, it becomes the group leader's function in this stage to help the group members negotiate relationships with each other. Based upon their own family of origin (what Yalom might call the corrective recapitulation of the primary family group), each adolescent approaches this dynamic differently. Some teenagers may be more timid with their peers. Others may demonstrate a strong need to control, lead, or dominate the group. It becomes the group leader's responsibility to facilitate this important group and developmental task. The way in which it is handled can seriously affect the ongoing development of all the group members.

3. *Development of cohesiveness.* Once the members have challenged the structure of authority and the group itself, they reach a point of relative cohesion. This is a time when the group experiences a sense of trust and safety. Members now begin to feel freer to express themselves. In a traditional psychotherapy group, it is the time in which the real work can begin. In other types of groups, achieving stage 3 allows the group to work on the task at hand, be it educational or recreational. Because of the nature, format, and time limits of many types of groups, stage 3 may be reached in a very

superficial manner. However, in order for any group to be successful, the members must have developed a sense of trust and ownership. This task may be greatly facilitated by the qualities of the particular group worker and the ways in which she uses them in the group process.

ANDREW MALEKOFF'S GROUP WORK APPROACH WITH ADOLESCENTS

A key figure in the adolescent group work literature is Andrew Malekoff. His well-respected book *Group Work with Adolescents: Practice and Principles* (2004) contains information on the fundamental principles of group work with adolescents, the role of the worker, group work techniques, and the many different types of group work with this population He defines the tasks of adolescence as: (1) separating from the family, (2) forging a healthy sexual identity, (3) preparing for the future, and (4) developing a moral value system. In addition, Malekoff defines group work as "one avenue for promoting the reflection and critical thinking necessary to clarify values and make healthy decisions" (p. 6). Malekoff's work is highly recommended reading for those looking to specialize in group work with adolescents.

THE ROLE OF THE GROUP WORKER

The role of the adolescent group worker is dictated by the type of group. In traditional psychotherapy or support groups, the worker's task is one of facilitation, empathic support, and emotional guidance. In educational, task-oriented, and recreational groups, the worker may assume more of a directive leadership stance. Each type of group requires a corresponding type of activity on the part of the group worker. However, there are certain elements of group leadership that are common to any type of adolescent group experience.

What is most important to remember when conducting an adolescent group is that you are working with adolescents. Keep in mind that adolescents are at different stages in their movement toward emotional autonomy and identity formation. Adolescents are also in a relative stage of rebellion from adult authority. This rebellion takes on many different forms, but it is important to remember that it is present in some form with all adolescents. It is their way of establishing a sense of identity apart from that of their primary caretakers. The worker needs to remember that challenges to authority, resistance to group structure, and ambivalence about the group in general are part of the adolescent phenomenon. They are not necessarily about the personality of the group leader, the content of the group, or even the group members. A firm and empathic approach to this resistance is necessary in working with adolescents in all types of groups.

Adolescents typically demand more self-disclosure from group leaders than do any other client population. This can be a double-edged sword. On the one hand, self-disclosure can enhance trust and help group members feel that they are not isolated in the group. On the other hand, knowing too much about the group leader can contribute to adolescent resistance and bog down the group process. The group worker needs to gauge when self-disclosure is appropriate and for what purpose. For example self-disclosing about one's own teenage marijuana use to an adolescent drug prevention group may create problems. If handled appropriately, this type of self-disclosure may generate a sense of trust in the group that sets the stage for greater self-expression. The key to self-disclosure is the ability of the group worker to understand its purpose. Self-disclosure should not be self-serving; it should be based upon the needs of the group. The group worker should ask himself, "Why would I want to self-disclose at this moment?" and "How will self-disclosing at this juncture in the group further or inhibit the group process?" These and other important questions need to be silently explored before the group worker utilizes self-disclosure in adolescent groups.

Finally, the group worker must remember that adolescents are still children; they are not adults. Part of one's role as a group worker with adolescents is to function in a quasi-parental role with them. This does not mean that the group worker exerts the same type of authority or control that a parent might; it also does not mean that the worker assumes the same type of existential role that she might assume with adults. Adolescents still need guidance. However, adolescents also need to be allowed to negotiate their sense of self with a certain degree of autonomy. The group worker's task is to decide the extent to which she should or should not intervene by sharing an adult perspective. One might argue that some adolescents are still struggling for answers. The group worker is a trustworthy adult who can help in that process in ways that parents cannot. They are seen as different from parents. They can serve as sources of support, modeling, twinship, and idealization that parents no longer provide. So sometimes sharing information, opinions, and guidance can be absolutely essential in working with adolescents. The difficulty once again is timing. The rule of thumb should always be: Whose interests are being served by intervening right now? Mine or the client's?

Of course all of the factors above are modified by the diversity of the group's membership. Racial, ethnic, and gender variables within the group's makeup must be understood in order to effectively approach the tasks at hand as well as deal with the challenges of the group stages (Brown, 1993).

TYPES OF ADOLESCENT GROUPS

Remember once again that few adolescents come to treatment on a voluntary basis. Groups are no exception. Later in this chapter I will give examples of purely voluntary adolescent groups, but they tend to be the exception rather than the rule. High school and junior high groups usually focus on mutual support and education. Teenagers having difficulty making friends may be referred to a socialization group. Adolescents struggling with decisions about relationships, including sex, may be referred to a psycho-educational group on dating. Adolescents who are in so-called behavior-disordered settings may be required to attend weekly or even daily groups to learn new behavioral coping mechanisms.

Psychiatric hospital settings provide another common type of imposed group experience. Most adolescents who are psychiatrically hospitalized are put there by their caretakers. Few of them decide voluntarily to enter hospital treatment. Self-injury, eating disorders, and many other mental health situations mandate group experiences as part of the overall treatment. These groups are usually *psycho-educational,* meaning that there are elements of education, support, and aftercare planning in all of these groups. The role of the group leader is typically a blend of education and supportive facilitation.

Youth and family agencies, YMCAs and YWCAs, park districts, and community-based youth development settings offer a variety of traditional and nontraditional types of group experiences. These can range from traditional activities such as sports activities and topical counseling groups to nontraditional group activities such as drop-in centers and on-the-street outreach groups. All of these activities are informed by the group principles mentioned earlier. All of them demand that the group worker assume a therapeutic stance in his role with the group. All of them are potentially therapeutic, if facilitated in a clinically informed manner. I have been involved in a variety of traditional and nontraditional adolescent groups over the thirty-plus years I have been privileged to work with teenagers. These groups have ranged from the very informal to the highly structured. The following examples help to illustrate this wide range and how they can be useful to the adolescent in negotiating his developmental journey.

The Adolescent Activity Group

There are many agencies that offer informal settings such as drop-in centers where adolescents can congregate with their peers under the loose supervision of an adult professional. Although the goal in these settings is prevention, they can also provide problem solving, modeling, support, and even intensive nontraditional counseling/psychotherapy. Some adolescents would never open up to an adult in traditional therapy but may develop a strong therapeutic alliance with a professional drop-in center worker. They may discuss family problems, drug issues, and peer situations in an informal setting such as this much more productively than if they were required to go to therapy.

In my early years as an outreach worker, it was my job to reach out to adolescents on their turf to help them stay out of trouble. As I began to engage teenagers in informal settings such as neighborhood hangouts, school cafeterias, and parks, I intuitively recognized that they needed places to congregate and hang out. The adolescents I met loved music. Music has been one of the universal themes for adolescents since the 1950s. When I asked them what they wanted to do most, they said, "Go to concerts." Most of them didn't drive, or their families wouldn't let them drive to concerts, so they needed a way to do that. I consulted with my colleagues at the agency, and we decided that perhaps we could develop an activity group whose purpose was to go to rock concerts. This would be the initial hook, but it would also be a vehicle through which these teenagers could consistently meet and discuss all types of issues. I did the initial screening, which consisted of gathering a clique of adolescents interested in going to concerts, and I set up weekly group meetings to discuss going to concerts, listen to music, and talk about all sorts of issues in their lives. We had to work collaboratively with parents, getting their permission to take their teenagers to the concerts, as well as assuring them that their adolescent's behavior would be monitored and supervised by professional counselors. The group was tedious logistically at first, but eventually turned into a very useful nontraditional therapeutic environment for these teenagers. Weekly group meetings centered as much on planning rock concert trips as on discussing family issues, relationship problems, and other crucial adolescent developmental dilemmas.

This decidedly alternative-type group went through all of Yalom's group stages and served as a therapeutic vehicle for many troubled teens who would never have initiated traditional counseling on their own. They also probably would have been highly resistant clients had they been referred to therapy by the school or their parents. Ironically, many of them did voluntarily ask for traditional therapy from our agency because they got to know us through the group. The group experience itself was therapeutic, but it also served as a mechanism for more intensive treatment if needed. This example demonstrates the real power of nontraditional group work in providing therapeutic support for adolescents in their journey toward adulthood.

The Psychodrama Group

The integration of psychodrama and Gestalt therapy principles can be creatively utilized with groups or families. Gestalt therapy was very popular in the late 1960s and early 1970s and has recently experienced a resurgence. Gestalt therapy was developed primarily by Fritz Perls (1969). It is a humanistic approach that emphasizes awareness and expression of thought and emotion in the present. Although Perls was psychoanalytically trained, his approach did not emphasize exploration of the past. Instead, Perls worked toward helping the client become aware of his emotional issues through a series of experiential techniques geared toward bringing the emotions to the surface in the here and now. For example, in the "empty chair" technique, a client who is angry with a sibling, parent, boss, or co-worker is urged to imagine that this person is in the chair beside her. She is next asked to express those ideas, thoughts, and emotions, that are troubling her in her relationship with that individual. Through this experiential role play of sorts, the client is able to safely recognize her struggle as well as practice or prepare for how she might like to deal with the issue in the future. It is a very freeing technique for many clients and has become so commonplace that many professionals do not know its origins.

Psychodrama is an individual (psychodrama) and group (sociodrama) treatment modality that was developed by Jacob L. Moreno (1970). It is a projective technique that allows the participant(s) to assume the role(s) of protagonists or antagonists from their lives in order to reenact experience and work through emotional conflicts. The main technique in psychodrama is to assign roles to groups or family members and direct them to act out key scenarios, conflicts, or interpersonal issues from the recent past in the therapy setting. The first task in psychodrama is called the "warm up" (Moreno, 1970). In the warm-up process there is specific assignment of roles, and the direction of the psychodrama enables all members to experience the thoughts and emotions surrounding the conflict of the entire family. The second stage is called the "action" stage. Insight is gained, conflict is reenacted, and the family or group is strengthened from the process. The final stage is called the "sharing" stage. It is here that the entire group explores and processes the psychodrama experience. This intense, immediate, and experiential process can be a powerful therapeutic outlet for adolescents and their families.

Many of the teenagers who came to our drop-in centers were experiencing family conflict. They talked about these issues informally in the drop-in setting with their peers as well as with the professionals who staffed the center. They were in emotional pain but not interested in coming to traditional therapy. Some were brought to therapy by their parents or referred by the school, but they were usually not willing participants in the traditional therapeutic process. Our staff, who had been certified in Gestalt therapy and psychodrama, decided that perhaps a creative group approach might help these struggling adolescents more effectively cope with their family problems.

We engaged, screened, and received informed consent to conduct a psychodrama group for several of these adolescents. All of them were clients of the agency, but they were also active in the agency drop-in center. Through our nontraditional relationship with them in the center, we were able to introduce the idea of a fun group in which they could play out some of the things that were bothering them in their families. It would be confidential, they would be with their peers from the center, talking and complaining about their families. The stage was set for the group.

I led this group with a co-therapist. We worked well together and had solid relationships with all the adolescent group members. We explained the process of psychodrama in the teenagers' language and created a safe and trusting environment in which to play out these family roles. The adolescents took turns creating the drama of their unique family situations. Group members were assigned family roles such as mom, dad, brother, sister, grandma, and so on. Each actor was also told how to interact with the others in the psychodrama. Finally, a scenario was reenacted in the group in order to allow the process to be experienced by all.

For example, a fifteen-year-old girl might be upset with her parents for not allowing her to stay out past midnight with her seventeen-year-old boyfriend. Group members would be assigned the roles of mother, father, and the adolescent girl (a different teenager); they would play out the discussion around why she was not allowed to stay out past midnight. As the roleplay unfolds, group members react to the process. Some members may side with the adolescent girl; some may side with the parents. The purpose is to create an experiential setting in which a variety of emotions can be experienced and to serve as a vehicle for discussion for all the group members. The psychodrama experience enhanced these adolescents' personal understanding of their family circumstances and the perspectives of all members of their family. In addition, the feedback from supportive peers enabled them to develop a broader viewpoint on their world. The experiences and insights gained from the adolescent psychodrama group were incorporated into the family therapy process for these teenagers. It often served as a pivotal point in the work with parents and their children.

The Deferred Prosecution Group

In the late 1980s I worked as the executive director in a very small community-based agency in the northern suburbs of Chicago. This was a grassroots organization dedicated to drug prevention for the youth and families of the community. One of the groups that we operated for first-time adolescent drug offenders was called the "deferred prosecution group." When a youth in this community was arrested for a first-time drug offense, he and his family were given a choice. Either pay the fine and serve time (if appropriate to the offense), or voluntarily participate in the agency's deferred prosecution program. The advantage to program participation was that the offense would be removed from the teenager's record. The group treatment program was time limited and geared toward education, prevention, support, and psychotherapy. This educational prevention group was helpful in reducing recidivism rates for drug arrests in the community. In addition, it served to engage adolescents in a supportive group dialogue with their contemporaries around issues related to drug use and values clarification.

Teenagers and their families were referred to the group through the local police department. There was an initial intake/screening interview in which an agency counselor explained to the adolescent and her family the purpose and logistics of the group. The deferred prosecution group met weekly for six weeks. The structure of the group was both educational and supportive. Trained agency counselors presented basic information about drug use, its effects, and its implications for adolescent and family development. Following each weekly informational segment, there was an opportunity for the group to discuss their thoughts, feelings, and reactions to the information. It was during this segment that the agency counselor attempted to encourage and facilitate honest and open group discussion surrounding drug use. The purpose of the group was not to use scare tactics or preach to teenagers regarding the evils of drug use, but to provide an atmosphere in which the decisions to use drugs could be discussed. The bias or belief on the part of the agency was that this type of opportunity was far more productive than punishment, especially for first-time offenders.

Even though the deferred prosecution groups met for only six weeks, all of the classic group stages inevitably surfaced. The development of trust and group cohesion was an ongoing challenge since most if not all of these adolescents were not self-referred. The challenge for agency clinicians was to find a way to engage these resistant teens in an honest exchange with their peers. The combination of traditional drug information and contemporary films depicting real life drug use helped the group to open up and honestly debate, dialogue, and examine the issues. The group was completely confidential, which served to encourage this type of frank discussion. For some of these adolescents, it was the first time they had ever discussed drugs or drug use with a nonjudgmental adult. The ultimate goal was to encourage these teens to begin to examine their life choices in a more informed manner. We knew we could not control their decisions, but perhaps we might enable them to develop the ability to explore them in a more thoughtful and objective manner.

Alternative to Saturday Detention Group (The Breakfast Club)

During my tenure at the agency mentioned above, I was able to influence the services provided in the community in a variety of ways. The deferred prosecution group was one of many we developed. Another project I helped develop was an alternative to weekend high school detentions. Part of the high school disciplinary system is school detentions. Depending upon the offense, high school students may be required to sit in detention for several hours after school, all day in school, or for more severe infractions, all day on Saturday.

I met with the high school deans to inquire about the ways in which our agency might interface with and provide services to the school that they were not able to provide. The deans felt that Saturday detention was not curbing these adolescents' behavior. There were many teenagers whose behavior problems seemed to worsen the longer they were required to attend Saturday detentions. It occurred to me that this would be the ideal group of adolescents to work with in group therapy. I spent some time brainstorming with my agency staff and came up with an alternative to this Saturday detention—a voluntary therapy group.

As with the deferred prosecution group, offending high school students were given a choice: either serve a series of all-day Saturday detentions or attend a weekly group at our agency. They were told that the purpose of the group was to help them discuss personal, peer, school, and family issues in a confidential group setting. The group met weekly for two- to three-hour sessions during an eight-week time period. Some of the adolescents decided they would rather not engage in any discussion about their thoughts or feelings. But many of these teenagers did decide to take advantage of this option rather than continue to serve Saturday detentions. One of the clear incentives was that it freed up their weekends, as well as requiring them to spend only two to three hours in a group dialogue as opposed to an eight-hour day in silent detention.

Many readers may remember the classic film *The Breakfast Club*, which came out in the 1980s. The film is one of the best representations of high school adolescent cliques and group interaction. It also captures many of the salient issues inherent in adolescent development. That film along with several others served as the impetus for discussion in the alternative detention group. Each three-hour session consisted of some type of group activity through which dialogue and group interaction occurred. For example, one week the group might watch all or part of *The Breakfast Club*, followed by group discussion facilitated by the group leader. Discussions were open-ended, geared toward developing a group atmosphere of trust and safety through which these clearly troubled teens could begin to open up and discuss their concerns.

Potential group members were referred through the high school deans and screened by the staff of the agency to ensure that the right mix of adolescents would be selected for the group. This group mix was usually a very resistant one, but its members seemed to quickly bond with one another around their mutual dislike for the high school and society in general. The agency counselor's role was to help them begin to explore some of the reasons and justifications for their behavior. This was no easy task, but the use of film depicting similar adolescent struggles and rebellion certainly helped. The group also worked because the group members realized that the agency had empathy for their plight. The counselor did not condone the adolescents' disruptive behaviors but tried to understand them in the context of each teenager's unique situation. The group also served as an important source of support and validation of twinship needs for all of its members.

BASIS OF PRACTICE

Group work with adolescents has been intuitively known about and practiced for decades. Theoretical knowledge from such masters as Yalom and more recently Malekoff has helped to improve clinicians' sense of practice wisdom beyond the mere anecdotal case study. Recent validated knowledge from such sources as Thomas O'Hare's *Evidence-Based Practices for Social Workers* (2005) and Malekoff's *Group Work with Adolescents* (1997) provides further comprehensive proof of the necessity of this form of treatment with adolescents.

SUMMARY

The groups mentioned above are but a few of the many different types of therapeutic experiences that can be provided to adolescents. Adolescent inpatient psychiatric settings thrive on the provision of educational and peer support groups. These groups, if managed well, become the glue through which disturbed adolescents begin to open up and dialogue about the important factors in their lives. High schools and junior high settings are often limited in the individual staff hours they can provide to adolescents in need. Groups for many schools are the only mechanism through which teenagers can receive psychological services. Topical groups such as socialization groups, divorce groups, ADHD groups, anger management groups, and drug education groups can be extremely helpful when provided in structured school settings.

Affiliation with others is an ongoing need throughout life. In adolescence it is especially important because of the ways in which the group experience shapes individual identity. In order to become an independent adult, most teenagers must first identify with a group. Group work services are important vehicles in that developmental journey.

RECOMMENDED RESOURCES

Readings

Jeffrey Applegate, "Transitional Object Reconsidered: Some Sociocultural Variations and Their Implications," *Child and Adolescent Social Work* 6, no. 1 (1989): 38–51.

Leonard N. Brown, "Groupwork and the Environment: A Systems Approach," *Social Work in Groups* 16, nos. 1/2 (1993): 83–95.

M. J. Hoag & G. M. Burlingame, "Evaluating the Effectiveness of Child and Adolescent Group Treatment: A Meta-analytic Review." *Journal of Clinical Child Psychology* 26 (1997): 234–246.

Andrew Malekoff, *Group Work with Adolescents: Practice and Principles* (New York: Guilford Press, 1997).

Thomas O'Hare, *Evidence-Based Practices for Social Workers* (Chicago: Lyceum Books, 2005).

Irvin D. Yalom, *The Theory and Practice of Group Psychotherapy* (New York: Basic Books, 1985).

Journal for Specialists in Group Work, Journal of Child and Adolescent Group Therapy, Research on Social Work Practice, Small Group Research, Social Work with Groups. These groupwork journals are excellent sources for contemporary scholarly writing on groups.

Film/Television/Media

The Breakfast Club (1985). This is the definitive film on the process and power of the adolescent peer group.

Internet

http://www.aaswg.org The web site for the Association for the Advancement of Social Work with Groups is the premier site for groupwork in the United States.

11

High-Risk Behavior,
Hospitalization,
and Medication

High-risk behavior is any type of maladaptive functioning that severely threatens the so-called normal process of adolescent development. This chapter deals with situations in which psychiatric hospitalization becomes necessary in order to protect an adolescent from herself or to protect others from her.

Suicide is more prevalent in adolescence than in any other developmental phase of life (Holinger et al., 1994). It is a time when, as Shakespeare's Hamlet says: "To be or not to be, that is the question." It is only when an adolescent comes to terms with who he is and is comfortable with that identity that he can move into adult life. Successful resolution of Erikson's identity vs. role confusion stage results in self-love and love of life. Lack of such resolution can lead to depression, suicidal ideation, and even death. Fortunately, the majority of teenagers do not attempt or commit suicide. However, many do question their existence and whether they want to live. Sometimes that questioning makes it necessary to hospitalize them for their own protection.

Another group of adolescents who definitely require psychiatric hospitalization are those who are a threat to others. Anger, frustration, and depression are emotional states that are interconnected. One might even characterize them as being on a continuum. At one extreme is depression. A depressed person is directing all of his emotions inward. Freud (1966) recognized that phenomenon in his early work. Derek Miller, in his classic book *Attack on the Self* (1994), examines at length how extreme depression in adolescence can lead to the ultimate attack on the self—suicide. At the other extreme is homicide. Homicide is anger turned outward. The angry adolescent may not feel good about himself, but the expression of that emotion is channeled outward toward others, not directed inward at the self. Fortunately these instances are quite rare.

There are a variety of psychiatric disorders that characterize these conditions, including mood disorders, psychotic disorders, and personality

137

disorders. Mood disorders range from extreme depression (major depressive episodes) to extreme elation (manic episodes in bipolar I). Schizophrenia and the range of psychotic disorders usually originate in adolescence or early adulthood. Teenagers who have a borderline personality disorder or an antisocial personality disorder are particularly vulnerable to extreme feelings of sadness and anger.

THE ROLE OF ACTING OUT IN ADOLESCENCE

Adolescence is a time of experimentation. This experimentation may take the milder form of joining different peer groups, trying out for a variety of extracurricular activities, listening to a range of music, or even registering for a unique combination of academic courses. On the other hand, it can take the form of drug abuse or dependence, self-injury, theft, reckless driving, or even violence toward self and others. The stereotype of adolescent acting out is the male juvenile delinquent. Adolescent females, however, are also capable of the same type of destructive behaviors. Teenage girls are cutting themselves with greater frequency than ever before. There are entire psychiatric programs devoted to managing self-injury. Adolescent females are also becoming more physically violent toward others. Perhaps that may be related to the expanding role of women in our society. Greater opportunity and equity for women may also create greater competition and with it a greater potential for anger and even violence in young women.

Winnicott (1992) understood that adolescent acting out was related to their search for love and structure not only in the outside world but within themselves. Neuroscience theory can now empirically demonstrate this fact (Cozolino, 2002; Greenspan & Shankar, 2006). If an infant does not develop the ability to self-soothe during critical periods of early life, the capacity for the management of emotions such as anger and frustration will be compromised throughout life. During the early stages of development this type of difficulty or impairment may not evidence itself in extreme violence toward self or others. However, the onset of adolescence intensifies not only the emotions but also how they are expressed.

SELF-INJURY

Self-expression seems to be one of the hallmarks of adolescence. I was a teenager in the sixties. Our form of self-expression was in our style of dress, the music we listened to, and how we wore our hair. In my late adolescence I wore my hair past my shoulders, dressed in gauze shirts and bell-bottomed pants, and listened to Jimi Hendrix, Led Zeppelin, and Frank Zappa. Today, teenagers still express themselves in all the forms mentioned above, but in addition tattoos and body piercing have become a common way to express one's individuality. It makes perfect sense, especially in adolescence. After all, Freud said, "The ego is first and foremost a body ego." That means that the body is the self. The self develops through the body's interaction with the world. As the adolescent comes to grips with his identity, he also comes to terms with his new body, its changes, sensations, hormones, and emotions. Tattoos and body piercing can be understood as dramatic physical expressions of self. That expression can also carry with it physical and sometimes emotional pain.

Many adolescents who cut or self-injure are doing so to experience and release painful emotions. They may not be able to feel their emotions unless they cut. Cutting themselves serves at least two purposes. First, it helps them see (the actual cut or blood) and feel (pain) their situation more clearly. Second, it directs a negative action upon the self. It is almost like punishing the self. The adolescent ego or self is a body ego. If the teenager has not been able to develop a form of self-expression that truly captures his identity and feelings, more severe measures of self-expression may become necessary. Cutting and destructive drug use serve that purpose. They are probably the most adaptive means these types of adolescents have to feel and express that feeling.

EATING DISORDERS

Another obvious way to use one's body for expression and emotional release is through eating. The etiology of eating disorders is still unknown. Theories about their origins have posited familial, psychodynamic, cognitive/behavioral, and sociological causes. There is no doubt that at least in more developed countries thinness is in. But this problem is not confined to females or Caucasians. There are increasing numbers of adolescent males as well as minority teens of both sexes who are struggling with eating disorders. In the United States especially, adolescents are encouraged by their adult role models to be as thin as possible. One only has to pick up the latest magazine to see many of the young Hollywood celebrities, male or female, looking like skeletons. This is not healthy, and it certainly is not a good message to send to our young people. However, I do not believe we can blame the entire eating disorder problem on Hollywood. There seem to be some clear psychological influences at work.

One of the most accepted explanations for eating disorders is the adolescent's need for control. If the self/ego is indeed a body ego, then controlling one's food intake, for whatever reason, controls the self. Most adolescents with eating disorders have extremely low self-esteem and poor body image. Psychologically we might say they also have a very poor observing ego. In anorexia, they see themselves as fat even if they are four feet ten and weigh seventy pounds. When they look in the mirror, they perceive and experience their bodies as fat. This distortion fuels their emotional insecurity and reinforces their need to further restrict eating as a way to control and manage the self. Unfortunately, it is a never-ending cycle. These types of teenagers can never be thin enough because the issue is not their body but their identity or self. If not treated in time, adolescents suffering from anorexia can experience shrinkage of the brain, organ damage, and even death.

Bulimia is another version of the same type of difficulty. There is usually the same type of distorted body image coexisting with an extremely low self concept. Binging serves to feed the self, and purging expels and punishes the self for that soothing. In many ways this is similar to cutting. Taken to extremes, bulimia can also lead to severe health problems such as heart arrhythmias, esophageal damage, electrolyte imbalance, and death. Psychiatric hospitalization is sometimes the only way to save these suffering teenagers.

OUTPATIENT TREATMENT

Although most adolescents dealing with these types of difficulties in the most severe forms will need inpatient treatment, outpatient therapy can be helpful and is certainly mandatory after a period of psychiatric hospitalization. The key factor in these types of life-threatening situations is ongoing assessment and careful monitoring of the adolescent. The practice formulation can be extremely helpful in giving the clinician in any practice environment a comprehensive picture of the adolescent. Remember, however, that assessment is always ongoing. With these types of adolescents, the true nature or severity of the high-risk behavior may not be apparent initially. Often these issues come out only after the clinician has developed sufficient trust with the teenager.

The decision to refer the adolescent and her family for more intensive treatment hinges on the extent to which the therapist believes the adolescent can control her behavior. If there is any doubt that the teenager can manage these complex issues on her own, parental involvement is absolutely crucial. If the family cannot manage the behaviors, then psychiatric hospitalization is a must. For example, in assessing suicidal behavior, the clinician should directly discuss the adolescent's thoughts and feelings about suicide. Avoiding the discussion will not make it go away. In fact it may exacerbate the problem. The clinician should find out what the reasons are for the suicidal thoughts and feelings, how severe they are, and most important whether the adolescent has a specific plan or means by which to kill himself. If he does, inform his parents immediately. Confidentiality is not an issue here. Suicide is an impulsive act. When in the midst of suicidal ideation, an individual is probably not thinking clearly and may react impulsively to manage the unbearable emotions. Self-injury is a mild form of that process. Suicide is the most extreme version. The most reassuring aspect of working with a suicidal client is that a meaningful relationship with a caring and empathic therapist is itself a deterrent. However, the relationship alone may not be enough. If the adolescent has a plan, or seems unable to manage her emotions in a healthy manner, psychiatric hospitalization may be necessary.

INPATIENT AND PARTIAL PSYCHIATRIC HOSPITALIZATION

There are a variety of specialized psychiatric hospital programs throughout North America. There are inpatient, partial, and outpatient programs for eating disorders, drug addiction, and general psychiatric conditions. Children and adolescents are kept in separate programs within these facilities, away from adult patients. The onset of managed care has dramatically curtailed the length of stay and services that one can expect from psychiatric hospitals. In the 1970s, for example, it was not unusual for a suicidal adolescent to spend several months in an inpatient psychiatric facility. At the present time, the typical length of stay is usually closer to 4–6 days, followed by either partial hospitalization or some type of intensive outpatient services. Unfortunately, the length of stay is usually based not upon what is needed but on what one's health insurance can support.

What types of services then, do adolescents suffering from these severe difficulties receive while they are in the hospital? An adolescent who is psychiatrically hospitalized is under the care of a psychiatrist. It is usually the role of the psychiatrist to evaluate the adolescent's psychiatric condition and prescribe some type(s) of medication for it. The advances in neuroscience and psychiatric medicine have been tremendous over the last decade. So much more is known about the brain and the way in which certain medications may help target areas to improve functioning. The hospital psychiatrist's job is to accurately assess the adolescent's need for medication, see that it is administered while she is hospitalized, and monitor the effectiveness of the medication during the hospital stay. Once the psychiatrist is certain that the adolescent patient is improving, through medication and other therapeutic treatment, he will look toward discharge planning.

While in a psychiatric setting, the adolescent probably sees her psychiatrist only once a day, for a very short period of time, usually less than a half hour. The psychiatrist will consult with the psychiatric unit staff to get a sense of how the teenager is doing, as well as read her chart before meeting with her each day. The success of such an effort depends on accurate and responsible reporting from the inpatient staff, including nurses, counselors (psychologists and social workers), and other key support members, and the extent to which they are able to work as a collaborative team.

In addition to seeing his psychiatrist daily, the adolescent patient is usually involved in a tightly structured routine of therapeutic inpatient services. There is a regular schedule that all patients are expected to follow each day. There are specific times for breakfast, lunch, and dinner, as well as scheduled break times throughout the day and into the evening. Adolescents will have time to socialize with other patients as well as interact informally with many of the inpatient staff. Depending on the adolescent's diagnosis, his behavior and interactions may be more closely monitored. Teenagers who are a suicidal risk will not be left alone for any length of time. Psychiatric patients are not allowed to have any possessions (including shoelaces) that might be used to hurt themselves. Their entire world is highly structured to increase their sense of safety and facilitate treatment aimed at helping them reenter their outside world once again.

The main therapeutic vehicle on most inpatient units is group therapy. Throughout their highly structured day, adolescents may attend three or four different groups. Some are educational, some supportive, and still some others recreational in nature. The goal is to help the adolescent patient learn about her problems, learn new ways to cope with her thoughts and emotions, gain support through listening and interacting with others who may have similar issues, and develop new practical coping skills that she may take with her when she leaves the hospital. Some psychiatric hospitals even have family therapy groups. This is an opportunity for parents and their teenagers to work together in an atmosphere of mutual support. Knowing that other families have suffered with similar problems can be a tremendous relief.

Most adolescents entering psychiatric inpatient settings are anxious and even resistant to treatment. But they are also safe. There is nowhere to go, and they will not be able to hurt themselves or anyone else. This is the unique and invaluable asset of an inpatient psychiatric setting. They are put through a rigorous yet individualized process through which they will regain their ability to manage their lives more effectively. Once the hospital staff in conjunction with the psychiatrist determines that the adolescent is ready, discharge planning begins.

DISCHARGE PLANNING AND OUTPATIENT FOLLOW-UP

The decision to discharge is a complex one, based upon a variety of factors. First is whether the adolescent is ready to resume her life outside the hospital setting. From a psychiatric standpoint, this is determined by the extent to which the medication seems to be not only working but helping. Unfortunately, most psychotropic medications usually do not take full effect for two weeks or more. Most hospital stays are less than a week. This can be a very tricky aspect of inpatient treatment. Careful monitoring of the adolescent by her family, outpatient follow-up therapist, and psychiatrist is crucial to the success of treatment.

If the adolescent has been experiencing anxiety, irritability, agitation, extreme elation, or depression, there should be a diminishment of those feelings prior to discharge. The medication can be a tremendous factor in helping the teenager get back on his feet. There will usually need to be some adjustment of the medication as time goes on, especially in the first few weeks or months after discharge. Families need to stay connected with a good psychiatrist in order to continue helping their adolescent.

In addition to staying connected with a good psychiatrist, the adolescent and her family must continue to be involved with a quality outpatient clinician. This therapist must be apprised of the hospital treatment and the medications the adolescent is taking and be committed to ongoing individual and family work. If the adolescent is going to be able to follow through on the changes that may have begun in the psychiatric setting, she will need to make a strong commitment to outpatient therapy. Often the family and the adolescent are relieved that she is home and out of the hospital. This sense of relief may lead them to hesitate in pursuing outpatient services. This resistance is probably normal, but it is incumbent upon the outpatient clinician to continue to engage the adolescent and her family in order to insure continued progress.

CASE EXAMPLE

Seth is a seventeen-year-old male who was hospitalized for extreme anxiety, agitation, depression, and suicidal ideation. He spent about a week in an inpatient psychiatric facility. The precipitating event was a breakup with a nineteen-year-old girlfriend, Jane, whom Seth had been seeing for a couple of years. The circumstances surrounding the breakup were extremely troubling to Seth. It appears that Jane's parents were fueling this breakup and not allowing Seth to contact her, even by phone. Seth and Jane had been having some difficulty of late but always seemed to be able to mend things if they could talk it over together. Jane's parents decided that the relationship with Seth was bad for her and put pressure on her to stay away from him. Seth did not seem able to tolerate or manage this anxiety and began to spiral into a panic. He began compulsively calling Jane. Jane's father threatened to put a restraining order on Seth if he continued to call Jane. Seth felt sure that if he could just talk with Jane everything would be all right. This very difficult emotional dance continued to spiral until Seth acknowledged that he was not sure he wouldn't hurt himself if left alone. With the help of his parents, Seth voluntarily admitted himself into a psychiatric facility.

Seth is an only child adopted at birth by his parents. His parents separated when he was eleven years old and divorced when he was thirteen. The divorce was extremely conflictual and may have contributed to some of Seth's emotional difficulties. His adoption may also have been a factor in the development of his symptoms. I will use the practice formulation with Seth to develop a comprehensive diagnostic assessment of his situation.

1. *Is there any evidence of constitutional factors that may have contributed to the present situation? If so, how have they affected the adolescent?* Seth was adopted by his parents at birth. He spent approximately 6–10

days in the hospital after he was born and before he was placed with his adoptive parents. Despite continued efforts on the part of his adoptive parents, there is virtually nothing known about Seth's constitutional predisposition. Seth's birth mother was sixteen at the time of his birth, and his birth father was apparently near twenty-one years of age. Besides these basic facts, little else is known about Seth's genetic constitution. Seth's extreme anxiety, depression, and agitation could be constitutional factors inherited from his biological parents (Cozolino, 2002; Greenspan & Shankar, 2006). It is well known that depression and bipolar disorders have a strong genetic predisposition. Anxiety as well may be inherited. On the other hand, many adolescents experience anxiety and depression during their crucial developmental years. Unfortunately it is not clear which of these factors is more influential in Seth's difficulties.

Attachment issues may also be a key factor in the etiology of Seth's problems. He was not placed with his adoptive parents until he had spent almost ten days in the hospital. Although the nurses who took care of him may have been extremely sensitive, caring, and focused on his needs, they could not have been consistent simply because there were so many of them. Each nurse handled Seth differently, even if in some small way. This inconsistency may have affected his ability to develop his early self-soothing capacities. It may also have affected the development of early neural networks associated with the management of anxiety (Cozolino, 2002). These constitutional factors cannot be ignored when examining Seth's behavior.

2. *What level of psychosocial development do you believe the adolescent has achieved? Do you believe the adolescent is fixated or regressed at all? What factors lead you to believe this may be the case?* Seth is chronologically in Erikson's stage of identity vs. role confusion. He is in the midst of ascertaining who he is in relationship to others. Seth had a difficult time finishing high school. He struggled with depression and a severe lack of motivation his last two years in high school. He barely finished his final courses. His father and new stepmother virtually wrote his final papers, which enabled him to graduate. Seth enrolled in college the fall after high school graduation but struggled not only in his academic courses but also with living on campus a short distance away from both his parents. He is extremely bright, scoring a 30 on his ACTs. This factor is probably a combination of heredity and environment. But Seth never seemed able to work up to his potential. He flunked out of college in less than a year. He failed to withdraw from classes, just didn't go to most classes and finished the year with a C, a B, and several Fs.

Seth seems to have been able to successfully negotiate some of Erikson's first few stages of development. He is and always has been a rather shy person but did seem able to experience the world as a safe place and initiate interactions with others in a normal manner. Seth walked, talked, and mastered toilet training all within developmental norms. He did experience some difficulty with bowel movements during early childhood but did not appear to evidence characteristic problems with control or anxiety related to this developmental period. Seth appeared to have successfully negotiated Erikson's stage of industry vs. inferiority well. During his early childhood he excelled in school and developed keen interests in science. He was and is still an avid reader. In his adolescence Seth began reading complex material on physics, especially as it related to astronomy. Seth recently has developed a strong interest in photography and has been involved in playing guitar for the last several years. Music is very important to Seth. He spends hours downloading and playing countless "alternative" types of contemporary music.

Seth is beginning to negotiate Erikson's stage of intimacy vs. isolation but is hampered by his lack of identity. Although this is true for many teenagers of Seth's age, he seems truly fixated in identity vs. role confusion. His intense involvement with Jane in some ways kept him from negotiating his identity. He appears to have been in a type of symbiotic merger with her. His entire life revolved around her. He, in a sense, had lost himself in her. This unfortunately came at the expense of his ability to define his identity. Complicating this situation is the fact that Jane is doing quite well in college and moving toward a much firmer resolution of her own identity. She seems to have been equally involved in the symbiosis with Seth, but because of her chronological age, her identity may be more firmly established. This is a potentially difficult situation for both of them.

3. *What type of attachment did the adolescent have with his primary caretakers, and how did these early developmental periods affect his present relationships with family, peers, and significant others, especially the therapist?* As mentioned earlier, Seth was adopted at birth. He remained in the hospital for approximately ten days before he was placed with his adoptive parents. The positive and negative repercussions of this time period cannot be fully understood (Greenspan & Shankar, 2006). What is certain, however, is that there was an adjustment period for Seth as he made the transition from a diverse group of nurses to his adoptive parents. There is no way of knowing how difficult this time period may have been for him.

Seth's adoptive parents report that he attached to them quite easily. He was a pleasant baby, eager to interact and play with others. His early childhood was uneventful, except for the fact that he developed childhood asthma at around the age of four. This medical condition was a source of anxiety for his parents, which may have been communicated to Seth in some subtle and not so subtle ways. Seth seemed to manage his asthma well, and it did not appear to interfere in his ability to form friendships or engage in activities.

Seth's parents separated when he was eleven. This was a very difficult and contentious separation and divorce. Seth was very close to both of his parents, and the separation was difficult. Seth was used to seeing his father day in and day out, and now he saw him only once a week and on weekends. It was at this time that Seth first saw a counselor. He appeared to adjust to the separation and divorce, but it is not clear how this situation may have affected his mood or identity. The one positive aspect was that Seth's father saw him consistently and never missed a visitation. Since Seth was an only child, however, the aftermath of the divorce left him alone with his mother. Their relationship may have naturally intensified with the physical loss of his father. Several years later, Seth's father remarried. This too may have been a difficult adjustment for him. Seth's mother hasn't remarried. The implications for Seth's relationship with his mother during adolescence are obvious.

Prior to his relationship with Jane, it appears that Seth may have had one other serious relationship. He dated and had his first sexual experience with a girl two years his junior a year or two before meeting Jane. Jane was very important to Seth. He seems to have channeled all his emotional energy into his relationship with her. It may have served to help him begin to separate from his family, particularly his mother. The abrupt ending of that relationship was something Seth obviously was incapable of handling from a psychological and emotional standpoint.

Fortunately, Seth does have a number of other peer relationships. He has friends of both sexes, and when not depressed, he spends time with them. He tends to be somewhat shy and withdrawn in his interactions with adults but is much more open and engaging in his relationships with friends.

In the therapy relationship Seth also tends to be rather quiet and withdrawn. His affect is slightly flat until he begins to talk about a subject that interests him. He can then become quite animated and engaging for brief periods of time. The therapist may feel as if he's pulling teeth when relating to Seth in session. This affective state, however, is related more to his anxiety than to true resistance. One might characterize Seth's attachment style as anxious/avoidant.

4. *Why is the adolescent in need of service right now? Is he self-referred, or does someone else believe he needs help?* Seth voluntarily hospitalized himself; however, he is extremely ambivalent about getting treatment. He does not open up easily and believes that talking about things only makes the situation worse. This may be characteristic of an anxious/avoidant attachment style. Seth was in therapy with several other clinicians prior to his hospitalization, all regarding his mild depressive symptoms and lack of motivation, but he was unable to sufficiently engage in therapy.

At the point of his hospitalization, both of Seth's parents are in agreement that he needs help. They are committed to working with professional staff in any way they can to help Seth get back on track. Their contentious feelings for one another have been put aside during this crisis in Seth's life.

5. *Does the adolescent see himself as being conflicted or in need of help, despite the fact that he may not be self-referred? To what extent can he see his part in the situation? Does the adolescent have the capacity to be introspective and/or to view himself objectively? What is the extent of his observing ego?* Seth recognizes that he is in emotional pain. He also realizes that he may not be in complete control of his impulses, which is what prompted him to voluntarily admit himself to the hospital. But he is extremely ambivalent about discussing his thoughts and feelings. He would much rather magically make these things go away. In addition, Seth does not clearly see his part in the events that led up to his psychiatric admission. He fails to recognize that Jane is no longer interested in having a relationship with him despite the fact that she has told him so. Seth believes that if he could just talk to her, everything could be repaired and things would go back to normal. He also believes that Jane's parents are controlling her. Although Jane's parents may have some influence over her, she is nineteen years of age and certainly capable of making her own decisions about her relationship with Seth.

Seth's observing ego is not being well utilized in this situation. He is very much in denial about how his behavior may be seen and understood by others. He wants to see himself not as out of control but rather as acting as anyone would to work things out with a girlfriend. He is extremely antagonistic toward examining his fragile self and utilizes primitive reality-distorting defenses as his main coping mechanism in this situation. In that way, Seth is highly resistant to introspection. He unconsciously utilizes projection, displacement, denial, and intellectualization as his main psychological defenses. Seth may be capable of introspection, but it is not a regular part of his psychological repertoire. He will need to develop this capacity further if he is going to be successful in managing his impulses in the future.

6. *Is the adolescent's defensive structure adaptive or maladaptive?* As with many individuals with extremely high IQs, Seth's main psychological defense is intellectualization. Intellectualization is a double-edged sword. On the one hand, it can be used to separate the self from painful and anxiety-producing emotion. On the other hand, if taken to the extreme, it can become a rigid impulsive mechanism that keeps emotion from conscious awareness. Seth falls on the negative side of that continuum. All his life he has relied primarily on his intellect to manage situations. For the most part, it has served him well. But the exclusive use of intellectualization has inhibited the development of Seth's ability to access emotion and self-soothe through the process of introspection. In this way, intellectualization has been a maladaptive defense. Seth's use of projection, rationalization, and denial also fall into that category. Prior to this crisis, Seth's defenses seemed to function in a mostly adaptive manner. This recent attachment dilemma, however, has stirred up more primitive impulses that Seth is not able to manage with his existing repertoire of defenses. In order to work through this crisis,

he will need to become more emotionally introspective and develop other, more adaptive coping mechanisms.

7. *How would you assess the adolescent's family system, and how does it affect his present situation?* Seth comes from a divorced family system. He is also an adopted child. Although it appears as if Seth's early development and childhood were in the realm of normal development, he clearly suffered a severe loss when his parents divorced. The contentious divorce may have contributed to Seth's further reliance on intellectualization as a means of coping. Seth had no control over the divorce. Intellectualization provided him an adaptive defense through which he could repress his overwhelming sense of anxiety, loss, and depression. This may have served him well the first few years after the divorce, but as Seth began his own journey toward intimacy, inevitable emotions surfaced once again.

His breakup with Jane is real, but the lack of control that accompanied it may be reminiscent of his experience not only with his parent's divorce but perhaps also with his being adopted. All three of those situations were beyond Seth's control. All three of them could stimulate quite a bit of anxiety and perhaps depression.

It is also understandable if Seth developed a more anxious attachment with his adoptive mother after the divorce. As he began to move toward emotionally separating from his mother, however, Seth may have experienced some understandable ambivalence. One might speculate that his relationship with Jane served as a convenient vehicle through which he could begin to separate. Seth was able to channel his need for attachment into his relationship with Jane. For two years it served him well. But the immediate crisis has stirred up intense attachment issues for him which have not been resolved.

Seth's relationship with his father was very close when he was a child. The divorce was an unexpected trauma for Seth. From that moment on, his relationship with his father changed. Although he saw him every week, his father no longer lived with him. Seth did not see his father every morning before school. He was no longer able to kiss his father good night. This was a huge loss. It was a loss that was out of his control. There is no doubt that it caused Seth to feel sadness, anger, anxiety, and depression. These are feelings that many children from divorced families experience (Nichols & Schwartz, 2006). Children from divorced families often do not feel able to express those emotions to the parent who has left the home. They may be afraid that the parent will leave them too. As a result, they may hide their feelings or, as in Seth's case, utilize sophisticated defenses such as intellectualization to cope with them. This very real loss in life was in many ways reenacted in Seth's breakup with Jane. Jane left Seth in much the same way that Seth's father left him. It was out of his control. It also triggered intense emotions reminiscent of his earlier life. These family systems issues may have been strong contributors to Seth's difficulties (Johnson & Whiffen, 2003).

8. *Are the adolescent's parents/caretakers invested and willing to recognize there might be a problem and help work on it?* Fortunately, Seth's parents have rallied around him in his crisis. They have both been actively involved in his psychiatric hospitalization. They seem to be presenting a united front and strong consistent support of Seth. They also both recognize the ways in which each of them may have unconsciously and unavoidably contributed to the development of Seth's difficulties. Seth's parents seem able to effectively follow through in a supportive manner with his aftercare. Both of them want to see Seth psychologically healthy.

9. *Are there particular issues of diversity that heavily influence the adolescent's situation?* As far as his adoptive parents know, Seth is a Caucasian adolescent. He is an adopted child and as such falls into that diverse category of children. Being adopted brings with it a myriad of challenges, including dealing with one's birth origins and understanding the circumstances surrounding the adoption. Seth does not know his biological parents. He has known of his adoption since he could speak. His adoptive parents discussed the fact of his adoption as a normal part of life. They told him that many children were adopted. They offered to answer as best they could any of his questions about adoption. Unfortunately, there was little to tell.

As a result of Seth's limited knowledge about his biological origins, Seth may be struggling with his identity in ways that nonadoptive teenagers do not. Adoption is an issue of diversity that complicates the adolescent's normal search for identity. Seth does seem curious about his birth parents. Exploring that history may help him achieve greater clarity about his identity in the future (Johnson & Whiffen, 2003).

10. *What environmental factors are relevant to this situation?* Seth's family is in the middle- to lower-middle-class socioeconomic bracket. In his early to middle childhood, while his adoptive parents were still married, Seth was quite well off. He was an only child and adopted, so understandably his parents showered him with toys and clothes. The divorce changed that situation. Although Seth's father contributed to his welfare through child support payments and maintenance, and Seth continued to live in the same home and go to the same school, he clearly did not have the same base of resources available to him. Furthermore, as in most divorce arrangements, Seth now received things from both parents. There were now two birthdays, one with mom and one with dad. This situation probably had both positive and negative aspects to it. On the one hand, Seth may have gotten more attention, but on the other hand, each birthday and holiday was a constant reminder of the divorce.

11. *What resources are available to the adolescent in dealing with this situation? What are the adolescent's strengths?* Although it has been mentioned as a maladaptive aspect of Seth's functioning, he is an extremely bright young man. Seth's intellect will probably be one of his greatest strengths throughout life. He can be a very polite and charming adolescent. He is physically attractive, creative, and resourceful. He is easily able to make new friends and can communicate well with adults when he must. Seth has the unconditional support of both his parents as well as extended family. He will not be alone in his emotional struggles. He was placed in a well-respected psychiatric hospital and is seeing some of the best professionals in the field. His parents' combined incomes will enable him to get the continued help he needs.

12. *Based upon all of the factors above, what is your intervention plan, and what do you think the outcome might be?* Seth clearly needs to be in a psychiatric facility at the present time. Although he continues to utilize some primitive and maladaptive psychological defenses, Seth recognizes that he cannot manage his emotions at the present time. It is to be hoped that a short stay in an inpatient psychiatric facility will help him develop some coping mechanisms. At the present time he seems to need a variety of medication to help him manage his overwhelming anxiety and depression. Once he is judged fit to leave the hospital, Seth will need ongoing individual therapy to help him understand his impulses and the factors that contribute to them. He will also need to utilize the therapy relationship to begin to develop the capacity to introspect and gain insight into his emotions. There may also need to be some family therapy should Seth decide that he needs to work through any unresolved issues surrounding his parents' divorce. Ongoing collaboration between Seth's outpatient therapist, his psychiatrist, and his parents is crucial for the success of his treatment.

TREATMENT SUMMARY/CASE DISCUSSION

After an initial resistance to the hospital environment, Seth began to examine his inability to adaptively manage his impulses and emotions. Prior to his hospitalization, Seth occasionally self-injured. He was not actively suicidal but did cut and burn his upper arms as a way to feel his pain and release it. Seth seemed incapable of handling these intense feelings of anxiety, as well as the loss of an important other. His fear of cutting himself was eventually what led to his hospitalization.

While in the hospital, Seth was encouraged to examine his thoughts and feelings surrounding his relationship with Jane. His psychiatrist was particularly adept at helping Seth explore the practical elements in the relationship. She was able to engage Seth's intellect in a healthier manner to help him recognize the destructive aspects of his behavior. Safe in the hospital and away from Jane, Seth was able to gain some emotional distance to explore the relationship, how it affected him, and what he wanted to do about it. In the meantime, he was put on several medications to help manage his overwhelming anxiety and depression. His psychiatrist prescribed Lexapro and Busbar for depression, Zyprexa for agitation and racing thoughts, Klonopin at night for anxiety and to help him sleep, and Ativan as needed throughout the day for anxiety. This psychotropic cocktail greatly facilitated Seth's ability to get his emotions under control.

The use of medication with all individuals, including adolescents, has become much more informed and sophisticated than it was even a decade ago. Brain research has been able to identify the neurotransmitters most clearly associated with anxiety, depression, and thought disorders. The so-called cocktail approach to medication management involves the use of several specific medications targeted at specific neurotransmitters in the brain to help alleviate severe symptoms of anxiety, depression, agitation, and obsessive thought (worry), as well as many other debilitating conditions. Seth was fortunate to have a very skilled and knowledgeable psychiatrist who was able to provide him with the optimal types and dosages of medications.

Seth was hesitant to become involved in the hospital groups initially. He was quite shy and anxious, and with his strong intellectualized defenses he convinced himself that he was above group therapy. However, as time went on and the medications began to work, Seth started to go to groups. He mostly observed others but began to engage in conversations with other patients outside the group. Through these dialogues, Seth came to realize that there were others like him and some much worse off. This form of twinship may have helped him feel less alone, less isolated, and actually more normal.

After about a week in the hospital, Seth was ready for discharge. He was referred to a therapist who specialized in working with adolescents. This new therapist was much closer to Seth's age than his previous ones and was similar to Seth in his interests and ideology. Seth's parents hoped that this new arrangement would prove to be what he needed to weather his relationship with Jane as well as get back on track in his journey toward identity achievement.

Basis of Practice

Utilizing the continuum of research knowledge discussed in this text, one might say that from an intuitive and practice wisdom standpoint, when adolescents are in serious physical danger owing to mental illness, hospitalization is key to ensuring their safety and to beginning to develop a process through which evaluation and successful treatment can occur. Theoretical knowledge, such as Derek Miller's, helps the clinician understand the inner psychological world of the adolescent and the myriad of emotional factors that can lead to self-destructive behaviors. Recent studies have demonstrated that inpatient psychiatric services can have a very positive effect on the outcome for these adolescents and their families (*Journal of the American Academy of Child and Adolescent Psychiatry,* 2001).

SUMMARY

Most adolescents never need to be psychiatrically hospitalized. Either their constitution or their life circumstances are such that they are able to negotiate their developmental journey without it. However, many teenagers get lost on that journey. Usually it is circumstances beyond their control that contribute to the necessity to hospitalize. It is the essential role of the clinician working with adolescents and their families to be able to determine when more intensive treatment is necessary. The sophistication of contemporary psychiatric hospitalization has made it an invaluable resource for adolescents, their families, and the clinicians who work with them. This chapter has given an overview of those services and shown the necessity for the clinician to be able to ascertain when they are needed. The skillful combination of therapy, medication, and family support is crucial to the successful treatment of adolescents who are suffering from severe emotional problems.

RECOMMENDED RESOURCES
Readings

Sonia G. Austrian, *Mental Disorders, Medications, and Clinical Social Work* (New York: Columbia University Press, 2000). This is an excellent source on psychiatric medication, although it is important to keep current with the latest information.

D. A. Brent, D. J. Kolko, B. Birmaher, M. Baugher, & J. Bridge, "A Clinical Trial for Adolescent Depression: Predictors of Additional Treatment in the Acute and Follow-up Phases of the Trial," *Journal of the Academy of Child and Adolescent Psychiatry* 38 (1999): 263–270. This is a good source for empirical data on treatment for adolescent depression.

Dwight L. Evans, Edna B. Foa, Raquel E. Gur, Herbert Hendin, Charles P. O'Brien, Martin E. P. Seligman, & Timothy Walsh, eds., *Treating and Preventing Adolescent Mental Health Disorders* (New York: Oxford University Press, 2005). This book offers a nice overview of the treatment of adolescent mental health disorders.

J. Garber, S. Little, R. Hilsman, & K. R. Weaver, "Family Predictors of Suicidal Symptoms in Young Adolescents," *Journal of Adolescence* 21 (1998): 445–457. This article provides some important information on suicidal predictors for adolescents.

Paul C. Holinger, Daniel Offer, James T. Barter, & Carl C. Bell, *Suicide and Homicide among Adolescents* (New York: Guilford Press, 1994). Although a bit dated, the statistics in this text are compelling.

Derek Miller, *Attack on the Self* (New York: Jason Aronson, 1994). This book is considered by many to be one of the definitive works on adolescent suicide.

K. B. Rodgers & H. A. Rose, "Risk and Resilience Factors among Adolescents Who Experience Marital Transitions," *Journal of Marriage and Family* 64 (2002): 1024–1037. This article examines the risk factors for suicide in adolescents who experience marital transitions.

Film/Television/Media

Girl, Interrupted (1999), *Prozac Nation* (2001). Both of these films depict the debilitating aspects of adolescent mental illness.

Internet

http://www.nami.org/ This is a very reputable source of information on mental illness, medication, and treatment.

12

Substance Use/Abuse/ Dependency and Adolescents

"Everyone does drugs!" That's what most of my adolescent clients tell me. Or, "Well, they may not smoke marijuana or do shrooms, but everyone drinks!" Those statements may or may not be accurate, but it is certainly common knowledge that many teenagers today use/abuse and become dependent upon drugs and alcohol (Doweiko, 2002). Drugs affect development on all levels, and deficiencies and difficulties in development may lead to drug use and dependency. This interplay is crucial to understanding and treating adolescents who may use drugs.

But why do adolescents use drugs and alcohol? Some believe that teenagers use because of peer pressure. To drink and use drugs makes one seem more grown up. Society in general is drug oriented, and perhaps many adolescents are influenced by the culture to experiment and use drugs to a certain extent. Many believe that adolescents use because their parents or family uses. Perhaps teenagers are genetically predisposed to become drug addicted. Adolescents may be drawn to use drugs as a substitute for emotional self-soothing mechanisms that never fully developed in infancy and early childhood. The environment and community in which a teenager grows up may exert undue influence on her decision to become involved with drugs or alcohol. Finally, perhaps the emotional struggle to achieve identity in adolescence itself becomes the impetus to use drugs as a means to help buffer the developmental process. These and many other factors all can help answer the question "Why do adolescents use drugs and alcohol?"

THE USE/ABUSE/DEPENDENCY CONTINUUM

The *Diagnostic and Statistical Manual of Mental Disorders*, 4th edition, text revision (*DSM-IV-TR,* 2000) defines substance abuse as "a maladaptive pattern of substance use manifested by recurrent and significant adverse consequences related to the repeated use of substances" (p. 199). Some might argue that this definition clearly describes the illegal use of substances of any kind for any duration by adolescents. But there are many teenagers who use illegal drugs recreationally and do not seem to have major difficulties in their lives. Is this possible? There have been some adolescents that have come to me for treatment whom I would consider recreational users. Without exception, however, I would argue that these adolescents have been affected developmentally by their recreational drug use. The key factor in assessment and ongoing treatment has to do with the extent of that drug use and how it affects their ongoing development.

The *DSM-IV-TR* (2000) describes substance dependence as "a cluster of cognitive, behavioral, and physiological symptoms indicating that the individual continues use of the substance despite significant substance-related problems" (p. 197). The problems referred to may include trouble in relationships, work, recreational activities, or in the case of many adolescents, school performance. The line between abuse and dependency is very fine. Adolescents can certainly become addicted, but determining the extent of that addiction can be very difficult.

All teenagers who use illegal substances are somewhere on the use/abuse/dependency continuum. But many teenagers appear to get through their adolescent drug use relatively unscathed. This chapter will review many of the explanatory theories of addiction as well as discuss a variety of treatment options based upon a thorough diagnostic assessment. In order to assess an adolescent's drug use, the competent clinician must place it in a comprehensive developmental context utilizing all the theories and concepts discussed in this text thus far. Only a comprehensive contextual assessment can lead to proper treatment for the adolescent and her family.

MODELS OF CHEMICAL DEPENDENCY
The Moral Model

For decades, many people, practitioners included, have believed that substance abuse and dependency are predicated upon poor moral character (the moral model). Only through strengthening his moral character can the individual stop using. This strengthening may include a twelve-step program, substance abuse/dependency treatment, church involvement, or any other type of interventions aimed at bolstering moral character. Although most practitioners recognize that teenagers who use do not do so because they have weak morals, values, and beliefs, these can certainly be factors in the etiology of drug dependence for some teens (Johnson, 2004).

The Community Model

The community model of substance abuse and dependency argues that individuals and families are a product of the community and that their drug use is a form of coping with their situation (Johnson, 2004). Although the community model is primarily meant to explain drug use in communities affected by social discrimination, it has some relevance to adolescent drug use in any community.

Clearly, those teens that grow up in oppressive and poverty-stricken environments are much more predisposed to use than those whose situation is not as threatening (Garmezy, 1991). But I would argue that the adolescent community in general exerts a strong influence on most teenagers to use as a way of coping with a difficult life stage. The sense of isolation that many teens experience is an inducement to using substances.

The Biological/Neuroscience Model

There is some evidence to suggest that some human beings are genetically predisposed to becoming addicted to substances. Adolescents who have this genetic predisposition may be in danger of becoming addicted, and recreational drug use on their part is much more likely to result in addiction. The explanation for this factor has to do with their brain chemistry.

Researchers have recognized that even so-called recreational use of drugs stimulates the limbic system in the brain, which results in an increased feeling of pleasure (Johnson, 2004). With continued drug use, the adolescent's brain can become dependent upon the use of drugs to feel pleasure. The normal and natural sources such as sports, hobbies, and lively conversation cease to yield pleasure owing to the body's reliance (dependence) on substances. With greater use come drug tolerance and a need for larger quantities of substances to achieve pleasure. Over time, the brain's natural ability to regulate the limbic pleasure center can become drastically impaired. Even when teenagers quit using, it takes some time before the brain can resume normal chemical management of emotions. Combined with the drug craving that accompanies cessation of drug use, this time lag can make sobriety a daunting task for the adolescent (Doweiko, 2002; Johnson, 2004).

The Social Learning Theory Model

Alfred Bandura and other behavioral theorists and researchers have helped practitioners to understand the behavioral elements that contribute to the development of drug use, abuse, and dependency in adolescents. Drawing from B. F. Skinner's original stimulus-response theory, social learning theorists explain adolescent drug use as stemming from the ways in which behavior is positively or negatively reinforced. In addition, the role models that adolescents look to for identity development may contribute to the teenager's interest in drug experimentation and eventual abuse or even addiction. The concepts of reinforcement, modeling, and other key behavioral factors may also be used to explain the adolescent's decision to use substances.

The Cognitive-Behavioral Model

Cognitive behavioral theory (CBT) examines the ways in which an individual's behavior is influenced by the values and beliefs that have shaped his or her identity since birth. CBT suggests that teens form certain self-defeating and self-destructive attitudes about drug use that not only contribute to their initial use of substances but also reinforce their continued use (Johnson, 2004). These attitudes, beliefs, and behaviors may be the result of growing up in a drug-using family or social environment.

CBT drug treatment programs target cognitive schemas and fundamental values in order to help teenagers change their thoughts and behaviors. Through intensive inpatient treatment, adolescents can begin to develop new cognitive and behavioral patterns that may lead to a less destructive lifestyle. Individual and group therapies are aimed at altering these patterns. Unfortunately, many inpatient programs are extremely time-limited, which does not lead to sustained sobriety for many adolescents.

The Disease Model

The best-known model for understanding and treating addiction is the disease model. This model and the twelve-step Alcoholics Anonymous (AA) recovery program have been widely accepted as a beneficial approach to helping addicts of all substances and ages deal with their illness. This model claims that addiction is a disease of body, mind, and spirit, that the addict is not able to control it, and that the only way to recover is through abstinence. Disease model advocates also believe that addiction (particularly alcoholism) is a progressive disease. Individuals move through a sequence of stages that ultimately result in severe drug/behavior dependency (Johnson, 2004).

AA was developed as a means of group support to help recovering addicts maintain sobriety. The addict must first admit that she is *powerless* over her substance/behavior and turn her fate over to a higher power in order to manage her disease. The twelve-step AA program is a personal process by which the addict examines herself, makes amends to those she has hurt, and continues toward personal growth and sobriety.

The Developmental Model

Throughout this text, the importance of understanding the adolescent's emotional development has been emphasized. Perhaps nowhere is this importance greater than in understanding why teenagers use substances. If the adolescent has been able to develop a relatively secure attachment in infancy and sustain those emotional gains throughout childhood, he may enter into adolescence with a relative ability to self-soothe (object constancy), a relative sense of autonomy, and a beginning sense of competent self-esteem. Most of us have some difficulty in at least one of those interconnected areas. Drug use can serve as a replacement, substitute, or adjunctive source of emotional support in development.

Self psychology, object relations theory, attachment theory, and neuroscience can all help us understand the pull that substances have for many adolescents. From a self psychology standpoint, those teenagers who did not receive enough mirroring, merger/idealizing, and twinship self-objects in early development may turn to drugs as a quick substitute for filling the those emotional gaps. Alcohol, marijuana, cocaine, and other drugs can simulate a consistent sense of well being that the adolescent is not capable of achieving at a particular point in her life. Use of these drugs can also serve as a buffer against many of the uncomfortable feelings and experiences that are part of being a teenager. The danger comes when these teenagers begin to rely on those drugs as an ongoing source of emotional sustenance. Drug dependency can circumvent the normal process of emotional development because it does not allow the teenager to naturally develop a sense of self. In addition, a heavy reliance on drugs may also thwart the normal process of "transmuting internalization" of self-objects. Instead of incorporating self-object experiences from others, the drug-addicted teen continues to rely on substances for that purpose (Levin, 1987).

Object relations and attachment theory, much like self psychology, would suggest that teens are predisposed to drug use if they have not developed the internalized object relations or neural networks that enable them to manage emotional life. During the "second individuation" of adolescence, the teenager revisits the tension of separation anxiety with few emotional tools to handle it. Drugs may seem a logical source of support if the adolescent is unable to manage extreme anxiety or depression on his own. The continued chronic use of substances replaces whatever neural networks the adolescent may have developed along the way. Many addiction experts suggest that addicts are emotionally stuck at whatever point they began to use chronically. A large part of their recovery is revisiting and developing the ability to manage their emotional life. These theories help to explain this complex emotional process.

The Multisystemic Framework

One of the most helpful ways to conceptualize substance use/abuse/dependency is through a multisystemic lens. A comprehensive assessment of any adolescent should incorporate all the theories and models discussed above. The competent practitioner can then begin to develop an informed intervention plan for the adolescent and his family. The treatment for adolescent drug use/abuse/dependency is difficult to manage and often meets with only limited success. The recovery rate in the general population is only about 20 percent (Doweiko, 2002; Johnson, 2004). For adolescents it is considerably lower. In order to have any hope in working with this population, the clinician must examine and understand the continuum of treatment for adolescents and the factors that influence success.

TREATMENT OPTIONS

Inpatient

When an adolescent's drug use drastically interferes in her normal developmental process, inpatient hospital treatment may be the only way to help turn a difficult situation around. Adolescents who are drug dependent/addicted are no longer capable of managing everyday tasks such as school, work, friendships, and family relationships. When this happens, their family members often resort to hospitalization as a means to stop the self-destructive spiral.

Inpatient programs for substance-abusing adolescents have been around for many decades. Adolescents are usually admitted to the hospital against their will. They are forced into sobriety, as well as the medical and psychiatric programs that the hospital provides. These programs usually include individual counseling, group counseling, family counseling, drug education, and comprehensive discharge planning aimed at insuring sobriety once the hospital stay is over.

The adolescent may be assigned an individual counselor and a psychiatrist, as well as several other mental health professionals during her hospital stay. The daily routine is usually tightly structured, with many educational and supportive group meetings and comprehensive individual and family counseling. The entire treatment program is geared toward helping the adolescent not only attain sobriety while in the hospital but also develop a comprehensive aftercare program that will enable her to maintain sobriety when she returns to her normal life.

While in the hospital, many teenagers learn a great deal about drugs, themselves, and their families. Strong group support from fellow teens who are dealing with similar issues can be a tremendous support for the individual adolescent while in the hospital (Smith, 1985). Many teenagers join adolescent AA or adolescent NA (Narcotics Anonymous) support groups. This new source of twinship can sometimes be very helpful in the recovery process. In fact, the entire inpatient substance abuse program is usually a strong source of education and support for teenagers suffering from severe substance abuse or dependency.

Unfortunately, most inpatient drug treatment centers are not able to provide extended treatment for the adolescent patient. The onset of managed care, although well intended and long overdue in many respects, has severely curtailed the amount of time most adolescents and their families can afford treatment. The skyrocketing cost of medical care has forced most insurance companies to limit adolescent inpatient drug treatment to three weeks at most. This is hardly enough time to get sober, let alone develop the internal resources and supports necessary to maintain successful sobriety on the outside. Fortunately, there are a number of alternatives.

Partial Hospitalization/Day Treatment

One of the newest drug treatment alternatives are day treatment or partial hospitalization programs. These programs offer almost the same array of ser-vices as the traditional inpatient programs, but the adolescent goes home at night. Some partial programs even have an initial inpatient hospital stay of several days or weeks, followed by a partial program lasting many more months. The advantage to this approach is obviously the lower cost, while still maintaining inpatient-like services for the adolescent. While this approach is certainly better than short-term inpatient programs alone, it also may fall far short of what the adolescent needs.

Perhaps the most difficult part of maintaining sobriety for any age group is altering the individual's lifestyle. For adults, it means drastically changing thinking, behaviors, and emotions. A key to maintaining sobriety is substi-tuting new behaviors for old addictive ones. This is an overwhelming task for even the most sincere and committed addict. AA can become a new social support that can assist in the process. Spouse, partner, family, and colleagues can also be crucial in the recovery work. For adolescents, however, this process is even more difficult.

Remember that adolescents need their peer group to help them sepa-rate from their family as well as define their own identity through twinship. Establishing a solid peer group can be difficult for even the most emotion-ally mature and well-adjusted teenager. Changing that peer group can be traumatic, especially if the change is imposed. Most adolescents who are in drug treatment return to their home environment, where they will find their old peer group waiting for them. The adolescent patient is still working through his development, only now without the help of drugs and alcohol. If a comprehensive aftercare plan is not developed and carefully adhered to, most teenage addicts are doomed to relapse.

Outpatient

The effectiveness of an outpatient approach to adolescent substance abuse depends upon a variety of factors, including the extent of the substance abuse problem, cooperation of family, resources in the community, and com-petence of the practitioner. Almost without exception, it is advisable for any teenager who has gone through hospital treatment to continue in some form of ongoing outpatient therapy. This adjunctive treatment may be in addition to AA/NA-type support groups, day treatment programs, and alternative programs aimed at helping the adolescent remain sober.

Outpatient therapy is the only place where the adolescent client can immerse herself in a safe, confidential, and empathic environment and get back on the developmental track. The outpatient therapist must not only be able to establish a therapeutic relationship in the manner discussed early in this book but also know when it is time to intervene in order to protect the adolescent client from further self-destructive behavior. All the knowledge, skill, and technique discussed earlier still apply to working with this particular adolescent population. What is important to remember is how stunted the adolescent's emotional life has been owing to her substance use/abuse/dependency.

Every adolescent substance-abusing client is different. Therefore, every approach to practice is different. But there are a few key generalizations. First, the competent clinician must be able to form an empathic relationship with the teenager in which she feels that her circumstances are truly understood. Only when the teenager believes this to be true will she allow herself to be honest and open in the clinical work. Second, the competent clinician must understand that this adolescent's emotional capabilities have been compromised owing to extensive drug use. The adolescent will probably have to rely on the clinician as a source of emotional support and sustenance in the process of recovery. This means that the therapist must be cognitively, behaviorally, and emotionally available. Third, the competent clinician can expect the adolescent in recovery to be resistant and prone to relapse. With each relapse, however, most addicts move toward a greater chance of ultimate recovery. Fourth, the competent clinician must work with the adolescent's family and community. This does not mean impulsively violating the teenager's confidentiality in the interest of maintaining sobriety. It means helping coordinate services for the teenager when she is not able to do it for herself. In order to be a successful practitioner working with substance using adolescents, the clinician must be aware of what the community has to offer.

PREVENTION SERVICES

Finally, a chapter on adolescent drug use would not be complete without some discussion of prevention services. Nowadays, most adolescents have been through some type of drug education program by the time they enter sixth grade. These programs range from primitive scare tactics to sophisticated values clarification education. Using drugs is a choice, yes, and perhaps "just saying no" is technically the answer. But the multitude of factors that contribute to drug use/abuse/dependency are extremely complex and interwoven. Therefore, drug education and prevention must be sophisticated.

Learning the straight facts about drugs is important. It is also important to learn why many people use drugs and to have key figures in one's life who model healthy approaches to managing thoughts, behavior, and emotions. Modeling is crucial for children and teenagers. The media have recently emphasized how talking to your kids about drugs helps. Research seems to indicate that it does. The reason is not the information that is shared; it is the relationship context in which that conversation happens. Children and adolescents need to feel cared about. The clinician too can play a crucial role in that process.

The clinician working with substance-using teens can become an important source of knowledge, support, and identification. Timely disclosure of the clinician's own drug usage can be a pivotal point for many teenagers struggling with substance use. Once the therapist can be trusted, many adolescents will listen to bits of information and education that the clinician might provide them. The only way adolescents will steer clear of self-destructive substance use is if they themselves have decided that it is not good for them. They may also discover in a helpful therapeutic relationship that alternative activities and interactions can be as fulfilling as drugs.

I would be lying if I said that I have had tremendous success in helping adolescent clients stay sober or never use drugs. Most teenagers I have seen in my thirty years of practice do use them at least occasionally. But I believe I have had an impact on their awareness of drugs and how they are affected by them. For many of my teenage clients, that has made a substantial difference in the nature and extent of their use.

It is also important to continue to bear in mind that family is a key factor in adolescent drug use. Even if parents or caretakers have used, or the family situation is such that teens have not developed adequate means to manage their emotions without drugs, the clinician must work with family if he is to be successful in helping the adolescent client. This is not a blame game.

CASE EXAMPLES

Several years ago I began seeing a fourteen-year-old client by the name of Jeff. He was referred to me by the school social worker; however, both Jeff and his father felt that it would be good if he got some therapy. Jeff had been injured in a bicycle accident the year before. He was attempting some stunts with his bike when he lost control and landed on his head. Jeff was in the hospital for quite some time. He was initially in a coma, but when he regained consciousness he realized that he was paralyzed from the neck down. Jeff told me that from the moment he got the news about his condition, he always thought, "I am going to walk again"; he never imagined any other possibility, even though the doctors were not sure if he would ever walk. It is very important to remember the type of person Jeff was and his attitude toward his circumstances.

Jeff's mother had been suffering from brain cancer, and coincidentally she died the same week that Jeff was hospitalized. Jeff knew she was very sick, but he was never able to say goodbye to his mother or attend her funeral because he was in a coma. Jeff was extremely close to his mother. This too is a very important thing to remember about this case.

Jeff's father was an unconditional support for his son. He was in his fifties and semiretired. From the time of Jeff's accident, he devoted his life to Jeff's recovery. He was supportive of Jeff's therapy and respectful of the confidential nature of the relationship. But with Jeff's approval he and I continually consulted regarding the progress of Jeff's therapy.

Jeff came from a large family of athletes of which he was the youngest. Many of Jeff's sibs lived across the country. Sports were a way of life for Jeff and his family. Even his mother had been a tremendous soccer player and marathon runner. Prior to his accident, Jeff was the star athlete of his class. He excelled in basketball, baseball, soccer, virtually any sport he tried. Jeff's self-concept and identity, developing both in Erikson's industry vs. inferiority and identity vs. role confusion stages, were shaped by sports and the social status and recognition that came from them. Jeff was the most popular kid in his class. He was recognized for his sports prowess, as well as his social abilities. His accident changed all that.

Jeff also mentioned to me that substance use and abuse were prevalent in his family. Apparently several of his sibs had drug problems growing up. Jeff seemed to realize that this was a family issue. This too is very important information for this case.

When Jeff first began therapy with me, he was struggling with understanding and coming to grips with the extent of his physical limitations. I came to understand that after a serious accident such as Jeff's, there is a two-year window of recovery. After that time, additional physical improvement is unlikely. Jeff was an exception to this rule from the beginning. This ability had both positive and negative elements for him.

Jeff worked a rigorous schedule of physical rehabilitation during the time that he saw me. He went to physical rehab at least three times a week. He worked on his upper body mostly, but also on all areas that had been affected by the injury. This task took a lot out of Jeff, both physically and emotionally. Jeff did not have much energy for anything else. As a result, his schoolwork suffered badly. He did not fail any classes, but he certainly did not get much more than a C in any of them. He felt that that part of his life was not important right now. He was trying to get back to his old self. Unfortunately, that would never happen. Jeff began to sink into an understandable depression as a result of that fact.

Jeff usually came to sessions in an up mood. Despite his difficulties, he always seemed to have a positive attitude regarding his condition and the future. But Jeff did not want to accept that his future could not involve participating in sports. His biggest emotional struggle in the early part of therapy was coming to grips with that fact.

My role as Jeff's therapist was complicated by the fact that I did not know if he would be able to return to his old athletic form. I was hesitant to confront Jeff about the true nature or prognosis of his condition. I did not want to suggest that he would never be fully healthy again if that was not true. On the other hand, I felt that it was important to discuss Jeff's physical limitations. Until he and I knew what the outcome would truly be, therapy was at a standstill. This dilemma was a major part of the therapy with Jeff.

To look at Jeff, one might not immediately recognize that he had any physical limitations. He could walk normally, and he could use his left arm quite well. He had poor upper body strength and very limited use of his right arm. He had to raise his right arm using his left in order to do anything with it. Jeff was extremely self-conscious about this and kept the use of his impaired arm to a minimum. For example, he would not raise his right arm to answer a question in class for fear that he would make an obvious scene. Jeff dressed and acted in a manner that disguised and covered up his physical limitations. But everyone knew he had difficulties. He was the most popular kid in school, and the whole community knew of his accident and subsequent injuries. This fact too was a major blow to Jeff.

Jeff still socialized with many of his former peers, but he was no longer the star that he was prior to his injury. Jeff had been top dog in junior high, and now he was in high school. He had been hospitalized for nearly a year before he regained much of his physical movement and was able to return to his life. He had been out of the loop for some time. As he struggled to come to grips with his physical limitations and the drastic change in his social status, Jeff began using substances to cope. His peer group used drugs and alcohol in a recreational fashion. Jeff informed me that "everyone uses" and that he used socially.

It seemed to me from the beginning of my relationship with Jeff that his use of drugs was a form of self-medication. Jeff was an extremely bright, introspective, and articulate adolescent, and our sessions were always filled with lengthy in-depth conversation about his life, emotions, family, and philosophy. Jeff seemed well aware of his plight, but he was not quite sure how he was going to handle it. It seemed to me that his drug use was a way of coping with an overwhelming situation that would have derailed even the most capable adult.

Instead of immediately intervening in Jeff's drug use, I decided to explore its meaning to him and perhaps, given his capacity for insight, help him understand it as well. Jeff seemed most drawn to mushrooms or "shrooms" as his drug of choice. When he was tripping on shrooms, Jeff became even more introspective and focused not only on his thoughts and emotions but also on his injured body. He spent hours contemplating his situation and imagining what his life might be like in the future. Yes, his drug use was self-destructive, but it was also in some odd ways therapeutic in its ability to help him cope with an unbearable situation.

During this period I seriously contemplated breaching confidentiality in order to help Jeff with his drug problem. I did consistently speak with his father about his progress. To my surprise, Jeff's dad knew or suspected that Jeff was using drugs. He and I both agreed that it was not time to intervene in any psychiatric sense but that I should keep working with Jeff to help him deal with his life. Fortunately, Jeff's bout with psychedelic mushrooms was very short lived. He used them for only about two months off and on. He decided on his own (with my support) that using shrooms was not really helpful and in fact was keeping him from facing his situation.

But Jeff's drug use was not over. His social group used continuously, and Jeff partied with his friends most weekends over the next year. This included primarily drinking and smoking marijuana. Jeff began to recognize that he did not really enjoy using drugs and alcohol with his peers. He would discuss his distaste for it in session. He realized that many of his friends used just to get wasted and that the continual use was affecting their lives. Jeff once again on his own volition stopped using.

During the time that I saw him, Jeff was also seriously involved with a girlfriend. They were intimate both physically and emotionally. Interestingly, Jeff seemed to be the one least invested in the relationship. He would tell me that he really liked his girlfriend and that she probably loved him but that he would probably not stay with her. Jeff also knew that his feelings about her had something to do with the loss of his mother. He really didn't want to become attached to any girl right now. This was an amazing insight for a fifteen-year-old male. As Jeff began to give up drugs, he also discovered new interests. He became adept at poker. Jeff found that he could emotionally read almost anyone he played with, and he was good at bluffing and betting. Jeff also started to develop an interest in writing. He had told me early on that he used to write poetry and that writing in general came very naturally to him. He was just not sure that he wanted to do that for a living. He wasn't quite ready to give up the idea that he would play sports again. This was Jeff's real struggle.

As he entered his senior year of high school, Jeff began to use the therapy to explore exactly what his new identity would be. He was able to get his driver's license without the use of any physical aids such as hand controls. He decided to stop using drugs altogether, except the occasional drinking party, because he recognized that they interfered in his ability to know himself. His therapy consisted of exploring his identity in what Erikson (1950) might term an atmosphere of "moratorium." Jeff realized that he would never be able to participate in sports like the rest of his family but that his contributions would be remarkable nonetheless. He received awards for his writing, both poetry and fiction, and Jeff knew that writing was to be his identity and future. His bout with substances was a detour along the way, but one that he was able to traverse through his therapy and innate ability and resilience.

Jeff was the type of client who turns to drugs as a temporary way of coping with a severe physical and emotional trauma. Could he have benefited from inpatient treatment? Probably. Would he have been able to gain the insights he did by working through his own drug use in his therapy with me? Probably not. It may have taken Jeff some time to come to these insights through imposed treatment. Jeff seemed to possess the innate core self necessary to utilize insight-oriented therapy to work through his developmental trauma. Most teenagers are not that resilient or insightful. Jeff was and is a unique and gifted individual. My hunch is that he got a lot of that innate ability from his relationship with his mother (and father?). Had he been a different type of adolescent, Jeff might never have been able to handle the emotional impact of his injury or pull himself out of drug abuse without serious intervention. Our second case example, Kelly, is that type of adolescent.

Kelly was also referred to me by her school social worker many years ago. She was having trouble academically and behaviorally in high school. Kelly was a sixteen-year-old girl from a blended family. Her parents divorced when she was eight, and her father remarried when Kelly was twelve. Kelly did not get along with her stepmother. Her birth mother had not remarried but lived with a man fifteen years younger. Kelly had an enmeshed relationship with her mom, even though she did not live with her. Kelly and her mom were more like friends than mother and daughter. Kelly was the youngest of four. Her older sibs were all in their twenties and lived outside the parental residence. Kelly was in many ways left on her own emotionally.

Kelly was immediately engaged in the therapy. She seemed to enjoy the attention and would spend sessions discussing all areas of her life, particularly her social life. Kelly felt disconnected and misunderstood by her parents. She also felt that they were much too strict with her. She wanted to be able to spend time with her friends and didn't think that her folks should interfere in any way whatsoever. Kelly didn't believe that she should have a curfew, and she also didn't see anything wrong with smoking dope all the time and drinking as much as she wanted whenever she could get it. School was not important, and Kelly failed to see why her parents were concerned about her failing grades and frequent trips to the dean for missed classes.

Kelly's father was very involved in the treatment. Family sessions occurred almost as frequently as Kelly's individual appointments. Although interested in Kelly's welfare, her father was extremely rigid and did not seem to understand her need for attention and support. He felt that Kelly should know what was expected of her and fit into her new family. He did not see any reason why Kelly should not like or get along with her stepmother and was not tolerant of Kelly's anger toward her. I had the sense that Kelly's father loved her but was not quite sure how to understand or support her. He seemed extremely rigid in his role as father and caretaker.

Kelly's biological mother came to a few individual appointments but spent the entire time narcissistically focusing on her own needs. She seemed interested in Kelly only insofar as Kelly could respond to her. I was left with the sense that Kelly must feel very alone with both these parents. She was struggling to survive in an emotional wasteland.

As time went on, I tried to engage Kelly in a therapy relationship aimed at meeting her tremendous insecurity, as well as helping her gain insight into her unsatisfying relationships with both her families. Although Kelly did seem capable of some insight and also seemed to benefit from the self psychology approach I used with her in therapy, it was not enough to alter her self-destructive drug abuse. Kelly began coming to sessions high, often with her girlfriends. I realized that she felt very comfortable with the therapy relationship and also enjoyed discussing many issues and concerns with me but that she was definitely getting worse. I decided that I must breach confidentiality and inform her father of her extensive drug involvement.

As I suspected, Kelly's father was not supportive of his daughter's severe problem. He immediately chose to involuntarily hospitalize her for her drug dependency. This in itself was probably a good idea, except for the fact that Kelly's two families continued their emotionally distant stance in their relationship with her. Kelly's father and mother viewed her as the problem, were extremely critical of her, and did not participate in developing a supportive and comprehensive aftercare plan for her recovery.

Not surprisingly, Kelly continued to relapse. She saw me for several months after her first hospitalization, but her father removed her from treatment after I began to urge him to become more involved in the therapy. He seemed to want to see Kelly's drug problem as a flaw in her and would not consider working on a plan that might involve the family in any way. I did not see Kelly again after that time.

These two cases demonstrate the dramatic contrasts in working with adolescents who are suffering from substance abuse issues. Both Jeff and Kelly might be described as drug abusers or even drug dependent. But they possessed very different constitutional factors and environmental supports.

Although Jeff's family history indicated that alcoholism might be a genetic factor in his drug use, he was capable of managing it better than Kelly. Jeff too had gone through some very extreme trauma and loss that certainly could have been a contributing factor to his decision to use substances. Yet Jeff did not struggle with substance use in the same way that Kelly did. Why not?

I cannot be certain, but it seemed to me that Jeff had a much stronger constitution than Kelly. I also think that Jeff had a much more supportive family system. Even though his mother had died, Jeff had internalized some very effective coping mechanisms from her. He clearly had internalized some healthy capacity for object constancy. In other words, he was already somewhat able to self-soothe in times of stress and loss. An example of that fact is that from the very moment of waking from his coma, he knew he would walk. I believe that this type of confidence comes from secure attachment and the proper constitution.

Jeff also had a father who was an ongoing support for him as he struggled with his physical and emotional losses and who was understanding of his possible use of substances. Had he been hospitalized for drug treatment, I am quite certain that Jeff's father would have been extremely supportive and that his family would have rallied around him to help him succeed. Jeff did not need that support, but it would have been there for him if he did.

Kelly appeared to be emotionally insecure from the start. Although I did not get a sense of her family's drug and alcohol history, I suspect that she too probably had some family history of it. Her relationship with her mother and father clearly indicated to me that Kelly was not securely attached, probably from infancy. She was a highly anxious teenager but also desperate for attention. I would argue that Kelly needed continual emotional support in order to feel safe and secure. Unfortunately, neither of her parents was emotionally available for her in the way she needed them. As a result, as she entered adolescence, the normal anxiety that comes from the search for identity and self-confidence was never managed successfully. Kelly did not have the tools to deal with her insecurity, and she was not able to self-soothe. She was also given the message from both her families that she was on her own. I believe that Kelly turned to drugs as a way of managing these feelings. The drugs gave her a sense of security but ultimately were destructive for her. Had she gotten more support early in life, I believe that Kelly might not have been as drug dependent. She still may have used, like many teens, but her use may not have been as self-destructive. She might also have been able to utilize the therapy as Jeff did and been able to find herself.

BASIS OF PRACTICE

Some of the references cited above indicate that the recovery rate for persons suffering from drug and alcohol problems is only about 20 percent. For adolescents it is even lower, given that they usually return to an environment in which many of their peers are continuing to use. Peer relationships form the core of most adolescents' world, and it is extremely difficult to modify those relationships during that developmental period. However, Thomas O'Hare, in his book *Evidence-Based Practices for Social Workers* (2005), states: "Effective substance-abuse intervention represents an array of supportive, coping-skills, and case management interventions that can be employed as specific strategies, as complete 'treatment packages,' or in eclectic combinations" (p. 144).

SUMMARY

This chapter has covered the complex and vitally important topic of drug use/abuse/dependence by adolescents. Adolescents use for a variety of reasons, and there are many complicated factors that contribute to whether or not they become drug dependent. The competent clinician is called upon to understand the myriad of etiological factors involved in adolescent drug dependence, as well as the multifaceted approaches to successful treatment. Working successfully with adolescent drug use is difficult. This chapter has attempted to equip the practitioner with the knowledge and skills necessary to handle it.

RECOMMENDED RESOURCES

Readings

Harold E. Doweiko, *Concepts of Chemical Dependency* (Pacific Grove, CA: Thomson-Brooks/Cole, 2002). This text provides comprehensive chemical dependency information.

Thomas O'Hare, *Evidence-Based Practices for Social Workers* (Chicago: Lyceum Books, 2005). This text provides a solid evidence base for studies of addiction practice.

T. Smith, "Group Work with Adolescent Drug Users," *Social Work with Groups* 8, no. 1 (1985): 369–376. This article examines therapeutic groupwork as an intervention with adolescents.

Film/Television/Media

The Breakfast Club (1985), *Dazed and Confused* (1993), *Thirteen* (2003). All three films present powerful and realistic drug abuse scenarios.

Internet

http://www6.miami.edu/ctrada/; http://www.drugpolicy.org/safetyfirst/adolescent/ These two sites provide good information on drug abuse and addiction.

13

Gender Issues and Working with Adolescents

The development of gender identity and gender orientation is one of the most pivotal aspects of adolescence. Although the sex organs develop during pregnancy in the uterus, the psychological manifestations of gender identity and orientation crystallize during adolescence. Research studies suggest that all human beings begin to develop with the same physical sex apparatus. It is only the timed release of specific hormones that dictates whether an infant will develop male or female sex organs. This indicates that all of us may have been capable of physically developing into either a boy or a girl (Pinel, 2006). Regardless of whether we are born with a male or female body, however, gender identity is a process shaped by social, cultural, psychological, and emotional factors throughout life. The combined interaction of all these elements shapes identity formation during adolescence.

Gender identity begins to take shape from the moment of birth. Long before a human being has language, he or she is being responded to as a specific gender type. Little boys tend to be handled more physically and to be spoken to in louder and more aggressive ways. Little girls are handled in a more delicate manner and spoken to in soft and quieter tones. In a study, adults who were given newborn infants to hold responded to them based on the gender they believed them to be. If the adult was told it was a boy infant he was holding, he handled it more aggressively; if he believed the infant was a girl, he was gentler. Even from the moment of birth, the insidious process of gender development is at work. It is inescapable, automatic, and unconscious.

Although there seems to be new evidence that suggests that there are differences in the brains of men and women, arguably the most powerful influence on gender development is the social context (Cozolino, 2002). Interactions with others dictate the way in which individuals come to know themselves, especially their gender identification (Floyd et al., 1999).

THEORIES OF GENDER DEVELOPMENT

There are numerous theories to explain the development of gender identity. Social learning theory and/or behavior theory might suggest that it is the ways in which a child's behavior is reinforced that dictate gender identification. A little girl who is praised and rewarded for acting like a sweet little girl may become one. If that same girl is punished or ignored for behaving like a tomboy, she may be less likely to continue that behavior. Cognitive theory would posit that our core beliefs or fundamental schemas regarding gender identification are developed in early childhood. For instance, a child may learn from his family that little boys are strong, do not cry, don't play with dolls, and don't show emotions. Little girls are caring, do not fight or show aggression, want to be mothers, are allowed to cry, and should want to dress up in pretty clothes. I am not saying that these are the correct values for little boys and girls to develop, but they are sometimes imposed upon them.

Self psychology would focus on the utilization of all three self-objects in the formation of gender development. Children are mirrored for their proper display of gender traits. They are emotionally validated for specific gender behaviors and interactions by their primary caretakers. Children idealize and merge with important others of the same gender. This merger process includes the internalization of a variety of aspects of the idealized other, including gender traits. Finally, children learn to feel a sense of sameness and similarity through the use of twinship self-object relationships with family, peers, and other important same-sex figures. These key relationships not only nourish the child's emotional self but help to form the core of his gender identity.

Freud's emphasis on the bisexual development of all children is often overlooked. In *The Ego and the Id* (1960), Freud discusses this important aspect of psychological development: "Closer study usually discloses the more complete Oedipus complex, which is twofold, positive and negative, and is due to the *bisexuality* (emphasis mine) originally present in children; that is to say, a boy has not merely an ambivalent attitude toward his father, and an affectionate object-choice towards his mother, but at the same time he also behaves like a girl and displays an affectionate feminine attitude to his father and a corresponding jealousy and hostility towards his mother" (p. 23). These are profound insights into the complexity of gender identity development.

Freud is mentioned here as an example of the ways in which gender identity was examined in the late 1800s and early 1900s by some of the most brilliant minds in psychological history. He is quite often misunderstood and summarily dismissed, but his early contributions on many fronts helped set the stage for meaningful and comprehensive discussion of these crucial aspects of identity formation.

Harold Searles has been one of the most courageous and prolific writers on the subject of countertransference. He dared to examine and write about the myriad of complex emotional reactions that he himself, and by implication, most sensitive and introspective clinicians experience in the intensive process of the therapeutic relationship. He highlights the diagnostic significance of these emotions in understanding the developmental needs of the client. The emotions a clinician is experiencing in session may be a signal about some psychological process within the client. If the clinician ignores these important signals, he may miss an opportunity to understand the client and her development.

Object relations theory would dub this emotionally charged process *projective identification.* Neuroscience recognizes that the origin of this nonverbal communication lies in early attachment. We are all capable of recognizing and intuiting intentionality from cells in our brain called mirror neurons. These cells enable us to anticipate and understand actions and emotions without language. They begin to operate early in life and aid in social adaptation throughout the course of development (Cozolino, 2002).

Searles's classic but perhaps now forgotten article entitled "Oedipal Love in the Countertransference" (1959) emphasizes the developmental importance of the parental validation of the child's sexuality and gender identity early in life. He argues that if a child does not feel attractive to his parents, he will not feel attractive to others later in life. If these important developmental needs are not met in the relationships with the primary caretakers, the child may continue to express them throughout life, most importantly in the therapy relationship.

> Not only my work with patients but also my experiences as a husband and a parent have convinced me of the validity of the concepts which I am offering here. Towards my daughter, now eight years of age, I have experienced innumerable fantasies and feelings of a romantic-love kind, thoroughly complementary to the romantically adoring, seductive behavior which she has shown toward her father oftentimes ever since she was about two or three years of age. I used at times to feel somewhat worried when she would play the supremely confident coquette with me and I would feel enthralled by her charms; but then I came to the conviction, some time ago, that such moments of relatedness could only be nourishing for her developing personality as well as delightful to me. *If a little girl cannot feel herself able to win the heart of her father, her own father who has known her so well and for so long, and who is tied to her by mutual blood ties, I reasoned, then how can the young woman who comes later have any deep confidence in the power of her womanliness?* (p. 186; emphasis mine)

This profound and deeply moving passage captures the essence of the developmental importance of early relationships in the acquisition of gender identity. Acceptance, nurturing, and love are integral elements in this process. If there have been major difficulties in the development of gender identity early in life, there will be even greater difficulties in adolescence. The development of secondary sexual characteristics, the onset of abstract thought, the emotional separation from primary caretakers, as well as the new investment in the adolescent peer group all become crucial factors in the further refinement of gender identity in adolescence. These important circumstances should always be taken into consideration when working with teenagers.

Searles experienced intense emotions in therapeutic interactions with heterosexual as well as homosexual clients. His profoundly important work underscores the necessity for all clinicians to allow themselves to experience, through vicarious introspection and empathic identification, the emotions and key aspects of sexuality inherent in all clients.

GENDER IDENTITY FORMATION DURING ADOLESCENCE

The development of gender identity and sexual orientation is shaped by a variety of physical and emotional factors. Early relationship with the primary caretakers is a crucial aspect of that process. The ways in which those experiences are internalized and understood by the child dramatically shape their sense of gender identity.

For example, I can clearly remember the drastically different ways in which my parents helped to shape my sense of self and gender identity. When I was around four or five years old, my mother would play Superman with me. I was Clark Kent, Superman's secret identity, complete with a Superman suit underneath my regular clothes. My mother was Lois Lane, Superman's girlfriend. We would play out scenarios in which Lois would tell Clark Kent that there was trouble in town and Superman was needed. I would cleverly go back to my bedroom, change into my Superman costume, and return to save Lois Lane from danger. I remember feeling not only very powerful in this play but also very loved and adored by my mother. It was an invaluable piece of early life experience and serves as a metaphor for the development of my early gender identity. My experiences with my father were much more negative. My father was an alcoholic. He rarely gave me positive validation, as far as I can remember. He was verbally and sometimes physically abusive not only to me but to my siblings. Here is an example of how this behavior affected the development of my gender identity. My father was an excellent swimmer. He constantly reminded all of us about how he held the record for underwater swimming at his high school. We went to the beach quite often in the summer when I was a child. My dad always drank and, at my mother's insistence, tried to teach my younger brother and me how to swim. I remember him aggressively holding us in waist-deep water (which was probably over my head) and yelling at us to "kick your legs, move your arms." I remember saying, "Don't drop me!" When we did not immediately respond to his angry commands by swimming proficiently, he became frustrated and angry and would say, "You'll never learn." We never did.

These two very different types of parental responsiveness obviously influenced my gender identity development in very different ways. From my mother I gained a sense of validation, power, and competence; from my father, a sense of insecurity, fear, and failure. This is an example from my own life, I know, but I cannot think of a much better one to emphasize the importance of those early life experiences in shaping the development of gender identity.

The identification with the peer group also strongly influences gender identity development. Each adolescent clique has its own style of dress, mannerisms, and language. In addition, it has implicit rules regarding how boys and girls are to be perceived and related to in a wide range of social interactions. This dynamic serves the purpose of helping the individual adolescent within the clique (group) to identify with others like himself (twinship) and in the process try on a possible identity that certainly includes gender roles and characteristics. I believe that this process goes on unconsciously, yet it is a necessary part of the development of gender identity.

An example from my own adolescence may be helpful here. I went to Catholic elementary school up through eighth grade. We all wore uniforms. The boys wore navy blue pants, light blue shirts, black dress shoes, and snap on criss-cross ties. The girls wore white blouses, with matching red plaid vests and pleated skirts, white bobby socks and black dress shoes. There wasn't much room for individuality or creativity. The move from that environment to a secular high school was traumatic. I had no idea except from television, what teenagers wore to regular school. I had a very steep learning curve to overcome in the transition.

My high school journey involved participation in at least three diverse cliques. I was first involved in the "jocks" or what might today be called the "preps." These were the adolescents who valued academics, sports, and traditional high school activities. They dressed in clothes that were considered to be the most popular and that were usually very expensive. Jocks did not smoke cigarettes, or marijuana for that matter. There was a clear hierarchy of popularity and status. For boys, the leader was the captain of the high school football team, usually the quarterback; for girls, it was the captain of the cheerleading squad. Boys should be strong, athletic, and successful. Girls were supposed to be pretty, soft-spoken, and gentle, adore their men, and not perform too well in school. Heterosexual couples went on official dates, and if they did have sex, it was covert and not discussed. In hindsight, this clique in many ways represented the adult establishment to me. My participation in this mainstream clique might even be considered a form of identity foreclosure from an Eriksonian standpoint. I tried my best to fit in, but something about this clique felt artificial after a while. The people in it seemed phony. They did not seem real. Staying in that clique felt like living a lie to me. I therefore moved to the other end of the continuum, the "greasers," or what might today be called the "gang bangers" or "burnouts."

The greasers were the enemies of the jocks. Their clique was the antithesis of the traditional establishment. Greasers hated sports as well as academics. They loved cars, drinking, fighting jocks and other greasers, and heterosexual sex. Greaser guys had slicked-back hair and wore baggy gray cuffed pants, steel-toed work boots for fighting, and short-sleeve shirts of stretch material, which accentuated their muscles and could hold a pack of cigarettes tucked in the sleeve. Of course greaser guys and girls smoked cigarettes. There was also a patriarchal hierarchy in the greaser clique. It was based not on mainstream achievements but rather on how tough you were. Greaser girls had no status except as sexual objects. They too were tough and would fight each other over a guy, but their main value to the clique was for sex. The greaser girls wore pumped-up ratted hair with lots of hairspray. They dressed in high heels, short, tight miniskirts, and tight sweaters. The greaser girls also wore lots of makeup, especially black eye shadow and dark lipstick. If you were a girl, your gender identity as a greaser was to be a slut and belong to a greaser guy. If you were a greaser guy, your gender identity consisted of being known for your sexual prowess.

At first, my involvement in this clique was exciting and served as an expression of defiance and rebellion toward the jock clique. After a while though, the greaser clique too felt empty to me. I began to realize that in the greaser clique as well, there was not much individualization. Everyone seemed the same. I was also not comfortable expressing my gender identity in such simplistic and drastic ways. I liked and respected women. Treating them as objects did not feel right. It also did not help me to develop any type of mutual respect and emotional satisfaction in my relationships with them. I soon came to realize that involvement in both the jocks and the greasers did not fit my gender identity or any part of my identity. There may have been elements in each of these cliques that rang true for me, but the rigid adherence to their specific ideologies was false.

This example is meant to help the reader recognize not only how the adolescent clique helps to shape gender identity but also its timelessness. Adolescents today discover their gender identity in large part from involvement in similar cliques. Whether the clique is called the preps, the skaters, or the goths, the function is still the same: to determine what it means to be a male or female through the association with others.

This process becomes even more complicated when an adolescent is struggling with issues of identification with being gay, lesbian, bisexual, or transgendered (GLBT). Although there is clearly greater tolerance and acceptance for being GLBT in our society today, gender identification and orientation for GLBT adolescents are much more difficult than for heterosexual teenagers (Ryan & Futterman, 1998).

*D*ATING

Another key aspect of the development of gender identity is the dating process. When I was an adolescent there seemed to be much more one-on-one dating. The guy asked the girl out, and if she said yes, the two of them went on a date to the movies or the burger place. Within the last couple of decades, the dating process seems to have evolved into a group activity. The purpose is still the same—to get to know someone the teenager is attracted to—but the circumstances are buffered by the presence of the peer group. Regardless of how many people are involved in the dating ritual, it serves the purpose of helping adolescents discover their gender identity through interactions with others. Eventually dating does become a one-to-one encounter. In that more intimate relationship, adolescents begin to discover their sexual identities.

Freud said, "The ego is first and foremost a body ego." Nowhere is that statement more accurate than in the discovery of sexual intimacy in adolescence. Through sexual experimentation with another partner, through the physical and emotion sensations of her body and that of the other, the adolescent discovers her gender identity. Many theorists believe that a hallmark of emotional maturity in adolescence is the ability to fall in love with another. First love symbolizes the end of childhood dependency. The child has found a love object aside from the parents. It is what Erikson means by the stage of intimacy vs. isolation. Although adolescents are not emotionally capable of approaching this stage with the maturity that comes a few years later, they are defining their gender identity through the experience. The give-and-take on all levels in a sexual relationship helps the adolescent know herself better. This is a crucial part of the formation of gender identity.

GAY, LESBIAN, BISEXUAL, AND TRANSGENDER ADOLESCENTS

There is not enough space in this book to give the topic of gender identity formation for gay, lesbian, bisexual, and transgendered adolescents (GLBT) the emphasis it truly deserves. But some discussion of this very important area is crucial for understanding and working with the adolescent population. From the discussion above one can certainly see that the process of gender identity formation is complex, even for heterosexual teenagers. When an adolescent is GLBT, the process becomes even more delicate, complicated, and confusing.

The suicide rate is highest among the adolescent age group. Within that age group, it is highest among the GLBT population. Adolescence is the search for identity. Gender identity is an integral part of that search. The journey toward gender identity in adolescence is dictated by adherence to discrete norms and ideology. Most teenagers, especially in early adolescence, want to know and be a particular gender. From my earlier examples the reader can see that this often means becoming what everybody else is. That kind of conformity may feel safe initially, but ultimately the adolescent must find his own unique sense of gender identity. There is confusion in that process for even the most clearly heterosexual teenager. If an adolescent is

GLBT, the process can be excruciatingly painful and isolating. Although our society appears to be more tolerant of the GLBT population, there is still prejudice and discrimination against that group. In adolescence, a GLBT youth may not be able to cope with those issues and turn to suicide as the only way out of what may feel like an unbearable situation (Morrow, 2004).

Fortunately, the situation seems to be improving. In my adolescence during the 1960s, I did not even know GLBT teenagers existed. Today, they are making out in the hallways of some high schools. It also seems to be more acceptable to "come out" in today's adolescent culture. Sexual experimentation has always been a part of adolescent development. Engaging in gay, lesbian, or bisexual behaviors does not necessarily mean one is gay, lesbian, or bisexual. Present adolescent culture seems even more accepting of sexual experimentation. But once an adolescent knows he is GLBT, the sense of social isolation, discrimination, and oppression becomes a real factor in his life. It is then that these youths need support and can truly benefit from connections with others who are like them (Fairchild & Hayward, 1998).

PRACTICE IMPLICATIONS AND RECOMMENDATIONS

Given the previous discussion, the astute clinician can imagine that attention should be paid to gender identity formation as an integral part of any therapeutic practice with adolescents. The delicate and multifaceted nature of this process calls upon the therapist to approach it with extreme care. Many adolescents in therapy will discuss their peer group, their families, sometimes even their most intimate sexual relationships. It is the clinician's responsibility to help the adolescent negotiate his journey toward identity formation and all the complex variables that are part of it. In this area, however, certain principles must be adhered to in the clinical work.

First, never assume that an adolescent you are working with is heterosexual, gay, lesbian, bisexual, or transgender until that adolescent has come to the certainty of it himself. This can be a delicate and lengthy process. The clinician should use words like significant other, special person, and so on in all preliminary discussions about relationships. This is not to be politically correct but rather to give the adolescent the opportunity to discuss his gender identity in an open, accepting, empathic, and nonjudgmental manner. If you ask a gay adolescent male "Do you have a girlfriend?" he may be much less likely to initiate discussion about his homosexuality, or even his confusion about his gender identity. The therapist should strive as much as possible to keep the door open for this discussion.

Many clinicians working with adolescents have the rainbow symbol hanging prominently in their office. This symbol does not mean the clinician is gay but rather that her office is a safe place in which to discuss issues related to the GLBT population. Displaying this sign may also frighten some more homophobic adolescents, especially those who are still struggling to feel comfortable in their gender role. The clinician must be sensitive to the complexity of these issues and be available in an open and nonjudgmental way to help adolescents discuss them.

Community resources can serve as an invaluable way to help GLBT teens feel less isolated. Some high schools have support groups for their adolescent GLBT population. Much like traditional cliques, these groups can provide a meaningful way to help this group find themselves by interacting with others who are like them (twinship). Clinicians should make it their standard practice to have a wealth of resources available to the GLBT youth with whom they work.

There are also some very standard approaches to helping all adolescents negotiate their gender identity. Remember that although the search for identity is individualized, it is common to all adolescents. All teenagers have formed a basis of gender identity through their early attachment relationships and childhood identifications in their families of origin (Johnson & Whiffen, 2003). The physical and emotional autonomy that an adolescent experiences as he separates from the primary caretakers thrusts him into exploring his gender identity through relationships with peers and other adults. The clinician can serve as an invaluable asset in that regard.

A same-sex therapist also functions as an important source of twinship for the adolescent struggling with gender identity. She becomes another valuable person whom the adolescent can internalize as she continues to shape her sense of self. The careful use of self-disclosure by the clinician may be a useful way in which to help some teenagers feel less isolated in their search for gender identity. Knowing that her therapist may have experienced similar thoughts and emotions during her own adolescence may not only be comforting but offer possible coping mechanisms for the teenager who feels isolated in her search for gender identity. This aspect of the therapeutic relationship enhances the twinship self-object needs of the adolescent.

Opposite-sex therapists can also serve an invaluable function for the teenager dealing with gender identity. Experiencing a sensitive, caring, and insightful adult member of the opposite gender can enhance the adolescent's understanding not only of gender but of gender relationships. The resulting mutually respectful dialogue can influence the nature of future relationships. Symbolically this central element of the therapeutic relationship also enables the adolescent to work through key transference issues from early childhood.

Finally, adolescents who are certain of their own GLBT identity may find comfort and support in a GLBT therapist who can tactfully utilize self-disclosure to help them work through their own process. Research indicates that especially with gay clients, the appropriate and therapeutic use of self-disclosure can be quite helpful in the therapeutic relationship (Perez, DeBord, & Bieschke, 2000).

CASE EXAMPLE

Sometimes a clinician's first cases are the most valuable experiences in his clinical education. Of course it is usually in hindsight that the therapist recognizes his errors as well as realizes what he may have done well. This case is such an example.

Becky was in therapy with another counselor at my agency. I saw her occasionally in my outreach work at the high school. She was an extremely extroverted fourteen-year-old. Becky did not appear to me to be a particularly attractive girl. She was overweight and had acne and crooked teeth. She was not the epitome of adolescent beauty. She dressed provocatively and was extremely aggressive and seductive in her behavior with almost any adolescent boy she liked; she was even seductive and flirtatious with me.

When I would visit the local high school at lunchtimes during my outreach shifts, Becky would usually try to cling to me. She was clearly hungry for attention. But she had trouble setting boundaries. I continually had to set limits with her. She wanted to constantly be by my side, touch me, hold my arm, and tell other teens that I was her boyfriend. I was around twenty-five years old at the time, and although I still wore my hair long and dressed much like the adolescents I worked with, it was clear that I was an adult, much older than Becky. Although I was sensitive to her obvious need for attention, I continually found myself tactfully setting limits on her physically aggressive manner. She truly was a challenge.

Sometime after Becky had developed a relationship with me through my outreach work, she happened to run into me at our agency after her counseling appointment with the agency's other therapist. A short time later I was informed that Becky was insisting that she be able to switch to seeing me in therapy. This caused a bit of a minicrisis in the agency. The clinical staff (all three of us) debated the value of this change and whether it was therapeutic, resistance, acting out, and so on. Although I believe it may have been a slight blow to her therapist's ego, the decision was made to allow Becky to see me in therapy. Her previous therapist would continue working with her and her family in family therapy. I was to consult with her previous therapist regarding my work with Becky to help coordinate the overall treatment.

Becky had been referred to therapy by her parents because of her impulsivity, unruly and defiant behavior at home and school, poor grades, and overall attitude. Diagnostically she certainly fit the *DSM-IV-TR* category for oppositional defiant disorder. She also had some traits of borderline personality disorder, and perhaps elements of ADHD. I didn't realize this at the time. I understood Becky to be a troubled teenager who was having difficulty in school and with her parents. I had only a BA in sociology and had not gone to graduate school. I was still very naive about clinical theory and practice, but so were many of us in the youth work movement at the time.

I was not sure what to expect from Becky in our first session together. This was the very first time that Becky and I were really alone together. It was just the two of us in a quiet, private counseling office. Becky seemed to be very anxious. She was extremely talkative and appeared to be very excited to be alone with me. I tried to engage her in discussion about her parents' concerns, as well as how her therapy had been going prior to the switch to me. Becky didn't want to talk about that. She wanted to talk about us. She became extremely provocative in the session. She said to me, "I'll take off my top if you take off yours." I was flabbergasted. How was I going to handle this? I couldn't believe it was happening. I realized that given my previous experiences with Becky, I should have expected this type of behavior, but somehow I had thought that once she was alone with me in therapy, she would open up about her feelings and troubles.

After what seemed like ten minutes but was probably closer to three seconds, I informed Becky very clearly and directly that I was not going to take my shirt off, nor would I allow her to undress in the session. Becky protested and continued to try to persuade me but finally yielded to my limit setting. She was obviously frustrated, but I also detected a little relief in her manner. It occurred to me from that moment on that Becky was looking for limits, as well as attention, appreciation, and validation.

I continued to see Becky for many months following that first harrowing session. None of our sessions were as intense or difficult as that first one. Becky seemed to settle down after that first appointment. She knew where the boundaries were with me. She knew that she was safe and that I would keep the therapy secure. This afforded her the opportunity to begin to discuss the feelings beneath her brash exterior. Becky was struggling with her identity. In particular she was struggling with her gender identity. She was compensating for her intense insecurity by displaying a provocative and seductive front to most of the males in her life. Her fragile self could be nurtured only by the attention she received through this inappropriate behavior. She thought that this was the only way she could be accepted as a woman. She actually did not feel particularly good about her appearance, I soon learned, but compensated for it through her sexually provocative behavior.

Gradually, Becky and I began to work on her underlying insecurity. She came from a family in which she experienced herself as unlovable and an outcast. Her father apparently wanted nothing to do with her once she began to physically develop into a young woman. Becky experienced this confusion and shift in her relationship with her father as an extreme personal rejection. There must be something wrong with her if her father no longer seemed to be interested in her. Understandably, Becky turned to others for validation. Unfortunately that validation took the form of impulsive and reckless acting out. Becky clearly had no other way of meeting her need for attention and validation.

CASE DISCUSSION

There may have been a myriad of other developmental issues that contributed to Becky's difficulties besides the rejection she experienced from her father. For the purposes of our work together, however, that insight was enough to help her. I became a mirroring self-object for Becky in therapy. I validated her for more than her seductive behavior. I helped her recognize that she had many qualities that defined her femininity. She was intelligent, witty, and creative, and she was very funny. As Becky learned to control her impulses with me and began to feel accepted and appreciated for more than her sexuality, she realized that she had many other qualities that defined her gender identity. Being a young woman was not about seducing guys or dressing like a slut, it was about who you are internally. As Becky came to realize this in our therapy, she was able to modify her behaviors. The therapy relationship served as a vehicle in which Becky began to experience a sense of validation and acceptance. The consistent mirroring self-object needed during adolescence came from the therapy with me. Becky gradually began to feel good about herself as a young woman and as a person in general. The therapy relationship was able to provide a safe environment in which Becky could discover herself and feel validated for that discovery.

From an object relations standpoint one might immediately recognize Becky's provocative behavior as a form of projective identification. The rejection that she experienced at the hands of her father may have helped to develop both a good and a bad object sense of father, as well as a bad internal self-representation. In her experiences with others, especially adolescent males who were symbolic of her relationship with her father, Becky wanted to feel loved, appreciated, and accepted. Unfortunately, her bad self was too powerful and reacted in relationships with others to preserve and protect for Becky whatever good object sense she had of her father. In other words, it was better for Becky to be bad than to unconsciously reject her father. Reinforcing her badness protected her good father. It was she who was bad, not her father.

Becky's provocative and flirtatious behavior was consciously meant to gain the favor of the boys she wanted. But her seductiveness was usually not experienced in a positive way by adolescent boys. They felt it to be obnoxious, overpowering, unattractive, and extreme. I experienced Becky that way myself, especially in our first session. By engaging her observing ego, I was able to help Becky realize that in actuality this type of behavior was leading to the very thing she was most afraid of: rejection. Ironically, her behavior reinforced Becky's sense of badness and kept her from feeling good about herself. It was only after she began to realize this fact through therapy that Becky was able to change her behavior and feel greater acceptance from others and begin to feel good about herself as a young woman. This intense and valuable transference/countertransference dynamic was crucial to the success of Becky's treatment.

The insight I was able to glean from my individual work with Becky was shared in the family therapy. With Becky's permission, information about her disappointment with her father was processed in the family work. This enabled the family to be a much better support to her and helped curtail her self-destructive behaviors.

As I got to know the real Becky, I came to experience what Searles discussed in his article "Oedipal Love in the Countertransference" (1959). I found myself realizing that Becky was a very attractive young woman. I believe that she recognized the fact that I felt positively about her during the course of our work together. It has always been my hope that such awareness helped Becky in her journey toward her gender identity. If I could appreciate the real Becky, it may have proved to her that others could as well.

The case example above highlights the complexities of working with a heterosexual adolescent who is struggling to feel comfortable with her sexual identity. The situation might have looked different if I had chosen to discuss a gay male or a lesbian or bisexual teenager. But the process would still be the same, that is, helping that adolescent come to terms with her own sexual identity and orientation.

The role of the therapist is to provide a relational context in which the adolescent can feel safe enough to find himself and feel comfortable with his sexual identity. With GLBT adolescents, it is crucial that the practitioner not judge or presumptively move the adolescent toward any definitive point in his search for sexual identity. The adolescent must be allowed to travel on his own journey and at his own pace.

Support groups can be helpful in that process. Fortunately there are more sources of support for the GLBT adolescent than there were even a decade ago. The list of recommended readings and Web sites can be a valuable resource for many adolescents challenged by this complex issue.

SUMMARY

This chapter has discussed the significance of the search for gender identity and sexual orientation in adolescence. The physical and emotional changes that occur during that developmental period have profound implications for adult life. Early family experiences help to shape the adolescent's sense of gender identity. Insidious societal influences certainly have an impact on that process. It is, however, the relationship experiences of adolescence that truly solidify that sense of gender identity. The clinician working with adolescents must be cognizant of this delicate and instrumental process. The therapy relationship can be a tremendous help to teens of all gender types as they struggle to find themselves in life.

RECOMMENDED RESOURCES

Readings

K. J. Bieschke, R. M. Perez, & K. A. DeBord, eds., *Handbook of Counseling and Psychotherapy with Lesbian, Gay, Bisexual and Transgender Clients,* 2nd ed. (Washington, DC: American Psychological Association, 2007). This is a comprehensive guide to counseling with this population.

B. Fairchild & N. Hayward, *Now That You Know: A Parent's Guide to Understanding Their Gay and Lesbian Children* (New York: Harcourt, 1998). This book may be helpful in working with parents of gay and lesbian adolescents.

F. J. Floyd, T. S. Stein, K. S. Harter, A. Allison, & C. Nye, "Gay, Lesbian, and Bisexual Youths: Separation-Individuation, Parental Attitudes, Identity Consolidation, and Well-Being," *Journal of Youth and Adolescence* 28, no. 6 (1999): 719–734. This article tackles a key issue in adolescent development as it is affected by sexual identity.

A. I. Lev, *Transgender Emergence: Therapeutic Guidelines for Working with Gender-Variant People and Their Families* (New York: Haworth Press, 2004). This is a good text for working with GLBT and their families.

V. M. Mays, L. M. Chatters, & S. D. Cochran, "African American Families in Diversity: Gay Men and Lesbians as Participants in Family Networks," *Journal of Comparative Family Studies* 29, no. 1 (1998): 73–87. This article explores gay and lesbian phenomena in the context of the African American family network.

C. Ryan & D. Futterman, *Lesbian and Gay Youth: Care and Counseling* (New York: Columbia University Press, 1998). This is a good source for therapeutic work with gay and lesbian adolescents.

Film/Television/Media

American Pie (1999), *Boys Don't Cry* (1999), *Raising Cain* (PBS, 2006), *The L Word* (Showtime, 2004–), *Queer as Folk* (Showtime, 2000–2005). All these films and TV series depict the challenge of being GLBT as an adolescent or young adult.

Internet

http://huizen.dds.nl/~klaver/index2.html This is the Web site of Klaver's Cool Queer Connections.

http://www.ngltf.org/ This is the Web site of the National Gay and Lesbian Task Force.

http://www.hrcusa.org/ This is the Web site of the Gay and Lesbian Rights Lobby.

http://www.contrib.andrew.cmu.edu/~nifty/lglv.html This is the Web site of the League of Gay and Lesbian Voters.

http://www.qrd.org/qrd/www/orgs/aja/ This is the Web site of the organization And Justice for All.

http://now.org/now/issues/lgbi/lgbi.html This NOW's Web page on lesbian rights.

http://members.aol.com/uloah/home.html This is the Web site of the United Lesbians of African Heritage.

http://www.lesbian.org/lesbian-moms/ This is the Web site of the Lesbian Mothers Support Society.

http://www.bsef.org/ This is the Web site of the Gay and Lesbian Prisoner Project.

http://youth.org/ This is Web site of the Youth Assistance Organization/Youth Action Online.

http://www.out.com/out-cgi-bin/page The is the Web site of Out.com, a gay and lesbian Web site.

14

DSM-IV-TR: *Mental Health Disorders/Problems/ Issues with Adolescents*

Adolescents experience a wide range of emotions as they struggle to find a true sense of identity during this crucial developmental period. Many teenagers suffer from anxiety, depression, mania, dissociation, even psychotic disorders. The consolidation of adolescent identity is a process that naturally requires most adolescents to think and feel very intensely about who they are, what they believe, what they want to become, and what life means to them. This can be a lonely journey. Despite the association with a strong peer group and even a supportive family, it is still a deeply personal and individualized path for every adolescent. Serious and milder forms of mental illness can often be a byproduct of that search. This chapter will examine the various types of mental illnesses that may develop during adolescence. It will focus on mental illness as defined by the *DSM-IV-TR* (2000), with discussion related to etiology and epidemiology, as well as the theoretical and treatment implications for adolescents and their families dealing with these difficulties.

THE DSM-IV-TR *AND ADOLESCENT DIAGNOSIS*

The *Diagnostic and Statistical Manual of Mental Disorders,* fourth edition, text revision, or *DSM-IV-TR,* is the mental health section of *The International Classification of Diseases Manual (ICDM).* These two reference guides are the global sources for classification and categorization of all physical and mental conditions throughout the world. They are based upon ongoing research and updated statistical information as well as collaboration among the medical experts of the international community. But one should remember that the *DSM-IV-TR* as well as the *ICDM* is a work in progress. Although the information is extremely credible and based upon strong empirical data, it is open to modification. This is a very important caveat to take into consideration when discussing mental illness in adolescents.

The naive undergrad and even the experienced graduate student begin to question their own sanity as they learn about abnormal psychology in the *DSM-IV-TR*. They may sometimes feel that they have every disorder in the book. In fact, we are all capable of experiencing some form of most of the disorders in the *DSM-IV-TR*. It is the extent or the severity of the symptoms that warrants a diagnosis, however. A diagnosis of generalized anxiety or major depression is warranted only if the condition is extreme.

Another important source of diagnostic information in both assessing and treating mental illness in adolescents is *The Psychodynamic Diagnostic Manual* or *PDM*, which sets a new standard in empirically based assessment and treatment recommendation, providing attachment-theory- and neuroscience-based empirical evidence for the assessment of the full range of psychiatric disorders. Its comprehensive diagnostic recommendations drastically expand the *DSM-IV-TR* and may well be the precursor to the highly anticipated *DSM-V.* New research in neuroscience and attachment theory can now validate psychodynamic-informed diagnosis as well as indicate the types of treatment that may be helpful. This information has the potential of revolutionizing the mental health field.

ANXIETY DISORDERS

All human beings experience anxiety. It is the body's primitive warning system. When the mind senses that a situation is dangerous, it sends out chemical and electrical signals that trigger an anxiety response. The body is then mobilized to handle the situation by either "fight or flight." Key to this process is the increased release of adrenaline, which enables the body to temporarily handle the situation. The stereotypical example of this process is the caveman who is confronted by a predator. His brain sets the process in motion so that he can either run or fight. His body is temporarily made much stronger than usual, allowing him to survive. Anxiety is a defense for all of us in times of perceived stress or danger (Elias & Saucier, 2006).

It is only when anxiety becomes debilitating or unmanageable that it is labeled as a mental disorder. The anxiety disorders range from the more diffused generalized anxiety disorder to more specific forms such as phobias and obsessive-compulsive disorders. Adolescence is a potentially anxious time in life. Increased anxiety is probably more prevalent during adolescence than most developmental time periods. Many teenagers worry excessively about their lives, their friends, their families, school, and so on. When that anxiety interferes with their ability to focus on their daily tasks, they may have an anxiety disorder and need some form of treatment.

More extreme anxiety may take the form of panic attacks, agoraphobia, and social phobia. These debilitating conditions may keep the teenager from going to school, socializing with peers, even interacting with family. If this should happen, there is no question that the adolescent needs help. There are a variety of ways to help an adolescent suffering with anxiety. Medication can be a miraculous immediate relief. Xanax, Klonopin, Ativan, and Valium are anti-anxiety medications that work quickly in the bloodstream to curb anxious feelings. In order to receive anti-anxiety medication, an adolescent needs to see a psychiatrist who can prescribe it. Clinicians treating this population should have a solid working relationship with at least one or two psychiatrists who specialize in working with adolescents. All psychiatrists understand anxiety disorders and their treatment, but adolescent psychiatrists are specifically trained to understand how anxiety affects that population.

MEDICATION MANAGEMENT AND OTHER ADOLESCENT DRUG USE

Many teenagers self-medicate their anxiety. Drug and alcohol use and abuse are factors in the treatment of not only anxiety disorders but all psychiatric conditions of adolescents. Throughout human history, people have used substances to make them feel better, take the edge off, and alleviate stress. Adolescents are no different. But if an adolescent is using drugs, the clinician and the psychiatrist treating her need to know that information. Chronic drug use may exacerbate or interfere with the effect of any drugs the adolescent has been prescribed. The chemical interaction of these substances must be closely monitored if the adolescent is going to improve. Substance use and abuse diagnoses often accompany many of the other diagnoses that an adolescent may receive. Knowing how a specific substance may interfere with prescribed medication as well as exacerbate a coexisting mental disorder is diagnostically essential for successful treatment of any condition.

Psychiatry today has become quite specialized and sophisticated in the management of mental disorders through medication. It is not unusual for an adolescent to be put on an anti-anxiety medication, a mood stabilizer, an antidepressant, and an atypical antipsychotic med to successfully manage his symptoms. This type of intervention has been informally labeled a cocktail approach, because of the mixture of medications utilized to target specific neurotransmitters in the brain known to be the sites for many of these emotional disturbances.

Psychiatry has come a long way in even the last decade. But one must still be extremely cautious in prescribing medications for adolescents. Before embarking on a regimen of medication management, the adolescent should have a complete physical examination. This will help identify any medical conditions that may influence which types of medication may be prescribed. Family history is also important. One of the first things a psychiatrist who is considering prescribing medication asks is "Has anyone in your family been on medication?" If so, the psychiatrist wants to know if it was effective and if there were any severe side effects or medical complications. The doctor will also want to know if anyone in the family has had depression, anxiety, drug dependency, suicidal ideation, or committed suicide. Heredity is a key variable in assessing for medication management.

Neuroscience theory also sheds light on this process. An adolescent's brain is still growing. The rate of growth is not as rapid as it was in infancy or even childhood, but growth in crucial areas such as the cerebral cortex is continuing to occur. All types of input, including social interactions, academic instruction, healthy diet, exercise, and unfortunately illegal alcohol and substance use and abuse can affect adolescent brain development. Many types of mental disorders are influenced by psychosocial stressors. Heavy drug and alcohol use can affect the body and mind in ways that may contribute to the development of or predisposition toward such disorders. It can interfere in the normal process of brain development and emotional adaptation necessary for functioning successfully as an adult. This probably more than any other factor is reason to caution teenagers about their drug use (Cozolino, 2002).

Besides being treated with medication, adolescents suffering from anxiety need to be in therapy. The clinical situation can help the adolescent not only identify the psychosocial stressors and developmental conditions that may be contributing to their anxiety disorder but also develop coping mechanisms to deal with it effectively. Neuroscience theory would suggest that therapeutic approaches that emphasize deeper ventilation of feelings may not be an effective approach to helping adolescents deal with an anxiety disorder (Cozolino, 2002). Cognitive therapy may be a better approach for teenagers suffering with severe anxiety. This approach will help adolescents identify the automatic thoughts and beliefs that may be contributing to their anxiety. The structured nature of cognitive therapy focuses on giving them the skills to identify their irrational cognitive processes and learn new coping behaviors to modify them and manage anxiety (Beck, 1995).

Some psychodynamic models may be a helpful addition to cognitive or CBT approaches in treating anxiety disorders (Cozolino, 2002). It is now well known that in order for the brain to develop successful coping mechanisms, there must be an optimal combination and interaction of cognition, emotion, and behavior. The client must feel safe and yet stressed enough to want to change. He must be able to learn to integrate his thoughts with their corresponding emotions in order to function most adaptively. Finally, he needs to practice these new ideas through interactions with others.

MOOD DISORDERS

The mood disorders consist of depression and the bipolar disorders as well as a range of other, milder forms of these two categories. Depression like anxiety is a normal emotional condition in life. All of us experience sadness from time to time. In fact, if we felt good all the time, how would we know what feeling good was about? It is only through experiencing the range of human emotions that one comes to appreciate both the good and the bad times.

Freud worked with many patients who were depressed. He theorized that depression was the result of turning anger inward onto the ego. According to Freud, anger can be directed either outward toward others or inward toward the self. Suicide is an extreme example of the latter (Freud, 1938). Cognitive theory would suggest that depression is the result of extreme negative thinking. According to Judith Beck (1995), the two core beliefs fundamental to depression are helplessness and unlovability. Neuroscience recognizes that severe depression is due to low levels of the neurotransmitter serotonin in the brain. Antidepressant medication aims toward controlling the optimal flow of serotonin in the brain, thus maintaining a sense of well-being. These three theories form the main basis of our understanding of depression.

Bipolar disorder is understood to be the result of a chemical imbalance in the brain. It is characterized by extreme mood swings from depression to mania. The individual with a bipolar illness cycles at varying rates between these two states. Extreme depression can become so debilitating that the patient is unable to get out of bed, has no appetite, or even attempts suicide. Mania, on the other hand, is characterized by extreme elation, high energy, and heightened creativity, among other things. This mood can also become debilitating because of its unceasing nature and the irritability that often accompanies it. The individual does not have control over these cycling mood states, nor do they seem to result from environmental situations or stimuli. They are automatic and unpredictable.

It is important to remember, however, that adolescence itself can be a bit of a bipolar state. Teenagers are understandably moody owing to their ever-changing physical, emotional, and cognitive makeup. Therefore, diagnosing an adolescent with true bipolar disorder may be difficult. To complicate this matter even further, the *DSM-IV-TR* has identified two basic types of bipolar disorder, bipolar I and bipolar II. Bipolar I is characterized by longer periods of major depression and mania, whereas in bipolar II the cycles may be only hours or minutes apart. These complex disorders are difficult for even the most skilled psychiatrist and clinician to accurately diagnose at times. In addition, irritability is both an aspect of the manic condition and a normal part of an adolescent's mood. Children and adolescents in particular may experience more irritability when they are depressed than adults. This factor as well can complicate the diagnostic picture.

Successful treatment for the mood disorders consists of a combination of therapy, environmental support, and medication. Depression is treated through the administration of antidepressant medications. These drugs target the neurotransmitters in the brain that affect the regulation of a sense of well-being. Serotonin, norepinephrine, and dopamine are the primary neurotransmitters affected by antidepressant medication. There has also been a tremendous increase in the types, quality, and combinations of antidepressant medications over the last decade. New antidepressants with fewer side effects are coming out every year. At the time of this writing, Lexapro is probably the most recent and progressive antidepressant available, with the fewest side effects. The psychiatrist decides which antidepressant medication or combination of medications is best for each patient. This decision is based upon the variety of factors mentioned earlier. The bipolar disorders are medically treated through mood stabilizers. These medications are aimed at chemically stabilizing the affective state of the patient, with no major fluctuations into depression or mania. Until quite recently, only lithium seemed able to manage the bipolar condition successfully. But recent advances in medications such as Depakote and Topamax have also provided relief without severe side effects such as weight gain and liver problems. An adolescent who is suffering from a debilitating mood disorder can experience welcome relief through these medications.

In addition to medication, however, adolescents suffering from mood disorders also need to be in therapy. Depression in particular, although influenced by hereditary factors, is also influenced by the psychosocial environment. If the factors that contributed to the onset of the depressive state are not worked on in therapy, the medication is only like a Band-Aid concealing a much deeper and more serious injury. Through discussing his personal relationships and life circumstances in therapy, the adolescent learns how to recognize emotional triggers and develop insight and greater coping mechanisms for the future. This may not be possible, however, until his mood has been successfully managed through the appropriate use of psychotropic medication. Once stabilized, the adolescent is more capable of working on the factors that contributed to the condition. Peer and family support is also an invaluable aid in this process. If the teenager has been hospitalized, he begins to experience group support in the inpatient setting. In outpatient work, family therapy is crucial to successful treatment. Parents need to be educated about their teenager's condition as well as be continually kept in the loop (confidentiality respected, of course) in order to be a source of support to him. A high school support group for teenagers dealing with these conditions is also a wonderful addition to treatment. Hospital day treatment or aftercare programs are also available in many areas to help adolescents in their recovery.

DISSOCIATIVE DISORDERS

Although certainly not as common as anxiety or mood disorders, dissociative disorders can be debilitative as well. Dissociation is a normal psychological defense that can develop into a mental disorder. It is an alteration in consciousness that allows the individual to psychologically remove herself from her emotions. In normal development this can be functional in order to get through traumatic situations such as car accidents or the death of loved ones. It becomes a problem when the individual continually dissociates at the expense of staying involved in her everyday life. The most common example of this in adolescence is the teenage girl who has been sexually abused. In order to deal with her trauma, the adolescent girl dissociates from her emotions. This is an adaptive way to protect the self from painful feelings, but taken to an extreme, it can interfere in the adolescent's ability to concentrate and remain emotionally present in her everyday life.

Harry Stack Sullivan (1953) believed that dissociation in general was a normal part of adolescence. Most adolescents "space out" from time to time in order to fantasize and daydream about their lives and identity. Sullivan believed, however, that extreme dissociation, especially dissociation not associated with specific trauma, may be a precursor to schizophrenia. Normal adolescents need to dissociate as part of their inward search for identity. Extreme and chronic dissociative functioning that is non-trauma-related should be taken seriously as a potential emotional problem.

Dissociative disorders may be treated through psychotherapy and perhaps medication management as well. In the case of trauma-induced dissociation, therapy aimed at helping the adolescent client uncover and explore the thoughts and emotions related to his circumstances can help him feel in control and resume normal functioning. This must be done at the client's pace. Timing is everything in working with abuse. Control is the key issue. The client needs to feel he is in control of his thoughts and emotions if he is to be able to resume a normal life. This process can take quite a long time depending on the nature and the extent of the trauma. In the case of sexual abuse, successful treatment can take years. The clinician working with these types of clients can utilize psychodynamic, cognitive, and even narrative approaches successfully in the course or treatment. Medication can be an adjunctive aspect of the treatment, particularly as emotions begin to surface. The adolescent client suffering from a dissociative disorder may eventually need anti-anxiety, antidepressant, mood-stabilizing, and/or even atypical antipsychotic medications to cope with emerging emotions.

SOMATOFORM DISORDERS

Eating disorders were touched on earlier in this text; however, some adolescents suffer from disorders related to their body-mind configuration. It is perhaps becoming a tiresome quote, but Freud said it best. "The ego is first and foremost a body ego." The adolescent's search for identity is intimately tied to her sense of a physical self. It is not uncommon for many teenagers to have distorted body images, especially if they have not successfully developed an observing ego. Body dysmorphic disorder is the result of that process taken to the extreme. It is usually associated with eating disorders such as anorexia and bulimia, but it certainly can exist independent of those disorders. Adolescents may also experience somatoform disorders related to bodily pain and fear of illness or disease. These are much rarer types of disorders than mood or anxiety disorders. But body dysmorphic disorders can occur in anywhere from 5 to 40 percent of adolescents with co-morbid anxiety and mood disorder conditions (*DSM-IV-TR*, 2000, p. 509).

The treatment for these disorders in adolescence is directly related to the teenager's self-esteem and self concept. Psychodynamic, cognitive, narrative, solution-focused, and even client-centered approaches can be quite successful in helping the adolescent modify his sense of self. This happens initially within the therapy relationship but is eventually applied to the adolescent's world in general. Coming to grips with one's body can be a lifelong process. Somatoform disorders are the extreme version of dysfunction in that process.

ATTENTION DEFICIT/HYPERACTIVITY DISORDER

It may seem odd to focus on attention deficit/hyperactivity disorder (ADHD) in a book on adolescence. This disorder is characterized by persistent hyperactivity and/or an inability to pay consistent attention to activities in life. The onset is usually identified in early childhood, and symptoms often diminish in severity throughout adolescence. ADHD is present in about 3–7 percent of the population (*DSM-IV-TR,* 2000, p. 90). Etiology suggests that, much like the bipolar disorders, ADHD is caused by a chemical imbalance in the brain. Medication is the main course of treatment along with supportive counseling. At the present time, Ritalin and Adderall are the main medications used for ADHD. Strattera and Concerta are also used for this condition. Proper use of these medications can help children and adolescents control their impulsivity and remain focused in their daily lives. Once proper medication levels have been established, treatment counseling can begin to focus on helping the child or adolescent and his family develop coping mechanisms to readjust to life without ADHD. Many of these individuals have effectively been out of the loop owing to the debilitating effects of their disorder. Counseling and therapy are aimed at helping clients catch up to their peers, as well as educating and supporting family members in the process. Close coordination with school personnel is crucial to the successful treatment of clients who suffer with this disorder. Often this adjustment occurs just prior to the onset of adolescence. Children who have suffered from ADHD in childhood may be at a much greater risk for problems in adolescence as a result of the social, cognitive, and emotional setbacks they have experienced. Therapy can be an effective way to help these youths adjust to their teenage years.

AUTISTIC SPECTRUM

The autistic spectrum of disorders, including autism and Rett's and Asperger's disorders, also begin and are identified early in childhood. These conditions are characterized most clearly by severe deficits in social interaction. The etiology of this range of disorders is still unclear. Many years ago it was presumed that children developed autism as a result of pathological parenting and attachment. Fortunately that explanation has been dismissed. It is now clear that the autistic spectrum of disorders are probably caused by brain abnormalities that develop in the first few years of life. Other, less popular explanations focus on hereditary factors and environmental influences. Whatever the causes, these conditions tend to run a chronic course and there seems to be only very modest improvement over the lifespan. Children experiencing these disorders have great difficulty fitting in with others, especially their peers. They often have difficulty with communication and may exhibit odd and repetitive behaviors. Adolescents suffering from this range of disorders may improve in the areas mentioned above, but their overall social functioning will be less adaptive than that of the general population. Ongoing therapeutic treatment is essential for this population. Efforts need to be collaborative and involve family, school, and other key resources in the community. The clinician working with clients who are experiencing these types of difficulties must be knowledgeable about them and recognize the clients' potential despite their obvious limitations. Helping this population develop adaptive and idiosyncratic social skills is the key to successful treatment.

ATTACHMENT DISORDERS

I have grouped a number of interrelated disorders in this section because all of them are etiologically related to problems in development. The most recognized cause for this range of difficulties, including reactive attachment, oppositional defiant, conduct, and key axis II personality disorders, is deficits in early emotional development. Emotional and developmental deficits can occur for a variety of reasons but most commonly are a combination of physical constitution and faulty caretaking. Even a constitutionally deficient child may function adequately if given "good-enough" caretaking. On the other hand, a constitutionally sound child may become developmentally deficient if he is chronically neglected and abused. It is not a simple matter of blaming the caretakers; development is a complex and individualized process influenced by a myriad of interlocking factors.

Psychodynamic attachment theories and neuroscience offer the most sophisticated and complex paradigms from which to understand the intricate process of emotional development. An attuned relationship with primary caretakers is crucial to successful development, but the success of that relationship is only as good as the physical constitution of the child involved in the process (Greenspan & Shankar, 2006). The disorders mentioned in this section are the result of difficulties in that developmental process.

According to the *DSM-IV-TR* (2000), reactive attachment disorders are the result of the combination of factors mentioned above. The diagnosis is made within the first few years of life. Children suffering from reactive attachment disorders experience difficulties in social relatedness characterized by failure to "initiate or respond in a developmentally appropriate fashion to most social interactions" (*DSM-IV-TR,* 2000, p. 127). In early childhood, this failure is represented by either inappropriate clinging and anxious dependency or marked avoidance of social interaction with others. On the attachment continuum, these children would be classified as either dependent or avoidant.

Many of these children are in the child welfare system. Some of them have been removed from their caregivers owing to chronic physical, sexual, and emotional abuse as well as neglect. As a result, many of them are institutionalized in residential facilities, group homes, shelters, and foster care. They may improve in their ability to attach to others through consistent and properly attuned caregiving over time. If this has not happened by adolescence, the teenager suffering from reactive attachment may continue to experience major difficulties in social interactions. In addition, the inevitable move toward autonomy during that developmental time period may be compromised by the deficits suffered early in life. These adolescents have not learned how to self-soothe or manage emotional autonomy as successfully as most teenagers. They may be more likely to experience a variety of psychiatric problems such as anxiety, depression, oppositional defiant disorder, conduct disorder, or even various personality disorders.

Treatment for adolescents who have been diagnosed with reactive attachment disorder is aimed at providing an empathic and emotionally attuned relationship with the clinician in order to help them develop *object and self constancy.* These object relations concepts refer to the ability to self-soothe in times of stress, to feel relatively safe when alone, and to experience the self and others as having both good and bad qualities. The early separation-individuation process helps the child to successfully internalize those ambivalent experiences with the help of attuned and empathic caretakers who are reliable and consistent in the provision of both love and structure, or more simply, in saying yes and no. The therapy is aimed at helping the teenager internalize these abilities through a long-term empathic relationship. Neuroscience helps us understand that this process involves the ability of the brain to reroute faulty emotional and cognitive functioning. This ability is called *neural plasticity* (Cozolino, 2002). As the adolescent experiences new and more reliable and consistent interactions both with the therapist and eventually in life, her brain is able to modify existing neurological pathways that manage thoughts and emotions.

Oppositional defiant and conduct disorder appear to be on a developmental continuum. Many adolescents are oppositional, and many are also defiant. Rebellion can be a normal part of the journey toward identity formation. It is only when this opposition is extreme that it warrants a diagnosis of oppositional defiant or conduct disorder. The major difference between the two is that adolescents diagnosed with conduct disorder usually have a history of aggression, destruction of property, and crime, while oppositional defiant youth do not. The behavior of oppositional defiant teenagers may eventually warrant the diagnosis of conduct disorder, but many adolescents who have conduct disorder never progress to that level of pathology. If the extreme pathology continues into adulthood, it may warrant an additional diagnosis of antisocial personality disorder. These individuals most often end up in the prison system where, unfortunately, their behavior only worsens.

The etiology of oppositional defiant disorder, conduct disorder, and antisocial personality disorders is also unclear. The developmental explanation mentioned above also applies to this group of disorders. There is also some indication, at least in antisocial personality disorder, that the individual may have abnormal brain development in those areas related to emotional functioning (Elias & Saucier, 2006). Behavior theory suggests that the capacity for violence and the lack of empathy are learned. Whatever the explanations for these disorders may be, this population can be quite challenging to work with in therapy.

D. W. Winnicott has written extensively on this population. A number of his key articles examine the development of conscience, the capacity to manage emotions, and the development and meaning of delinquent behavior. He and his wife took in many adolescents during their lifetime in England. They provided what today would be considered foster care for many a wayward youth. In addition to being a trained psychoanalyst, Winnicott was also a pediatrician. His object relations theories came from the integration of all of his work with children, adolescents, and adults. In his article "The Development of the Capacity for Concern," Winnicott (1992) describes the development of conscience as a process in which the child internalizes the emotional representations of the primary caregivers. Moral behavior, he argues, comes from a fear of losing the love (and person) of these primary relationships through actions that may be disappointing to them. That fear can only happen once the child has been able to internalize the other. Conscience cannot develop, according to Winnicott, if the child has not successfully internalized an emotional other who is invaluable to him. In "The Absence of a Sense of Guilt," Winnicott (1992) points out that it is the young child's right and responsibility to test the limits of her world. It is only through that process that she learns what is acceptable behavior. It becomes the caretakers' responsibility to provide that structure. If they don't, the child will test out those limits in the environment. This may lead to juvenile delinquency or other forms of self-destructive behavior. A further elaboration of that theme is discussed in the article "The Anti-Social Tendency" (Winnicott, 1992). Winnicott believed and experienced the fact that adolescents who were moving toward delinquent behavior were actually looking for love and structure that they had not received enough of early in life. Stealing, for instance, is not necessarily about getting the "thing" but about getting love. The stealing itself often feels empty to the teenager because the object is not what he really wants or needs. It is symbolic of a deeper need. Delinquent behavior is also, according to Winnicott, a reaching out for limits and structure. Children who do not receive adequate limits on their behavior do not learn or internalize a sense of their own boundaries. If this structure is not provided successfully in the home in early childhood, adolescents may look toward society to give it to them. These themes have considerable validity in understanding delinquent behavior even today. One merely has to look at the different types of delinquent teens and their difficulties to recognize the applicability of these concepts to treatment. Remember, of course, that it is not caregiving alone that is responsible here; it is the unique and idiosyncratic combination of constitution, quality of caregiving, and environmental influences.

Treatment for these adolescents needs to focus on the right combination of what Winnicott referred to as love and structure. A careful balance of empathic support, firm structure, and adult guidance is crucial for successful work with adolescents suffering from delinquent disorders such as oppositional defiant and conduct disorder. Education and rigid structure alone are not enough. If these adolescents are to begin to function more successfully in life, they will also need to become more empathic and caring in their relationships with others. That process takes time. Neuroscience has demonstrated that fact. Unfortunately, the ability of these types of adolescent clients may be limited owing to the chronic nature of deficient development. Accurate assessment is necessary in order to ascertain the nature of the treatment. Some teens may be better off in a more secure therapeutic environment, such as a psychiatric hospital or residential facility; others whose difficulties are less severe may benefit from traditional outpatient therapy. These decisions are probably the most important to successful management of this range of disorders.

The diagnosis of axis II personality disorders is recommended in the *DSM-IV-TR* only once an individual has reached the age of eighteen. But many adolescents begin to exhibit prominent traits of these disorders well before then. Labeling can be controversial with adolescents, but the accurate and timely recognition of a budding personality disorder can be invaluable to the psychological health of many youth. Axis II personality disorders represent pervasive, chronic, and inflexible patterns of enduring behavior that "deviate markedly from the expectations of the individual's culture" (*DSM-IV-TR*, 2000, p. 685).

Personality disorders are generally considered to be of developmental origin. Similar to reactive attachment disorders, personality disorders take shape through a combination of constitutional predisposition, developmental relationships, and environmental influence. From a psychological standpoint, psychodynamic theories, particularly object relations theory, help to explain this process. A sense of emotional self and the ability to manage one's emotions are acquired through the internalization of the physical and emotional interactions with the primary caretakers in infancy and early childhood. Neuroscience theory would say that these internalizations lead to the development of neural networks in the brain that help the child successfully adapt to stressful situations. The more consistent the infant's care early in life, the more successful she will be in developing self and object constancy, and the greater will be her ability to manage stress in adolescence and adulthood.

From this developmental perspective then, the personality disorders can be understood as inflexible and pervasive defensive structures and adaptations that were developed in response to the inadequate mix of constitution, environment, and early caretaking relationships. Each type of personality disorder can be understood as a unique but rigid and dysfunctional style with which to manage life. For instance, the individual with paranoid personality disorder approaches all interactions with mistrust. One might speculate that early development for this individual led to the internalized sense of self as unsafe. In order to survive, he came to rely on paranoia for protection. Extreme hypervigilance is relatively adaptive for this type of individual. It is an attempt by the self to remain emotionally safe. Unfortunately, it also may keep him socially isolated and unhappy. The extent to which this form of functioning is inflexible and pervasive dictates whether or not it constitutes a diagnosis of personality disorder.

The entire range of personality disorders may be understood from this developmental vantage point. Neuroscience theory would suggest that strong dysfunctional neural networks were developed that led to this rigid style of functioning. Remember that this is not blaming the caretakers; constitutional predisposition as well as environmental factors also plays a key role in the process. We also do not understand how or why an individual makes sense of his world. Siblings within the same family who experience the same situations at the same time may have dramatically different understandings of self in relationship to that world. We must try to understand each unique individual's developmental perspective based upon the multitude of factors that contribute to his view of self and other.

Because identity formation is the crucial task of adolescence, it is not surprising that personality disorders have their onset during adolescent development. The seeds of that process were probably sown in early childhood, and there may have been some indication of rigid personality disorder traits even then, but more obvious manifestations of these disorders usually surface during adolescence. Common personality disorder traits seen during adolescence are conduct disorder, borderline, narcissistic, and histrionic. These character disorders in particular are related to difficulties in interpersonal relationships. We do not have the space here to cover these disorders in detail. What is important to remember is that the onset tends to be during adolescence, and the astute clinician must include assessing for budding personality disorders as an integral part of her ongoing diagnostic work with adolescents and their families. Early identification and treatment of person-ality disorder traits can be invaluable in helping the troubled teenager make the adjustment to adulthood.

Treatment for personality disorders depends upon the category involved. Successful treatment for most, if not all, personality disorders requires longer-term, relationship-oriented psychotherapy. Adolescents in need of this type of treatment will begin to modify their personality structure as they engage in an empathic, attuned, and structured relationship with a knowledgeable professional. They can begin to modify their view of self and other with their therapist and eventually transfer that knowledge into new behaviors and relationships in their world outside of the therapeutic setting. Technically this process is accomplished through working with transference and countertransference. An adolescent suffering with a personality disorder will distort her view of the therapist based upon her rigid and defensive per-sonality structure. Over time, these distortions and defense maneuvers can be modified as the teenager recognizes the dysfunctional aspects of them. The adolescent also begins to form a new, attuned, and empathic relation-ship with her therapist with whom she begins to feel safety, trust, empathy, and support. This process eventually modifies her rigid personality structure so that she can begin to have a more satisfying view of both self and other. There are various approaches to working with this group of clients, but the goal is the same: to modify the existing entrenched personality constellation to help the adolescent function better in life.

SCHIZOPHRENIA AND OTHER PSYCHOTIC DISORDERS

The final category covered in this chapter is the psychotic disorders. Schizo-phrenia and other disorders of a psychotic nature also usually have their onset in adolescence. Although there does not appear to be a universally accepted definition of the term *psychotic,* it is usually understood to mean a mental condition in which the individual experiences a disorder in thinking characterized by delusions (bizarre and extremely irrational beliefs) and hal-lucinations (usually these consist of hearing voices, but they sometimes can be tactile and visual in nature) (*DSM-IV-TR,* 2000). These disorders are thought disorders. The etiology of schizophrenia and the other psychotic disorders is also unclear. Theories about schizophrenia suggest that there may be faulty communication networks between the right and left hemi-spheres of the brain. The left hemisphere of the brain is generally consid-ered to control the more logical aspects of mental functioning, while the right hemisphere is in charge of emotional functioning. Difficulties in the communication between these hemispheres through the brain's corpus cal-losum are considered to be a probable cause of schizophrenia (Cozolino, 2002). Not only the mismatch between thoughts and emotion but the mis-interpretation of both is theorized as a probable factor in schizophrenia.

Julian Jaynes's classic book *The Origins of Consciousness in the Breakdown of the Bicameral Mind* (1976) explored the anthropological development of the human mind. He hypothesized that the early human brain had not fully developed the corpus callosum. As a result, emotional warnings coming from the right side of the brain were perceived as "voices" from others rather than as coming from the self. Early societies, Jaynes speculated, did not need sophisticated neurological networks because of the closed nature of their social structure. The corpus callosum developed further as human society evolved. People suffering from schizophrenia today, Jaynes argued, are perhaps limited in their brain development. These hereditary neurological deficits may be the cause of schizophrenia.

The individual diagnosed with a psychotic disorder is usually considered to have been constitutionally predisposed to it owing to heredity. The onset of the disorder, however, seems to be strongly influenced by psychosocial and environmental stressors. Studies of identical twins constitutionally predisposed to schizophrenia (from families who also had this disease) indicate that the likelihood of acquiring schizophrenia is strongly influenced by the amount of environmental stress and situational developmental factors they are exposed to throughout their lives. The incidence of schizophrenia in the general population is from 0.5 to 5 per 10,000 people. That incidence can increase up to ten times for relatives of those who have schizophrenia. Family incidence is a strong indicator of the possible occurrence of this disorder. Clinicians working with adolescents should certainly be careful to gather a comprehensive family mental health history if they suspect any psychotic disorder.

Schizophrenia and the other psychotic disorders can be managed quite well through medications. Decades ago the major medications used for managing psychotic disorders such as schizophrenia alleviated the debilitating symptoms but produced severe and sometimes irreparable side effects. Medications like Thorazine and Clozaril certainly help reduce or even eliminate delusional thinking or hallucinations in individuals suffering from schizophrenia, but they can cause extreme drowsiness, dizziness, dry mouth, and constipation. In extreme cases, individuals may even develop a neurological condition called tardive dyskinesia, whose irreversible neurological symptoms include involuntary facial tics, jaw movements, tongue thrusting, eye blinking, and other body movements. These side effects occur in only 20–30 percent of cases of prolonged use of the medications mentioned above, but they can be quite a concern for those taking these types of medications. Fortunately, there have been some newer developments in antipsychotic medication. At the time of this writing, Risperdal is probably the newest medication for the symptoms of schizophrenia and other psychotic disorders. Risperdal is as effective as the older medications, can be given in smaller doses, and does not have the same number and severity of side effects (Austrian, 2000).

The problem for adolescents on any medication is getting them to consistently take it. Even adults who begin to feel better often choose to stop taking their prescribed medication because they feel they no longer need it (feel better), and/or they are tired of the annoying side effects. For adolescents this type of behavior is even more frequent. Besides the subjective feelings about and physical reactions to taking medications, adolescents often forget to take them. The clinician working with adolescents on psychotropic medications of any sort should coordinate efforts with the family in closely monitoring the consistent use of them. Abruptly ending the use of certain medications can cause uncomfortable and even dangerous side effects. Cessation also brings back the psychological and emotional symptoms and behavior. Ongoing education for parents and teenagers should be part of the overall treatment approach, especially with adolescents suffering from schizophrenia and other psychotic disorders such as schizoaffective disorders, delusional disorder, and so on.

In addition to medication management of the psychotic disorders, adolescents dealing with these diagnoses also need ongoing therapy as well as family and community support. The use of insight-oriented approaches such as the strict forms of psychodynamic models is usually contraindicated in working with adolescents who have schizophrenia. Delving into deeper emotional layers of the mind may exacerbate the psychotic symptoms for adolescents dealing with these disorders. Emotional and empathic support, however, is crucial. Ego supportive interventions and client-centered therapy can be effective and helpful interventions with this population (Walsh, 2000). Staying focused primarily on the surface level of thoughts, emotions, and behavior can help adolescents with these difficulties learn to manage their lives more effectively, recognize the destructive quality of their symptoms, and ultimately lead more adaptive and functional lives. Adolescents suffering from schizophrenia need to remain focused on the tasks of daily living, reality checking, and symptom management. These are key factors for the person with schizophrenia.

Cognitive-behavioral therapy or CBT approaches are also valuable in working with adolescents suffering from schizophrenia. The structure and consistency of these approaches combined with their inherent educational aspect help the adolescent dealing with psychosis not only to learn about her particular version of the disorder but also to develop concrete coping mechanisms to deal with it. Homework assignments, both in and out of session, keep the adolescent focused on her disorder and consistently monitoring it and improving her functioning. Keeping track of things like automatic thoughts or images can help these teenagers recognize the dysfunctional and functional elements of their thinking. Learning to pay attention to the more adaptive processes in their minds through a structured therapy such as CBT can help these adolescents remain emotionally healthy and relatively functional.

The course of the psychotic disorders unfortunately is uncertain. Some adolescents who experience a psychotic break or incident may recover completely and eventually resume their normal lives. Other teenagers may not. Schizophrenia in particular can be a lifelong debilitative disorder. It can also lead to deteriorated functioning even with the use of medication and therapy. The early identification and treatment of schizophrenia can be crucial to the successful future of these adolescents. There is some evidence to suggest that overall functioning deteriorates with each subsequent psychotic break (*DSM-IV-TR,* 2000, pp. 298–311). If that is the case, then early intervention can make the difference in many teenagers' lives.

Collaborative efforts are essential in therapeutic work with all clients, especially children and adolescents. Teenagers suffering with psychotic disorders especially need the continued support of their therapist, psychiatrist, family, friends, and relevant community resources including their school, church, park district, community centers, and so on. Confidentiality is extremely important in these situations because of the tendency of many to misunderstand and discriminate against people with mental illness in general. The tactful involvement of concerned others, however, can help adolescents struggling with these potentially debilitating disorders feel safe, secure, and supported.

Psychiatric aftercare support groups can be helpful with these adolescents. Being with others who are like them, sharing and discussing mutual concerns, worries, successes, and failures can make a difference in how they perceive themselves and function in life. High school support groups can provide the same type of psycho-educational help. Staying involved with people and limiting the tendency to isolate are crucial to successful recovery with this population.

CASE EXAMPLE

In my thirty years of professional practice I have worked with a variety of clientele who have suffered with severe mental illness such as schizophrenia. Most of my professional experience prior to graduate school was in a youth and family agency. Although we occasionally saw adolescent clients who were dealing with psychotic disorders, it was very rare. Our role tended to be one of referral for hospitalization. We did provide a great deal of outpatient aftercare therapy and support for these teenagers, however.

My most intensive experience working with persons suffering from schizophrenia came during my first-year MSW graduate placement at the state psychiatric facility. I worked for an academic year on the adult female ward. I was privileged and fortunate enough to work with adult women who had experienced psychotic breaks that had led to criminal behavior, usually murder of a loved one. These women were judged not guilty by reason of insanity (NGRI). These women were almost without exception quite likable.

I came to realize that their offense was an isolated incident due to the symptoms of their illness. They were not in their right minds when they committed these crimes. For instance, one young mother had truly believed that she and her daughter were possessed by the devil and that the only way to save them both was to commit murder and attempt suicide. This woman killed her baby daughter but was unsuccessful in her suicide attempt. While in the state hospital she received comprehensive treatment that included medication, therapy, group education, and support. This type of work enabled me to learn firsthand about severe mental illness, medications, and psychiatric treatment, as well as aftercare planning and community placements. That experience has been invaluable to me in recognizing and treating these disorders in adolescents.

John was a self-referred client in my private practice many years ago. I will never forget the experience I had in working with him. Unfortunately John's story does not have a happy ending, but it is a very good illustration of the onset and debilitating effects of adolescent schizophrenia. John was seventeen years old when he first came to see me. His presenting concern centered on his desire to have a more satisfying social life. He was an only child from a modest middle-class family living in the suburbs of a large metropolis. John was not particularly close to his parents, nor did he have many friends. He seemed to move in and out of many jobs and had difficulty initiating as well as maintaining friendships. He hoped that I could help him develop the skills to do so. I will use the practice formulation to assess John's situation as well as discuss his course of therapy with me.

1. *Is there any evidence of constitutional factors that may have contributed to the present situation? If so, how have they affected the adolescent?* In hindsight I can clearly recognize that John was probably genetically predisposed to developing schizophrenia. In my initial and ongoing discussions with his parents, I had no indication of any family history of severe mental illness. As mentioned earlier, schizophrenia is generally considered to be strongly influenced by hereditary factors. John's awkward and socially isolated early childhood and adolescence may have been warning signs about his impending condition.

2. *What level of psychosocial development do you believe the adolescent has achieved? Do you believe the adolescent is fixated or regressed at all? What factors lead you to believe this may be the case?* John is chronologically in Erikson's stage of identity vs. role confusion. He seems to be in a perpetual state of moratorium, perhaps bordering on confusion. At the heart of his identity crisis seems to be his inability to find a sense of comfort and security with peers. He is certainly unable to develop any type of romantic or dating relationship with women. He seems to be clearly identified as a heterosexual adolescent but has tremendous anxiety in making contact with females his own age. These difficulties would seem to indicate that

John has encountered problems in the successful resolution of earlier developmental stages. John does seem to struggle with trust. Early in our work together he discussed his suspicions about the trustworthiness of his mother. He wondered whether she was making him proper lunches, specifically whether she used fresh ingredients or put spoiled ingredients in his sandwiches. He realized that these were probably paranoid worries, but he had them nonetheless.

In my discussions with his parents, I came to realize that John did not have many friends in childhood. He did well in school but remained relatively socially isolated. He was recognized by his family and teachers to be an introvert. John did develop hobbies and interests in childhood and adolescence, but these also tended to be of the solitary variety: reading, playing with toys, building models, and so on. He never developed the ability to socialize with others despite his parents' encouragement and support. One might say that John appeared somewhat schizoid in his mannerisms, that is to say, distant and flat in his affect and somewhat aloof in his interactive style. Still, he initiated therapy to help him work on this issue. John himself saw this as a problem that needed fixing for him. That was an encouraging and positive sign.

If John is suffering from any type of developmental fixation or regression, I would venture to say he is fixated in the stage of trust vs. mistrust. Although he recognizes that he needs help, his overall functioning is strongly influenced by his mistrust of others, even family. This mode of adaptation tends to be John's worldview. That factor could cause problems in any type of therapeutic work.

3. *What type of attachment did the adolescent have with his primary caretakers, and how did these early developmental periods affect his present relationships with family, peers, and significant others, especially the therapist?* According to his parents' reports, John exhibited an avoidant or even disorganized style of attachment in early childhood. He tended to keep to himself and did not seem to have a strong need to develop friendships. In adolescence as well, John focused more on his schoolwork, not social activities or friendships. Now that he is nearing the end of his adolescence, it appears that John recognizes his social isolation and that at least a part of him wants to do something about it. Unfortunately, he has not developed the skills necessary to help him to accomplish that task. In his interactions with me, his therapist, John is also rather distant. He comes across as enthusiastic in his interest in learning how to find a girlfriend, but I never feel a sense of emotional connection with him. He is a bit robotic in his mannerisms and his affect. There is something a bit contrived or inauthentic about him. He seems awkward and anxious about being in the room with me. He seems disorganized. There seems to be a disconnection between his agenda and his emotional capabilities. I realize that this is a countertransference

feeling that probably comes from John's early attachment style. His presentation does not generate a sense of warmth, empathy, or engagement, but instead I feel distant toward him. I believe that emotional configuration comes primarily from John, not me. How do I know this? I usually feel a strong sense of connection with my adolescent clients, regardless of their difficulties. My experience with John is dramatically different.

4. *Why is the adolescent in need of service right now? Is he self-referred, or does someone else believe he needs help?* John's presenting concern is primarily about helping him get a girlfriend. He is not entirely sure why he wants a girlfriend, but he knows it's important, and he is not sure how to accomplish the task. John approaches this problem almost robotically as well. He believes that there must be certain techniques and skills he can develop that will accomplish this task. In a sense he's right. Developing a romantic relationship does entail utilizing a variety of interpersonal skills. But developing a romantic relationship is also an interpersonal process. It takes time and there are numerous intangible factors, conscious and unconscious, that contribute to it. John does not seem to understand this sophisticated and elusive aspect of relationship development. He wants me to give him the skills to make it happen now. Despite recognizing John's limitations in both his thinking and his emotional capabilities, I believe that his presenting concern is legitimate and something we can work on together.

5. *Does the adolescent see himself as being conflicted or in need of help, despite the fact that he may not be self-referred? To what extent can he see his part in the situation? Does the adolescent have the capacity to be introspective and/or to view himself objectively? What is the extent of his observing ego?* This question really cuts to the heart of the matter with John. I believe that John recognizes that he has a dilemma in his inability to find a girlfriend, but he does not tend to see himself as deficient or responsible for problems in his life in any way. Most difficulties that John experiences he thinks are the fault of others. He has not developed an observing ego to any extent. He is egocentric and narcissistic in his interactions with all others. This is a severe emotional deficit for John that has had a great impact on his emotional development since his adolescence in particular. Any attempts on my part to engage John in a more introspective examination of his part in human relationships or situations is met with a strong insistence on the fault of others. I soon recognized that this psychological deficit was going to be a severe detriment to treatment and might take some time to remedy even in therapy.

6. *Is the adolescent's defensive structure adaptive or maladaptive?* John's defensive structure is a strong mixture of mostly maladaptive primitive and sophisticated psychological defenses. He utilizes projection and denial to blame others for his difficulties as well as protect himself from any

sense of ownership of emotional deficits. In addition, John's use of intellectualization and rationalization helps him to stay removed from his feelings and the sense of anxiety, helplessness, and fear they might have generated.

As a result, working with him in therapy is quite a challenge. As time went on in our work together, I realized that John's reality testing and judgment were also becoming increasingly impaired. He began to develop subtle paranoid delusions that became more and more bizarre over time. For example, as we discussed his plans for the future, John informed me that he wanted to work in government. He is quite bright and actually very savvy about the political arena. He wanted to work as a presidential advisor. Initially his discussions about this interest centered on how he would develop the skills necessary for this work through a college education. As time went on, however, John began to elaborate on how he already had these skills and in fact there was a job waiting for him in Washington as a presidential advisor. He believed that if he went to Washington, he could meet with the president or some other important advisory figure who would hire him immediately. This is very dubious thinking that also affects his ability to discuss his interest in women. Over time I began to recognize that John might be beginning to experience the signs of a psychotic disorder.

7. *How would you assess the adolescent's family system, and how does it affect his present situation?* As an only child, John is the center of attention for his parents. They both seem to be conscientious and concerned about John, but the family in general appears to be a relatively closed system. There tends to be little involvement or encouragement to be involved in the outside world. John's parents, through no fault of their own, are comfortable in allowing John to remain socially isolated with them. The family seems to be enough for all of them. They function as a self-contained unit. Unfortunately, this closed style of adaptation seems to contribute to and exacerbate John's tendency to isolate himself and negatively affects his ability to develop proper social skills.

8. *Are the adolescent's parents/caretakers invested and willing to recognize there might be a problem and help work on it?* John's parents were initially supportive but removed in their investment in his therapy. John insisted on his independence and discouraged them from collaborating with me in his therapy. Because of this, my initial work with John involved his parents only in a peripheral way. As his psychotic symptoms emerged, however, I insisted with or without John's approval or consent on involving them in the process. Once involved, John's parents could not have been more dedicated, concerned, or cooperative in the therapy situation. They were willing to do whatever it took to help their one and only son.

9. *Are there particular issues of diversity that heavily influence the adolescent's situation?* Although there do not appear to be any issues of

diversity related to race, ethnicity, culture, spirituality, or even socioeconomic class that influence John's situation, persons suffering from mental illness are a vulnerable population. Mental disorders are often a misunderstood phenomenon, and individuals with a mental illness can be discriminated against because of ignorance and fear. As he continues his life journey and struggle with schizophrenia, John will be affected by this dilemma.

10. *What environmental factors are relevant to this situation?* John lives in a fairly affluent environment. There are many community resources that he can rely on in his struggle with schizophrenia. The area is rich in mental health services. John's school personnel are well equipped to understand and help him deal with his mental illness. His parents, although not involved intimately in their community, are certainly aware of its services and can help facilitate John's involvement in them. This is fortunately an enriched environment.

11. *What resources are available to the adolescent in dealing with this situation? What are the adolescent's strengths?* There are a multitude of community resources available to John. In addition, his parents are probably the most reliable and valuable ongoing resource for him as he struggles with the onset of schizophrenia. John's most valuable strength is his motivation to be in therapy. He may not be able to see his part in or contribution to his emotional difficulties, but he is at least willing to come to therapy to find the answers to his questions. John is very intelligent. He seems capable of comprehending the reasons for his difficulties if he becomes capable of allowing himself to look at them emotionally. John's strength and weakness is his own mind.

12. *Based upon all of the factors above, what is your intervention plan, and what do you think the outcome might be?* John's treatment was actually in two phases. The details will be discussed in greater depth below. The first phase of treatment focused on John's concern with finding a girlfriend. As we worked together on this problem, however, he began to develop the signs and symptoms of schizophrenia. The onset of this condition drastically altered John's interest in and motivation for therapy as well as affected how he approached his life in general. Treatment for adolescent schizophrenia should ideally include a course of medication combined with inpatient psychiatric treatment as well as outpatient follow-up therapy and comprehensive community support.

CASE DISCUSSION

John's therapy, as mentioned earlier, evolved in two distinct chapters. I first understood and accepted John's need to work on developing his social skills as a very legitimate request for service. I recognized, however, that owing to his clear emotional deficits, lack of insight, and poor social skills, the work would be challenging. As I empathically challenged John to begin to examine his part in the difficulties he experienced in life, I recognized that he was becoming more and more delusional and irritated with the process. His delusions began to center on not only his grandiose career aspirations but his perceptions of potential women he wished to date. John began to imagine that women whom he found attractive also believed he was special. In exploring these ideas further, it became clear to me that there was no real evidence to validate John's impressions. His beliefs and certainties about these women were all in his mind. They were delusions. In addition, John began to imagine that other potential male suitors were out to get him or to diminish him in the eyes of the women he admired. I began to realize that John was beginning to experience the signs and symptoms of a psychosis.

From the time that John began to see me until the onset of his schizophrenic symptoms, perhaps two months had elapsed. Initially I tried to encourage John to seek out psychiatric help to deal with what I told him were some distortions in his thinking. As he became more agitated, I also mentioned to John that seeing a psychiatrist could help manage the tension he was experiencing through the use of medication. John became very defensive and paranoid about this suggestion. He began to accuse me of being against him and in league with "others" who were envious of his obvious talents. I believed that it was fruitless to try to persuade John to seek out psychiatric help and decided to contact his parents against his wishes to help protect him from himself.

Before I could reach John's parents, he had left town. His parents and I had no idea where he was, if he was safe, or if he was even sane. Several months went by before I heard from John's parents again. John had been found wandering the streets of a Virginia town. He was clearly delusional and rambling on about how he would be a government representative if he could just see the right people in Washington. John was uncooperative with authorities, irritable, and mildly combative. He was returned to his hometown, and his parents involuntarily hospitalized him in a reputable psychiatric inpatient facility. John remained in the hospital for several months while he was assessed and treated for paranoid schizophrenia. He was put on antipsychotic medications and released to his parents' care. Eventually John came back to therapy with me.

Upon his return, John resumed his interest in finding a romantic interest as well as becoming more social. He acknowledged that he had a psychiatric disorder but continued to move in and out of his delusional thinking for the remainder of the time that I saw him. John ended therapy with me because, as he put it, I could not find him a girlfriend.

Although he never returned for ongoing therapy, John still occasionally contacts me, even fifteen years later. Now an adult, John still struggles with the symptoms of schizophrenia and is still focused on his delusions regarding women. These are not dangerous or threatening delusions but certainly are not helpful to John. Most particularly I am reminded of the last time I saw John in person. He called me and asked to come in for a session. When he arrived, we began to catch up on how his life was going, where he worked, his social life, and so on. John still lived with his parents but was able to hold down some meager jobs for modest pay. He seemed to be functioning marginally well, and I could not detect any obvious signs of delusional thoughts or psychotic behavior. At the end of the session, however, John asked me about a young woman whom he was interested in dating. I told him that I didn't know whom he was speaking about. John looked at me curiously and stated that of course I knew her and why wasn't I going to help him date her? I strongly challenged John's delusion, but he refused to believe otherwise. Although he had improved, John was still suffering from schizophrenia.

I would like to share one final note about John and his sad story. Although I have never seen him again since that last disappointing session, John occasionally calls my voice mail and leaves me messages. The last one went something like this: "This is John. I want to thank you for ruining my life. Never call me again!" It's important to know that I never did call John unless he asked me to contact him. This most recent voice mail came probably a year prior to the writing of this book. I had not seen John for five years before that time.

This sorry case illustrates the dramatic and challenging dilemma of working with adolescents who are undergoing the beginnings of schizophrenia. The horribly debilitating effects of this disease can wreak havoc on the normal process of adolescent development. The clinician working with adolescents must be continually hypervigilant about the possibility of the onset of psychotic disorders. Early detection, assessment, and comprehensive treatment can make a tremendous difference in the outcome of this crippling disorder.

SUMMARY

This comprehensive chapter has discussed the myriad of mental illnesses that can beset adolescents. Normal adolescent development is a time filled with a wide range of emotional, cognitive, and behavioral experiences. The search for identity is fraught with challenge, doubt, excitement, worry, elation, and the whole range of human emotions. Clinicians working with adolescents and their families must be good diagnosticians. They must be conversant with the conditions described in the *DSM-IV-TR* as well as the theories and methods that are utilized in understanding and working with them. Treatment for each disorder needs to be diagnostically specific to that condition. Medication and psychotherapeutic treatment combined with comprehensive community support are the method of treatment for this population. The clinician is urged to keep continually abreast of the literature and methodology for working with adolescents suffering from mental illness.

RECOMMENDED RESOURCES
Readings

D. A. Brent, D. J. Kolko, B. Birmaher, M. Baugher, & J. Bridge, "A Clinical Trial for Adolescent Depression: Predictors of Additional Treatment in the Acute and Follow-up Phases of the Trial," *Journal of the Academy of Child and Adolescent Psychiatry* 38 (1999): 263–270. Adolescent depression is a key area of treatment.

E.V. Brestan & S. Eyberg, "Effective Psychosocial Treatments of Conduct-Disordered Children and Adolescents: 29 Years, 82 Studies, and 5,272 Kids," *Journal of Clinical Child Psychology* 27 (1998): 180–189. This study provides useful information on an important area of work with adolescents.

Diagnostic and Statistical Manual of Mental Disorders, 4th ed., text revision *(DSM-IV-TR)* (Washington, DC: American Psychiatric Association, 2000). This is the standard international diagnostic manual.

J. J. McEachin, T. Smith, & O. I. Lovaas, "Outcome in Adolescence of Autistic Children Receiving Early Intensive Behavioral Treatment," *American Journal of Mental Retardation* 97 (1993): 359–372. This study provides important treatment information on this group.

Thomas O'Hare, *Evidence-Based Practices for Social Workers* (Chicago: Lyceum Books, 2005). This text is an excellent evidence-based study guide to practice.

Psychodynamic Diagnostic Manual (PDM) (Silver Springs, MD: Alliance of Psychoanalytic Organizations, 2006). This text provides useful, expanded, and empirically validated information on emotional disorders.

Film/Television/Media

Equus (1977), *Girl, Interrupted* (1999). Both of these films depict serious adolescent mental health issues.

Internet

http://www.nami.org/; http://www.nimh.nih.gov/ These two sites provide comprehensive and contemporary information on mental health issues.

15

Residential and Group Homes and Shelter Programs for Adolescents

For many adolescents, the developmental journey is a difficult one. Whether they are deficient in developmental capabilities owing to hereditary factors, have been raised in an abusive or neglectful family situation, or are the product of an oppressive and depleted environment, many adolescents grow up needing help with the development of their identity and their journey to adulthood. This chapter will address working with those types of teenagers through the use of residential facilities, group homes, and temporary shelter services.

There are a number of reasons and situations that can warrant placing adolescents in these types of settings. There is a wide range of both positive and negative case scenarios, from that of the mildly oppositional teenager whose behavior parents are unable to manage, to that of the adolescent who has been in the child welfare system since birth, resulting in inadequate and inconsistent caretaking, which has led to the development of more severe emotional and behavioral problems. In order to negotiate the developmental challenges of childhood and adolescence, these individuals need attuned, consistent, and reliable caretaking in some form or another. The range of professional services discussed in this chapter is aimed at meeting those needs from a variety of perspectives. Whether one is either working in these settings, or referring adolescents to them, it is important to understand the developmental needs of these teenagers, as well as the capabilities of the settings in which they may be placed.

REVIEW OF BASIC DEVELOPMENTAL NEEDS FOR CHILDREN AND ADOLESCENTS

Before discussing the specific nature of residential, group home, and shelter programs, a review of the basic developmental needs of children and adolescents is in order. Children who end up placed in the child welfare system have been removed from their families owing to a variety of circumstances.

210

Sometimes it is because they have been physically or sexually abused by their caretakers. Other times it is because their caretakers have been judged unable to meet their children's needs. This may be because the parents or caretakers are suffering from severe mental illness, drug addiction, or even severe mental retardation, among many other things. Most often the child is not given a choice about whether or not she wishes to stay with her family. That decision is made by the child welfare authorities. "The best interest of the child" is a phrase often used to describe this situation. Usually removal is a better environmental solution for the child than remaining where she is. Unfortunately, that physical removal may not adequately take into consideration the child's emotional and developmental needs. Abrupt removal from even a severely abusive home can have negative effects on the child's emotional development.

CASE EXAMPLE

Several years ago I received a good deal of child welfare referrals from an agency that provided child protective services to its community. This agency was under contract to the state child welfare department to do follow-up work with families who had been indicated for abuse or neglect. Many times the children from these families were temporarily or permanently removed from their homes and placed in what were determined to be safer environments. Sometimes this was with a family member or friend; other times the children were placed in temporary shelters or group homes. Some of these children and families were referred to my private practice for ongoing treatment aimed at helping them adjust to their situation as well as working toward some type of permanency planning.

A case that stands out in my mind among the many I have seen over the years is that of the Smiths. Mrs. Smith and her two boys were referred to me for follow-up counseling. Mr. Smith had been indicated for sexually abusing his two boys, ages five and seven. He was also arrested and convicted for this crime and was serving over ten years in prison. My job was to help this family cope not only with the repercussions of the sexual abuse of the children but also with adjusting to a new life without a father or husband. I had dealt with sexual abuse cases before, so I assumed that I understood some of the emotional factors that might be integral to this case. I realized how traumatic sexual abuse can be to a child's development, especially a young child's. I also recognized how traumatic it can be for a parent or spouse to realize that her children are being abused by her partner. These dynamics I understood and could certainly handle in treatment. What I was not ready for were the ways in which the removal of the father/husband emotionally affected both the wife and the children.

I was horrified to hear about the specific nature of the sexual abuse of these children. The mother spoke in great detail about how their father had admitted to engaging in anal sex with his two little boys. He had apparently been doing so for years before he was caught. She was shocked to discover these facts and understandably felt tremendous guilt for not realizing what was happening. She also was depressed and angry with herself for not protecting her sons. She also, however, missed her husband. She still loved him and wished they could be together. He was the primary wage earner in the family, and his abrupt departure had caused considerable stress and financial hardship for the family. These were some of the main issues the mom was dealing with in therapy.

The truly amazing and at first shocking insight for me, however, was realizing how the boys felt about their father. I expected them to be relieved that their dad was gone and that they were finally safe from his sexual behavior and abuse. The boys admitted that they were glad that their father was no longer forcing them to engage in anal sex, but they really missed their dad. Despite the sexual abuse, which they experienced as extremely uncomfortable physically and emotionally, they really enjoyed time with their father. He was their playmate. He didn't just sexually abuse them; he played all sorts of legitimate games, sports, and other recreational activities with them. They cried when they talked about not being able to see their father again. They wanted him back in their lives. They were really grieving his loss. I could see that this loss was a severe emotional trauma for them. How is it possible that they could feel this way about a man who had continually forced them to have anal sex with him?

I use this case to illustrate a point. I was given the opportunity through this case to learn that even in the most severe abuse situations, children may still be emotionally attached to their parents. Physically removing the abusive parent from the home and forbidding further contact with the children will certainly stop the abuse. But they also create a rupture in the emotional relationship that the children have with the parent. The legalities that are put in motion to protect the children may not adequately take the children's emotional needs into consideration. They are now physically safe, but they may have been emotionally traumatized by that very act of protection.

There is no question that this father's behavior was wrong and that it needed to be identified and stopped immediately. But the children's emotional needs must be taken into consideration. The best interest of these children may have been met, for instance, in allowing them to continue to see their father in a professionally supervised situation. Abruptly cutting them off from a father whom they loved may not be the best way to help in their emotional development. These children will probably not be allowed to see their father until they are adults. Is that in their best interest? My best clinical and professional judgment tells me that these children are going to have some severe emotional deficits if their relationship with their father is abruptly terminated. There must be a better way to meet the best interests of the child than this. Looking into their sad eyes as they cried about missing their father was an eye-opener for me. It made me realize how complex these child welfare situations are and how important it is to find developmentally informed ways to resolve them.

I could have discussed a case example in which an adolescent was removed from a sexually abusive home and how multiple placements had a negative impact on her ongoing development, but I wanted to emphasize the emotional impact of misinformed and misguided child welfare and public laws. Children's and adolescents' needs are far too often ignored or not taken into consideration in cases of abuse and neglect. The focus tends to be on dealing with the offense or even on parental remediation at the expense of the child's mental health. Far too much time is taken in moving children back and forth between multiple caretakers while the parent is getting treatment to help him return to his role of caretaker for the abused child. While this process goes on, children are not frozen in time developmentally; they continue to grow and develop in whatever placements they may be given. If there is no attachment established, and no consistency and reliability in that setting, these children become even worse. When they finally are returned to their parents, who may be ready to parent more effectively, too much time has gone by for them developmentally. They are damaged not only from the initial abuse but from the process that focuses more on the parent's needs than on the child's. Children are not property; they should have rights as well, particularly a right to decent and normal emotional development. This is not happening in our society at the present time. An adolescent's developmental needs must be taken into consideration when making decisions about any type of placement outside of the home.

RESIDENTIAL FACILITIES

When it becomes necessary to remove children or adolescents from their homes owing to the variety of circumstances mentioned above, a decision has to be made regarding what type of setting or facility is best for that child. Placement in residential facilities is usually made when it is determined that the child or adolescent is in need of a highly structured, self-contained therapeutic environment where he can live while his emotional and physical needs are addressed in intensive treatment. The most stereotypical example of this type of facility is Boys Town.

Father Flanagan established Boys Town in 1917 in Omaha, Nebraska, as an orphanage for boys. Children placed in this self-contained residential community lived there until they were either adopted or became legal adults. Boys Town was the prototype for many therapeutic residential facilities today. Children placed there were able to develop new emotional attachments to adults and as a result continue their developmental journey in a safe and effective manner. Residential facilities such as Boys Town aimed at meeting the physical and emotional needs of the entire child. Children

placed in these facilities lived there, went to school there, received therapeutic treatment there, and most important found a new and emotionally
healthy home there.

Today there is a wide variety of residential facilities for children and adolescents throughout the world. Many of these programs are highly specialized
and geared toward specific types of child and adolescent problems such as
sexual abuse, physical abuse, neglect, eating disorders, drug addiction, attachment disorders, and a multitude of other circumstances. The advantage of
these types of settings is their self-contained nature, which allows the child to
develop attachments to significant others, thus enabling them to recover and
lead normal lives. Children and adolescents placed in residential programs
usually live there for several years. The purpose of such a system is to give
them the time to attach to therapeutic professionals who can help them work
through their emotional difficulties by being a part of a residential family.

Youth in these programs get the love and structure that Winnicott refers
to in his article "The Anti-Social Tendency" (1992). An ideal residential setting is one in which there is a mixture of both that is appropriate to the
developmental needs of the child and adolescent. Some adolescents need
more structure and some need more nurturance. A well-run and professional staffed residential facility develops a comprehensive treatment plan
for each child based upon a thorough and ongoing psychosocial assessment.
These types of programs should be staffed with psychiatric, medical, psychological, and social work professionals. In addition, they must have highly
trained technicians whose job is to work with the youth on a day-to-day
basis, helping them go to school, do their chores, get along with peers, and
so on. It is essential that these professionals be thoroughly trained in child
and adolescent development; as well as aware of the specific developmental
needs of each child they are working with in the facility.

A residential program is only as good as its professional staff. Ongoing
professional collaboration among all of the professional staff is the key to a
child's recovery. Medical staff attends to the child's physical needs. Psychiatrists evaluate and focus on the need for medication. Psychologists utilize
sophisticated testing to measure cognitive and emotional factors relevant to
the youth's needs. Social workers and other mental health professionals usually provide the ongoing counseling services deemed appropriate to the specific individual's problems. Day staff or technicians must be in the loop
regarding all these factors in order to be sure that the needs of the adolescent are being met in a way that is appropriate to their development. Finally,
the case manager must coordinate the permanency planning for all children
and adolescents in these types of facilities. This means making sure that the
individual is ready to leave a facility and that her placement is likely to have
a successful outcome.

Clinicians working in these environments must have a thorough understanding of the adolescent's history as well as how that history has affected

his development. Remember that adolescent development is affected by earlier developmental factors. Teenagers placed in residential facilities have often had a disrupted life prior to their placement. They may have been in multiple foster or adoptive homes prior to a residential placement. This will have undoubtedly affected their capacity to attach to others, as well as their behavior. These adolescents may be very oppositional, conduct disordered, depressed, anxious, irritable, bipolar, or a combination of all these things. They are not an easy group to work with in treatment. They can be highly resistant and understandably defensive.

Adolescents placed in residential programs have usually been through a tremendous amount of inconsistency, abuse, neglect, and uncertainty. It is the job of the clinician working with these adolescents to help restore their emotional competencies. This can take time and a great deal of patience. It is in many ways analogous to parenting a two- or three-year-old child. They need the caregiver's love, but they also need environmental structure.

Most residential programs operate on a behavioral point system. Adolescents earn privileges by accumulating points for good behavior. There are many variations within programs, but a typical example is one in which the teenager is given a point card. They have a running total of points either positive or negative depending on their current behavior. The more positive their behavior, the more privileges they will receive. It is one of the main jobs of the regular staff to help "teach" the teenager about his behavior. Moment-to-moment instruction with these youths can help them realize the consequences of their actions. This can also be accomplished through day-to-day interactions with staff, their counselor, their teachers, and in groups with their peers.

The pivotal aspect of this comprehensive approach is the optimal balance between behavioral management and an empathically attuned emotional relationship. Love and structure are the key elements in development and in the successful outcome of a residential placement. Many facilities are not able to achieve this balance. Part of the reason is the lack of understanding and coordination among the therapeutic team. All members of the professional staff, especially support staff who work with adolescents day to day, must understand this important developmental concept. The failure to do so can lead to faulty interventions and perhaps even exacerbate the adolescent's problems. This breakdown in professional continuity is far too common in many residential facilities.

GROUP HOMES

Group homes are a form of residential placement as well. What primarily distinguishes them from residential facilities is that they are typically not locked facilities, they provide shorter stays, and they are usually located within communities. The professional staff at group homes is usually not as comprehensive as that of residential facilities as well. Group homes do not usually have a psychiatrist on staff, and psychological services, if needed, are provided away from the facility through referral. The professional staff at most group homes is a two-tiered system consisting of counselors and support staff. The counselors provide therapy and case management services to the adolescents placed in the group home, and the support staff manages the teenagers' day-to-day behavior.

Group homes are typically either all-male or all-female programs. The purpose of these types of settings is to provide temporary housing and structure for adolescents until they are deemed ready for permanent placement in either foster homes or their families. Group home facilities were not originally designed to work with adolescents with severe developmental problems. They were developed to work with children and adolescents who needed a safe and secure therapeutic setting for three months to a year.

The length of stay as well as the structure of the program has implications for the nature of the therapeutic services offered in a group home environment. In residential facilities, the child or adolescent has been placed for long-term services aimed at modifying and repairing his developmental deficits. These facilities are usually locked and often located in rural areas. Adolescents in particular are not as capable of or interested in running away from residential facilities. Most group homes are not locked facilities. The adolescents within them are free to leave if they choose. The legal mandates limit the constraints of these facilities for the protection of the adolescents' civil rights. This is an odd policy from a developmental standpoint, even with adolescents who may be psychologically healthier than the teenagers living in residential placements.

Many of the teenagers placed in group homes have a history of running away from home as well as placement facilities. These are adolescents who are struggling with emotional, psychiatric, and developmental problems. Placing them in facilities that are not locked can offer a dangerous temptation and a strong deterrent to therapeutic services. If a teenager knows she can walk out of a facility at any time, it may be difficult to motivate her to remain when her situation becomes conflicted. It is strange that all adolescents living with primary caregivers can be restricted or physically stopped from leaving, but group home staff is legally not allowed to restrain adolescents unless they are a physical threat to themselves or others. There are some serious flaws in this type of policy. How are these adolescents going to learn the limits of their oppositional behavior if the adults who are supervising them are not legally allowed to set physical limits? Teenagers placed in group homes are encouraged to adhere to the behavioral point system within the group home, but most adolescents living in group homes know that they will not be stopped from running away and that the worst that can happen to them if they leave is that they will get some negative points and perhaps have to sit in a timeout for a day or two. This type of behavioral modification philosophy may be ineffective for teenagers who want to leave a group home to smoke a cigarette, do drugs, have sex, or simply stay out for a night. Primary caregivers of most children would bar the door or even physically restrain their teenagers from such impulses if they felt that their adolescents could not manage their own behavior. Staff in most group home settings are legally not allowed to provide adolescents with that type of safety. This policy is developmentally misinformed and emotionally destructive in my opinion.

These comments may sound disparaging of group home facilities. I highlight them here to illustrate an important point. Adolescents who are in greater danger of running away or who have severe difficulty managing their impulses should probably not be placed in a group home setting. Such a facility is not equipped or legally allowed to handle this type of acting-out behavior in a developmentally effective manner. These adolescents need a more restrictive setting like a residential facility or even an inpatient psychiatric setting.

Unfortunately, public policy and fiscal management in today's child welfare arena are not always conducive to ensuring that adolescents are placed in settings appropriate to their developmental needs. Cost management is a key variable in child welfare. Residential placement is much more costly than placing an adolescent in a group home. The cost per day of a residential setting can sometimes be more than double that of a group home. Public child welfare in most if not all areas has a limited amount of dollars to provide therapeutic services to the children and adolescents who need them. To save dollars or perhaps more correctly preserve funds for more children and teenagers, many adolescents are placed in therapeutic settings that are far beneath their developmental needs.

On the brighter side, many adolescents placed in group home settings do quite well. Many of these teenagers have been removed from abusive and neglectful homes. Some of them have had a relatively successful and good enough early developmental history. They already have the cognitive, emotional, and behavioral skills necessary to function in a relatively adaptive manner in adult life. They are not in need of a long-term therapeutic environment to help mend severe developmental issues. These adolescents can benefit from the less restrictive structure of a group home setting. The group home setting can serve as a temporary moratorium or transition to the next step in many of these adolescents' developmental journey.

Living in a group home environment with adolescent peers who have struggled with similar difficulties can be a tremendous emotional support for many teenagers. Because of its less restrictive environment, the group home can seem like living in a family. Professional staff and adolescent residents operate together like a real family. Teenagers living in group homes make meals together, do daily chores, go to school in their community, develop friendships in and outside the group home setting, and live a relatively normal teenage life while they await a new permanent placement or return home.

Most group home structures operate on a behavioral point system similar to that of residential programs. Adolescents earn points and achieve behavioral levels that allow them to have privileges such as time away from the group home and greater flexibility in using their allowance. The support staff works with these adolescents to help them learn better ways of managing their behaviors, while the professional counseling staff helps them through more traditional psychotherapeutic services such as counseling. Even in group home and residential settings, the principles and techniques of both traditional and nontraditional types of therapy are essential for successful outcomes. Many of these adolescents cannot engage in talk therapy. They may function much better if approached through more nontraditional clinical work.

Clinicians working with these more challenged and dysfunctional adolescents need to have a thorough understanding of their developmental history. These teenagers have fallen off the developmental track, many of them through no fault of their own. They need the support, structure, and guidance that a professional therapeutic environment can offer. Treatment plans are specifically aimed at helping these teenagers develop and maintain the cognitive, emotional, and behavior abilities necessary to function effectively once they are placed back in the community.

Permanency planning with adolescents placed in group home settings is an important part of the treatment process. If the goal is for the teenager to return home, work with the family is in order. Family therapy while the adolescent is in the group home, as well as regularly scheduled home visits, helps these teenagers make the transition back to their homes. If the return home is going to be successful, the family and their teenager need to develop a plan to ensure that whatever progress the teenager has made while at the group home is maintained. Premature placement or return home can have disastrous results.

For those adolescents placed in new foster homes, the situation can be much more complex. Not only must the adolescent be helped to adjust to a new home, but she must grieve over leaving and losing their previous one. As I mentioned in the case example at the beginning of this chapter, even the most abusive relationships can still be experienced by the adolescent as having some positive elements. Object relations theory reminds us that infants, children, and adolescents internalize a sense of self and other that is both good and bad. The achievement of object and self constancy enables those children to experience themselves and prominent others in shades of gray. But termination and disruption of even the most abusive home environment can be experienced as a loss and is an extremely stressful event in life.

Helping adolescents who will be placed in new homes must be done in a timely, sensitive, and therapeutic manner. This, too, is a process. As the hour of termination from the group home approaches, many adolescents regress in their behavior and feelings. This is normal. Professional staff, both counselors and support staff, must be knowledgeable about this predictable situation. The sensitive and therapeutic handling of this stressful time can help the adolescent experience the loss as a necessary and normal part of life rather than as another disruptive and traumatic event.

Finally, the key element in the success of any group home setting is the extent to which counselors and support staff cooperate in the treatment of the adolescents placed there. In most group home settings, the professional counselors have professional master's degrees and have been educated in the theories essential to understanding child and adolescent development. They also are well versed in the skills and interventions necessary to work with that population. The support staff may not have such an extensive background. Most support staff have bachelor's degrees in sociology or psychology or some other liberal arts degree. Some do not have even a bachelor's education. Although these essential staff members receive on-the-job training through their agency, many of them do not have the level of knowledge and sophistication of the group home counselors.

This disparity has the unfortunate potential to contribute to agency infighting as well as inhibiting the therapeutic effectiveness of the group home. The key to managing this potential discrepancy is communication. Ongoing collaboration among all group home staff is crucial to the effectiveness of the program. When conflict splits the staff, the adolescents are in the middle. This situation is not unlike living in a family with extreme marital conflict. It is imperative that professional staff working in these types of settings be aware of these possibilities, work collaboratively together, and receive outside consultation to help them better manage these potential problems.

SHELTER PROGRAMS

Shelter programs are the shortest and least restrictive of the service programs discussed in this chapter. Some of the adolescents who are placed in shelter programs are returned home, but many are not. Once again, the circumstances and background of the adolescent placed in a shelter program dictate the type of treatment he should receive. Staff of most shelter programs is similar to that of group homes. Support staff are usually bachelor-level professionals, and shelter counselors have their professional master's degree. Shelter program are also usually operated on a behavioral point system similar to that of group and residential facilities.

A key difference lies in the nature of counseling services the adolescent may receive while in a shelter. Many adolescents placed in shelter programs do not come with an extensive packet of information about their psychosocial history. As a result, it can be difficult to make an accurate assessment of them. In addition, even if an extensive psychosocial history accompanies them to the shelter, their stay will presumably last perhaps a little over a month or more; therefore treatment should be aimed not at long-term change but rather at short-term stabilization.

Shelter programs were designed to be a short-term respite for adolescents. It is the job of the professional staff to help quickly stabilize the teenager so that she can be placed in a more appropriate permanent setting. There usually is very little time or opportunity to do extensive clinical work in a shelter program. Often it is merely a holding tank for adolescents while a child welfare worker or supervisor determines where they should go next. Many times the decision is made to return the adolescent home to her family. Frequently the teens are placed in temporary foster homes. Sometimes they are placed in group home settings for further assessment and treatment while awaiting a more permanent home.

For adolescents who are living in an abusive or neglectful environment, placement in a shelter facility can be a quick and effective relief. If run effectively, shelter homes can be a therapeutic environment for these adolescents. Supportive professional staff and peers can help many of these youths feel less isolated. While they await a more permanent placement or even the return home, these adolescents are usually involved in counseling that is aimed at preparing them for their immediate future. Clinical work with teens living in short-term shelter programs is usually time-limited supportive therapy, group therapy, and CBT-like models. There is no time to pursue more complex issues related to developmental problems. These adolescents need to be stabilized and placed elsewhere as quickly as possible if they are to begin to function better in their lives. Time is the essential therapeutic factor for adolescents in a shelter program.

Shelter homes may suffer from the same difficulties that group homes can experience. Only those adolescents who need and can benefit from a short-term stay should be placed in a shelter program. Adolescents with severe developmental issues should not be placed in these facilities. They should be sent to group or residential programs for the treatment they need. Even a short-term stay in a shelter program while awaiting group or residential placement can have detrimental effects for adolescents who are struggling with more severe emotional and behavioral difficulties. The less restrictive environment of shelter programs makes them more susceptible to adolescent runaways. Even adolescents who are experiencing minor difficulties that necessitate shelter placement need to be in a secure environment. Open-door policies, even in shelters, are in my opinion a mistake. This policy sends the wrong message to teenagers at risk. Parents would restrain their children from leaving home. Shelter staff legally cannot. I cannot emphasize enough the danger of this type of policy from a developmental standpoint. Adolescents who are appropriately placed in residential and group homes and shelters need secure structure as well as consistent and reliable emotional support. These teens are not getting that in their lives. There is no point telling them they can't leave the shelter when the staff lacks the power and authority to keep them. But many of these programs function just this way with their adolescent clientele. This is an unfortunate aspect of the child welfare system.

CLINICAL ISSUES

Although the three types of facilities discussed above may operate differently depending upon their setting and the specific nature of the adolescents seen within them, there are some strikingly similar clinical issues that are common to all of them. Even the most psychologically healthy adolescents may occasionally try to pit their parents against one another in order to get what they want in life. From a psychological perspective, this phenomenon might be labeled *splitting.* One parent is the good parent, and the other is the bad parent, depending upon the extent to which they meet the adolescent's needs. If mom doesn't let the teenager stay out later, maybe dad will agree to it. The key to successfully managing any adolescent is for both parents to be consistent in their parenting as well as continually communicate with each other about their interactions with their teen. It is not helpful for parents to give mixed messages to their teenagers, for one parent to be consistently experienced as the disciplinarian while the other is seen as more supportive of the child's behavior as well as more lenient.

This same dynamic crops up frequently in residential, group, and shelter facilities. Support staff, who are most often in the position of needing to set limits with these adolescents, can be labeled as the bad staff in the program. The professional counselors tend to focus more on emotional support than on behavior management, and as a result are often experienced as the good staff by adolescent residents. It is important for the emotional development of the adolescents within these facilities to recognize that support staff and the counselors are in agreement about the rules and requirements of the setting. This can happen only if there is ongoing collaboration as well as honest and open communication among all professional staff. Remember that consistency in particular has usually been lacking in many of these adolescents' backgrounds. It is important to ensure that it is happening in these types of settings.

Adolescents placed in many of these settings have also experienced disruptive, unreliable, and inconsistent attachment relationships early in their lives. As a result, they may have developed attachment styles that elicit strong emotional reactions on the part of the professional staff within the program. These extreme emotional states have both *transference* and *countertransference* components. On the transference side, many of these teenagers are acting out their anger, avoidance, or dependency needs in inappropriate ways. They may be excessively clingy or seductive or disregard emotional boundaries. They may also react in strongly oppositional ways in order to avoid emotional attachment with another. The range of emotions and the resulting reactions of the professional staff vary depending upon the developmental background and needs of the particular adolescent. From a countertransference standpoint, clinicians as well as support staff need to remember that the way they emotionally react to these troubled adolescents is usually a diagnostic indication of the teenager's deeper developmental issues. It is important not only to recognize these reactions within oneself but also to have an open dialogue with all program staff in order to understand the extent to which these feeling states are a part of all of the staff's reactions. If there seems to be a common emotional reaction among the majority of professional staff, it may signal something more troubling within a particular adolescent. Ongoing communication and collaboration among all professional staff is essential in not only understanding these complex emotional features but developing consistent and appropriate therapeutic interventions to manage them and help the adolescent function more effectively.

CASE EXAMPLE

Nearly fifteen years ago I was hired as a part-time social work consultant for a pilot program aimed at providing diagnostic and treatment services to adolescents in the child welfare system. The child welfare system of the state I practice in had determined that it needed to do a better job in early assessment and treatment intervention for the adolescent wards of the state. This new pilot program was unique in its design, the makeup of its professional staff, and the services it provided.

The operation was housed in a large older home located in an urban setting. The home was uniquely coed and could house up to fifteen adolescents. Adolescent wards of the state between the ages of twelve and seventeen were eligible to be placed in this setting. Violent teens as well as those who were suicidal or a sexual abuse risk were not allowed in this program. It was designed for youth who were in need of comprehensive assessment before being placed in the appropriate therapeutic setting. While that assessment was being completed, these adolescents lived in this group home setting, went to school in the community, and developed relationships with other teenagers placed there as well as with the professional staff.

The professional staff of this diagnostic program was quite diverse. There were two clinical consultants: myself as the social work consultant and a Ph.D. psychologist. The psychologist performed psychological testing on all youth placed in the program. This testing was designed to gather important information on IQ and other emotional and psychological factors relevant to determine placement. The psychological testing was one of several elements in this comprehensive diagnostic evaluation. My role was at least twofold. I was to serve as the ongoing clinical supervisor for the professional counselors in the program, as well as function as the social work consultant to the program. Integral to that role was overseeing the content and writing of the comprehensive diagnostic assessment and placement recommendation.

In addition to the social work and psychology professionals, this program retained its own psychiatrist as well as a consulting nurse. These two professionals were in charge of overseeing the physical and psychiatric needs of the adolescents living in the home. There were several masters-level counselors in the program, as well as a large group of support staff who managed the day-to-day functioning of the adolescents living in this program. The program operated on a behavioral point system, and every member of the support staff received comprehensive training in that behavioral model. The model utilized for this program was in fact a derivative of the original behavioral model used at Boys Town.

Each adolescent placed in this diagnostic program went through a 45–90 day comprehensive diagnostic assessment that was to culminate in a professional recommendation for permanency planning and ongoing treatment. The professional counselors were each assigned about five teenagers to their caseloads. It was their main task to provide therapy to these adolescents while in the program and oversee the development of their comprehensive assessment. They were to make certain that all elements of the assessment were completed in a timely fashion and write the final assessment document. It was my job to review that final assessment, making certain that it contained what the professional team proposed, and put my signature of approval to it.

This process was quite intricate and comprehensive from the onset of the program. The entire clinical team met weekly to discuss each adolescent case. The clinical counselors, select support staff, the psychiatrist, psychologist, and nurse all contributed to the weekly case discussions. This was truly a collaborative effort from a multidisciplinary team. Every week as the comprehensive assessment developed, the clinical team discussed each adolescent client from a variety of theoretical and practical viewpoints. Psychological, behavioral, and developmental theories were combined in these discussions in order to develop the best professional decision about the needs and future placement of these youths. Family histories were gathered through extensive contact with previous caregivers and important others involved in the adolescent's life. The professional counselors also utilized their ongoing clinical work with these youths to further refine their diagnostic picture. Support staff were able to augment this clinical picture through their feedback on how the adolescent was performing in the program on a day-to-day basis. To my knowledge, this type of comprehensive diagnostic program had never been done before. It seemed that these adolescents might truly get the services they needed through our help.

Once the final comprehensive assessment was completed, it was forwarded to the adolescent's child welfare caseworker. This caseworker was then charged with following through on the recommendations of the diagnostic team. Initially this arrangement seemed to work well. The entire diagnostic team and professional staff took its work quite seriously. The recommendations that were made came from a dedicated and conscientious group of professionals who felt passionate about their work and believed that the child welfare system was finally getting adolescents the services they needed. Understandably, many of our assessments recommended residential placements for these severely disturbed adolescents. Our team did not take fiscal policy or politics into consideration in making our recommendations; we were acting, we believed, in the best interests of the teen, based upon the best clinical judgment from a group of highly experienced professionals.

More and more of our assessments began to recommend residential placements. The costs of these services must have been very high. As a result, not long after our program started to send in recommendations, we were told that they would have to be reviewed by a professional called a gatekeeper. The qualifications of this gatekeeper were nowhere near as extensive as those of the members of the clinical team. Curiously, more and more of our recommendations were denied. We were told that we were making too many recommendations for residential settings and that the child welfare department didn't believe they were necessary. It began to circumvent our recommendations and placed many of these teens in foster homes and other less therapeutic environments. Many of the adolescents in our program failed in their placements because they were not psychologically or emotionally ready for them as we had predicted.

The deterioration of this diagnostic program continued as the child welfare department intervened in its management. Fiscal management took precedence over the developmental needs of these adolescents. As a result they did not receive the services or placements that were crucial to their developmental success. What had started as a tremendously optimistic program for adolescents in need became a victim of the system.

CASE DISCUSSION

I am not using this example to criticize the child welfare system of my state. I am sure that this type of situation and political maneuvering happens throughout the U.S. child welfare system. What I am hoping to do is impress upon those clinicians working with this adolescent population the importance of advocating for their clients. Faulty and inappropriate services are no better than no services at all. The comprehensive developmental needs of adolescents must be taken into consideration so that they are placed in the most appropriate setting and receive the treatment they so sorely need to succeed in life.

SUMMARY

This chapter has addressed that segment of the adolescent population who are need of placement and comprehensive services outside of their homes. These youths may need placement owing to severe abuse or neglect or simply because they do not have the emotional and psychological skills to function without intensive therapeutic help. Residential and group homes and shelter facilities serve to bridge that developmental gap. They are a valuable part of the array of professional adolescent services. Unfortunately, there are many problems with the operation of these facilities, whether it is the bureaucratic policies that impinge upon effective service provision or the inherent challenges of collaborative service provision. Clinicians working in these settings must be cognizant of those factors in order to insure that the effective and therapeutic provision of services can be maintained.

RECOMMENDED RESOURCES

Readings

John F. Curry, "The Current Status of Research into Residential Treatment," *Residential Treatment for Children and Youth* 12, no. 3 (1995): 1–17. This is a good review of residential treatment research.

Daniel L. Davis & Lucinda H. Broster, "Cognitive-Behavioral-Expressive Interventions with Aggressive and Resistant Youth," *Residential Treatment for Children and Youth* 10, no. 4 (1993): 55–68. This is an interesting study on resistant teens.

Eileen Gambrill & Mary Ann Mason, eds., *Debating Children's Lives: Current Controversies on Children and Adolescents* (Newbury Park, CA: Sage, 1994). This work highlights the fact that not all teens cope in the same ways.

Film/Television/Media

Boys Town (1938), *Antwone Fisher* (2002), *White Oleander* (2002). These three films depict adolescents in residential settings.

Internet

http://www.therapeuticmilieu.org/ This is a helpful site on inpatient programs.

16

Working with Community/ Collaterals

In order to provide the most effective treatment to adolescent clientele, the clinician must work with the social service agencies and community organizations that serve them. Some communities are rich in resources, while others have virtually none. The extent to which adjunctive services and opportunities are available to adolescents and their families has a direct impact on the developmental process. The practice formulation asks: *What environmental factors are relevant to this situation? What resources are available to the adolescent in dealing with this situation? What are the adolescent's strengths?* The more enriched an adolescent's environment, the greater the opportunities for her to discover her talents and identity.

Identity is shaped by three main elements: hereditary constitution, developmental caregiving, and the environment. Deficits in any one of these areas can be detrimental to an adolescent's development. Even with the healthiest constitution and the most attuned parenting, an adolescent may not develop a healthy identity if he grows up in a deprived environment such as a high-crime urban community. The lack of community resources as well as a funding base in which to develop those resources can compromise and limit the opportunities available to adolescents and their families. Rural areas as well often do not have the fiscal capability to develop sorely needed community resources. This is a much larger problem than the individual clinician can solve. But understanding the strengths and limitations of the adolescent's community is an essential part of the assessment as well as the treatment plan.

Part of a comprehensive approach to working with adolescents can include developing the community in which they live. Preventative community development work can be as important a therapeutic variable as traditional clinical intervention. Enriching communities through the construction of programs and services aimed at enhancing adolescent development can help prevent problems for many teenagers. In order to accomplish this task, however, one must understand the needs of the adolescents within a community, the nature of the community, and the opportunities for the development of new programs (Meenaghan, 2005).

DEVELOPMENTAL IMPLICATIONS OF COMMUNITY PRACTICE

As an outreach worker in the 1970s, I was hired not only to provide concrete services to teenagers but also to assess their needs. Our agency's advisory board, called the Committee on Youth, consisted of concerned citizens from the community who were dedicated to helping prevent so-called juvenile delinquency. This well-meaning committee was made up of teachers, parents, business people, and other social service professionals. They were knowledgeable about adolescent development and recognized that their community was deficient in the resources necessary to help their youth negotiate the adolescent journey successfully. Hiring an outreach worker like me was an attempt to remedy that situation.

My job was to hang out with the adolescents who were on the edge. I didn't really engage much with the mainstream teenagers. Those adolescents were for the most part involved in traditional school and community programs such as sports, extracurricular activities, and park district programs. The adolescents I attempted to engage were much more isolated and in need of nontraditional opportunities to augment their developmental process. Through interacting with many of these youths in informal dialogue on their own turf, I was able to develop a trusting relationship in which these teenagers could communicate their concerns.

By building a trusting relationship in my role as an outreach worker, I was able to ascertain that these adolescents felt isolated. They had nothing to do that fit with their interests and needs as they understood them. These adolescents were on the fringe of the mainstream culture. They rebelled against traditional programs and services for teenagers, yet they had nothing else to fall back on. As a result, many of them turned to activities that got them into trouble such as drug use and even crime. Fortunately I was in a position to do something about that problem.

My involvement as an outreach worker with those adolescents led to the development of a teen drop-in center as well as a myriad of nontraditional adolescent programming such as the activity group I mentioned in chapter 10 and other quasi-therapeutic recreational opportunities. Although at the time I didn't fully realize the psychological significance and developmental importance of these programs, I instinctively knew they were necessary and would be helpful to the teens I was working with. Community development work can be instrumental in providing resources that are crucial to a successful developmental journey for many adolescents. This type of practice is as therapeutic and important as any form of traditional clinical work. Developing a community suitable to meet the specific developmental needs of the adolescents within it can be one of the greatest sources of prevention in adolescent mental health. If done successfully, community development practice can offset the need for traditional psychotherapy services for many adolescents and their families.

COMMUNITY COLLABORATION

Even in those communities in which there are a plethora of services, there can still be problems. Most agencies are also struggling for survival. Many agencies within the same community provide similar services. This can create unhealthy competition and interfere in the provision of quality services to adolescents and their families. Two very different scenarios help to illustrate this point.

When I worked as the executive director of a small community-based agency in the 1980s, we were the only counseling agency that served adolescents. All adolescent programming came through our agency. We weren't concerned about competition or survival. When it came time to secure funding for an adolescent program, I merely needed to convince my board of its importance and viability. Even acquiring funds from the local area United Way was easy because my agency was the only show in town serving adolescents.

In my outreach days from the 1970s, our agency was in direct competition with the local community mental health center, as well as a variety of community-based social service agencies. In order to survive, we had to carve out our professional niche. In contrast to the agency mentioned above, we had to be able to demonstrate that our services and programming not only were justified from a developmental standpoint but could not be better provided by another agency in the same community. Competition and agency survival were ongoing factors that figured prominently in the service provision of that agency.

Fortunately, the agencies in question worked quite well together. Ongoing collaboration helped ensure that services were not duplicated and were complementary in nature. For example, my agency provided nontraditional service programming such as outreach services, the agency drop-in center, and a variety of therapeutic group activities. The community mental health center offered comprehensive psychiatric services that in particular provided assessment for medication as well as more in-depth psychotherapy for severe mental illness. Our agency offered counseling services as well but utilized the mental health center in circumstances that warranted more comprehensive psychiatric involvement. This is the ideal picture in comprehensive service provision and coordination of professional programming.

ADVOCACY AND REFERRALS

Most community-based agencies, schools, and mental health centers have developed a comprehensive list of referrals to meet the needs of their adolescent clients and families. The therapist working in these settings must become familiar with those resources in order to make certain that adolescents and their families receive the services they need.

It behooves the practitioner to get to know the agencies and the specific personnel within them in order to help expedite service provision, as well as see to it that the adolescent in question gets the kind of help or resource he needs. This means spending time interacting with agency personnel and developing a relationship with key people in order to smooth the referral process. Many social service agencies are busy and understaffed. The referral process may not move along as quickly as one might like. Having an ongoing professional relationship with key agency personnel can be an invaluable help to the clients that the clinician sees in practice.

The clinician in private practice or working in a more isolated or deprived environment must be diligent and creative in developing a resource and referral base for her clientele. Nurturing productive relationships with necessary referral sources may be secondary to simply finding them in many communities. Effective clinicians are those who have been able to develop a comprehensive repertoire of community resources and referrals.

In my thirty-plus years of clinical experience I have been involved in several private practices in very different communities. Each time I have settled into a new area, I have made a point of exploring the availability of community resources. It is very helpful to know who the best psychiatrists are in the area. Although many general practitioners can and do prescribe psychotropic medications for their adolescent patients, they are not specialists in psychiatry and can't possibly be as knowledgeable and comprehensive in their understanding of these types of medications. There is no substitute for a quality psychiatrist who specializes in working with adolescents.

Once the clinician has been able to identify a quality psychiatrist in her area, it is essential to develop a solid working relationship with him. Even the best adolescent psychiatrist probably sees his clients perhaps once a month for maybe fifteen to thirty minutes. This brief snapshot can't possibly give a comprehensive picture of the adolescent's condition. The clinician must have ongoing dialogue with the psychiatrist about the client. The level of respect and cooperation between the clinician and the psychiatrist determines the quality of service the adolescent receives. This relationship building takes time, but it is crucial to the successful treatment of many adolescent clients.

In addition to psychiatric referrals, the practitioner should have access to resources for psychological testing. I have been fortunate enough to be located within a hundred miles of several key universities that can perform low-cost comprehensive psychological testing for my adolescent clients and their families. This has been an invaluable addition to my practice. Although psychological testing has its limitations, it is one very valuable lens in gathering a comprehensive diagnostic picture of the adolescent and identifying or ruling out certain clinical phenomena. For example, knowing that an adolescent's behavioral difficulties in class stem from a discrepancy between his verbal and performance scores on the IQ test can be an invaluable piece of the diagnostic picture. That type of information can help rule out or modify such diagnoses as oppositional defiant and even ADD.

In addition to psychiatric and psychological referral sources, the clinician should be in close contact with school personnel, particularly the school social workers, psychologists, and guidance counselors. Strong ongoing relationships that have been developed through mutual collaboration and dialogue can make a crucial difference in the successful treatment of most adolescents. Whether one is working in an agency, school, or private practice, mutual collaboration around the adolescent's functioning in the school setting is important. This means spending time communicating about the teenager and his difficulties. Confidential communications must be respected, but communication about the adolescent's life in school is essential. Over the thirty years I have been practicing, these mutually respectful collegial relationships have been an invaluable source of support for the adolescent clients I have seen in therapy.

In addition to the collaterals already discussed, the clinician should also develop strong relationships with the juvenile probation officers, local police, park district personnel, youth ministers, private tutoring centers, and other resource personnel who can be useful to the adolescent. It takes time and energy, but advocating for the adolescent client becomes much easier when the clinician has developed ongoing relationships with these key personnel.

CASE EXAMPLE

I learned a great deal about working with adolescents in my first agency. Most social service professionals don't stay in agencies much longer than three to five years. I stayed fifteen years. I moved from outreach worker, to agency counselor, to clinical director of the agency. In between, I learned to do informal youth work, traditional clinical practice, nontraditional recreational services and group work, parent education, community development work, clinical supervision with both professional staff and a variety of graduate and undergraduate student interns, and even some fiscal management that included fundraising. I grew up as a professional in that setting. I was twenty-four years old when I started and thirty-nine when I left to become executive director of a small community-based agency some twenty-five miles away. During that time, I developed the knowledge and acquired the skills to run my own agency.

It was also during that time period that I went to graduate school, developed my first private practice, and began teaching as an adjunct professor for several MSW programs. The development of my private practice gave me the opportunity to put much of what I had learned at my agency (much of it the hard way through mistakes) into practice. I worked hard to make contact with all the people connected with the types of resources discussed above. I learned about that new community, developed strong professional relationships, and was able to maintain a very successful practice for over twenty years. Through my teaching experiences, which continue to this day, I began to truly understand the relationship between theory and practice. I have taught not only traditional clinical theory and skills but also community organization and macro-level theory and practice with the adolescent population. I have learned through this ongoing process that proficient teaching of theory requires a solid understanding of practice, and that to practice effectively requires a solid basis in theory. The two go hand in hand. By the time I began to run my own agency I had learned a great deal and had grown as a comprehensively knowledgeable professional. I was ready for the challenge.

I was hired as the new executive director of a small community-based youth and family service agency. This new agency had been established in the late 1960s to deal with the problems of juvenile delinquency and adolescent drug abuse. The agency was the only community-based family service agency in the town. It was quite small, with two staff members, an administrative assistant, and the executive director. In addition to my administrative duties as the agency director, I was also the clinical director for the staff, provided therapy for adolescents and their families, and supervised graduate student interns from several nearby universities. Our agency was located in a small house in the community, near the downtown area. The agency owned the house, having purchased it many years before I was hired. This gave the agency a rather comfortable and homey atmosphere for both the staff and all who came to visit or for services. It also meant that the executive director shoveled snow in the winter (among other things) and was responsible for the general upkeep of the house.

As the executive director, I was hired by and responsible to the agency's board of directors. These individuals were for all intents and purposes my bosses. The board members of most social service agencies have terms of service, much like a senator or representative in the U.S. government. These terms usually run from three to five years. It is unusual in social service agencies for board members to have lengthy terms of membership. I was surprised to find that my board was composed of members who had served twenty years or more. Most of them had outlasted any of my predecessors. These individuals, I soon realized, were used to being in charge of things as well as micromanaging agency operations. Agency management is supposed to be the director's job, not the board's. The director must consult and work with the board to make certain that services are congruent with the agency's mission, but the board should leave the day-to-day operations to the director and the professional staff.

This very powerful board scrutinized my ideas, work, and overall running of their agency. They were quite protective, which was both a good and a bad part of my position. Two key board members served as my orientation team when I was first hired. They were the two members who had been there the longest. I knew the lay of the land in this agency when during my first week one of these board members told me the history of all their past executive directors. It seems all of them had either been fired by the board for not adequately following through on the agency's mission or outlived their usefulness to the agency and the community, or left prematurely for positions elsewhere. This little talk let me know implicitly that I would be watched closely and asked to leave once I was no longer of any use to the board. I decided that very week that I would need to make things happen in this community if I was going to survive. I did just that.

Having painted a rather negative picture of this agency, I must say that my tenure there was exciting, educational, and successful. I developed many wonderful professional relationships and brought tremendous program growth and increased funding to the agency. The two board members mentioned above introduced me to the key people in this small community. I quickly learned that the business breakfast or lunch was the way things were done in this community. So I had lunch with the unit school district superintendent, township supervisors, police chief, village mayor, president of the women's club, local United Way chairperson, and so on. These initial meetings were quite productive. I learned a great deal about these powerful community individuals, especially their personal ideologies and vision of their community. Most important, I learned what their expectations were for our agency. For instance, the school superintendent informed me that his school district did not have school social workers within its schools. Instead, when needed, social workers were hired on a temporary basis from a local consortium. Politically this meant that he wanted my agency to provide social services within the schools of the district. The police chief was concerned with the growing number of first-time arrests of adolescents for drug possession and abuse. He and his chief juvenile officer were particularly concerned with the way in which the parents of many of these teenagers reacted to their arrests. Apparently in this upper-middle-class community, many parents wanted to look the other way. They would rather pay the fine and ignore or minimize the problem. What was even more troubling to these police officers was that many parents allowed their teenagers to have drinking parties when they were out of town. They would even buy the kegs of beer. Our agency was expected to help solve this growing community problem. These were but two of the concerns I was expected to deal with in my role as the new executive director.

As exciting as these opportunities were, they were also daunting challenges for me. I was but one of only three professional staff in an agency that served an entire community. I realized that I would have to hire additional professionals, but I did not have the funds to do so. If I was going to respond to the needs of these community leaders, I would have to find a way to increase agency funding. First of all, however, I would have to develop an overall service plan to meet the expectations of the community.

At my board's request, I made a point of meeting with the principals of all the schools in the community. Each of these individuals had his own unique personality, as well as a different set of problems he felt needed to be addressed. I also met with the director of special education for the district, whose job was to oversee the social service needs of all the schools. From my meetings with her I learned that the middle school and high school were fairly well staffed with counselors but that the elementary schools were sorely in need of help. In particular, the director wanted our agency to consider providing counseling services to this population. I brainstormed with the individual principals and staff of each school about the types of programs and services our agency might be able to offer.

The middle and high school personnel had other needs. As I mentioned earlier, our agency developed the alternative to Saturday detention groups through my collaborative efforts with the high school deans and counselors. Our agency already had a strong presence in the middle school through our "Operation Snowball" drug prevention program. One of the agency counselors spent most of his time in providing drug prevention services, either through direct counseling at the agency or through groups in both middle and high school settings. We were asked to increase our presence in both of these settings.

The director of the community park district informed me that she was extremely understaffed in her summer youth programming. She wondered whether our agency might be able to work with her to find an answer to her staffing problems. The community's juvenile officer wanted our agency to work more closely with his staff to expand our deferred prosecution program as well as provide counseling services to adolescents who had recently been station adjusted (referred for counseling services in lieu of being arrested for a crime). The social service agencies of the community, including the Women's Club, Kiwanis, and Rotary Club, wanted more community education regarding the needs and problems of the community's adolescents. These were just a few of the challenges facing me immediately as I entered into my new role of executive director.

After developing my initial thoughts surrounding this community needs assessment, I approached my board with an initial plan. I proposed that we hire an agency consultant to help us develop programs to meet the needs of the school district and other community organizations. The board was open to my proposal, and the planning began. In the meantime, I was informed that the local-area United Way was looking for funding proposals for new and creative social service programming. I worked with my board and key United Way officials to map out an initial grant proposal.

Working with our new agency consultant, we were able to develop a variety of programs aimed at working with the schools, police, park district, and other key elements of the community. My United Way proposal laid out the details of this new comprehensive service plan, which would require hiring new agency staff. Unfortunately, whatever monies we might receive from the United Way would not be nearly enough. I would need to sell this idea to our other funding sources as well as do some additional fundraising in the community. In addition, even if we received the funds necessary to hire new staff, we would be able to afford only one. I knew the demand for services was far beyond the capabilities of four staff members. I would need to find more help in order to carry out this new initiative.

It seemed my only option was our agency's graduate intern program. I began meeting with the universities with which we already had relationships to inquire about increasing the number of graduate students placed at the agency. In addition, I contacted new universities to further increase our pool of graduate students in social work and psychology. The agency was used to having perhaps two or three interns a year. That number was increased to eight to ten in order for our agency to provide the types and numbers of groups and other services proposed. My duties now also included supervising these ten interns. In less than a year, the agency's staff and budget had more than doubled, and so had its services to the community.

I was fortunately able to secure an enormous grant from the United Way, as well as incremental funding increases from the local townships and civic organizations. A new full-time staff member was hired (the first new position in many years), and I worked with our consultant and interns to develop specialized group programming for the elementary and middle school populations. We were able to provide the high school with the alternative to Saturday detention groups, which also dramatically increased our counseling load in general. Agency staff and interns worked more closely with the juvenile police officers, and our deferred prosecution program as well as response to station-adjusted teens significantly increased. The increase in professional staff and interns enabled the agency to meet the needs of this community in a much more comprehensive manner than it had ever done before. When I was hired as the executive director, the agency's annual budget was around $150,000; it had doubled by the time I left in two short years.

CASE DISCUSSION

This is an example of how community development can happen and how comprehensive services can be identified, created, and provided through hard work, determination, and community collaboration. The changes in this community were not a result of my work alone, although the fact that our agency was the only service provider in this community certainly helped. Open and honest communication with community members was a key factor in the success of this project. It was a collaborative effort of all involved.

BASIS OF PRACTICE

The effectiveness of community work must be assessed through an examination of trends in the population over time. The reduction in juvenile crime rates might indicate that comprehensive community programming is paying off. But validating this knowledge would require a longitudinal study taking account of a myriad of intervening variables and multiple methodologies. This type of work aims at prevention, not direct treatment. It has been my practice wisdom experience as an agency administrator, consultant, and private practitioner that collaborative efforts can lead to healthier communities.

SUMMARY

Although the overwhelming majority of material in this text focuses on individual, family, and group work with adolescents and their families, community development and collaboration cannot be overlooked. The myriad of developmental needs of adolescents cannot be met through traditional psychotherapeutic interventions alone. Communities must provide a variety of recreational and preventative programming aimed at meeting normal developmental needs. The clinician working with adolescents can be instrumental in helping to shape the development of these sorely needed services. He must also be keenly aware of the resources within the community in order to assist his clients in getting competent, comprehensive, and timely service.

RECOMMENDED RESOURCES

Readings

Thomas M. Meenaghan, *Generalist Practice in Larger Settings* (Chicago: Lyceum Books, 2005). This text is an excellent source of basic information on communities and organizations.

Internet

http://www.acorn.org/index.php?id=2716; http://www.idealist.org/ These two sites provide good sources of information on organizations.

17
Implications of a Comprehensive Approach

This final chapter is intended to illustrate the complex integration of the theories, concepts, techniques, and principles discussed throughout this text. Adolescence is a developmental period influenced by numerous physical, emotional, social, cognitive, and behavioral factors. The journey toward identity formation is filled with challenges that are influenced by all of these factors. In order to work successfully with adolescents and their families, the practitioner must understand the multitude of concepts and issues discussed throughout this text. The clinician must be flexible, knowledgeable, empathic, and above all creative in facilitating an effective therapeutic relationship. The wide range of theories and methods covered in this book, as well as the numerous case examples, have been designed to give a sense of that process.

In order to illustrate the complex integration of the multitude of principles put forth in this text, I will once again present a case example.

CASE EXAMPLE

Taylor is a sixteen-year-old female referred to me by the local high school social worker. She has just been released from an inpatient psychiatric treatment center that specialized in adolescents who self-injure, in other words, cut themselves. Taylor is the older of two siblings in an intact nuclear family. She has a younger sister who is ten years old. Both her parents work outside the home. Her mother is a physician and her father a very successful business person. The family lives in a metropolitan suburb and would be characterized as in the upper-middle socioeconomic income range.

Taylor is a good student. She received all As throughout elementary school, but since middle school has begun getting some Bs and occasional Cs. She talks about wanting to go to medical school but at the present time is not very conscientious in her school work. Taylor is of normal weight and height and does not evidence any type of thought disorder. Her affect, however, comes across as particularly anxious. Taylor can be engaging at times but shifts to a more removed and emotionally distant stance even within the same session. In her anxious states, Taylor moves frequently in her chair, fidgets with her hands, and shows some signs of nervous facial tics. She is an intelligent, independent, and creative young woman. Taylor is attractive and dresses appropriately for her age. In many ways she comes across as quite normal in her presentation.

Taylor's parents are very concerned about her recent cutting behavior. They have very different personality styles. Taylor's mother is a visibly anxious woman in her early forties. She is extremely bright, engaging, and cooperative in family therapy but strongly affected by her innately anxious character style. Taylor's father, also in his forties, seems to be the complete opposite of his wife. He is also extremely intelligent, cooperative, and engaging in therapy, but in complete contrast to his wife, he is laid back and relaxed. This interesting couple's dynamic is a complicating factor in their parenting of Taylor and will be discussed in greater detail below.

Beyond their concern about Taylor's self-injury behaviors, her parents have always felt that she is odd and moves to a different drummer. Ever since birth, according to her father, Taylor has been extremely independent and insistent on having things her way. This character style is most upsetting to her mother but does occasionally irritate her father as well. They have agreed to bring her to therapy on the recommendations of both the psychiatric hospital and the school social worker. They would like Taylor to be happy, less withdrawn, and more engaged with the family. She has been in therapy with three other clinicians, but to no avail. According to her parents, Taylor will engage in therapy for a while until she becomes bored with it and feels it is no longer helpful to her. This usually means that Taylor doesn't see the point of therapy or the benefit of just talking.

Taylor is open to beginning therapy once again, especially since she has just been released from the psychiatric hospital. She is uncomfortable with her self-injury behaviors, her mood shifts, and overall sense of worry about life and her future. While in the hospital, Taylor received CBT and liked the concrete structure of the approach. It helped her feel more in control and gave her some skills that seemed to help her manage her ruminative thoughts and emotions. She wants to continue some form of that type of therapy with me. Taylor was diagnosed as having bipolar II disorder and was on a variety of medications including Depakote for mood stabilization, Prozac for depression, and Risperdal for her ruminative thoughts. She seemed to feel that these meds were working for her and took them regularly. Taylor started therapy enthusiastically. Here is the practice formulation for Taylor.

1. *Is there any evidence of constitutional factors that may have contributed to the present situation? If so, how have they affected the adolescent?* There seem to be several possible constitutional factors contributing to Taylor's situation. Taylor is an anxious adolescent. Her mother comes across

in session as very anxious. In fact, Taylor's mother acknowledges that she has always been anxious and that there is no doubt in her mind that Taylor has inherited this quality from her. This anxious predisposition has been a debilitating condition for Taylor's mother throughout her life but one that she has learned to manage with some success.

Taylor does not seem to have inherited her father's more relaxed manner. In fact she doesn't seem to have many of the emotional qualities of her dad. Both her parents are intelligent and successful in their professional careers, and Taylor has demonstrated some of that potential in her educational career thus far.

Taylor's mother recognizes that Taylor also seems to have inherited her grandmother's uniquely independent personality. Both of Taylor's parents discussed at great length how much Taylor and her mother's mother are alike. Taylor was extremely attached to her grandmother, who died a few years ago. Like her grandmother, Taylor, according to her parents, will not hesitate to speak her mind or argue any point that she feels strongly about. Although they are not severe enough to warrant a *DSM-IV-TR* diagnosis of oppositional defiant disorder, Taylor clearly evidences some of its traits in her relationship with her parents in particular.

Taylor's mildly nervous facial tics may also have been inherited, but I was not able to ascertain from her parents whether there is a family history of them. Many adolescents are anxious and display that anxiety in a variety of affective and physical ways, so I was not extremely concerned with Taylor's nervous gestures. The reader may recall that one of the side effects of psychotropic medications such as Risperdal is involuntary facial tics and body tremors. I would keep this possibility in mind as I worked with Taylor.

2. *What level of psychosocial development do you believe the adolescent has achieved? Do you believe the adolescent is fixated or regressed at all? What factors lead you to believe this may be the case?* In the interest of demonstrating the complexity of this important diagnostic question, I will discuss my understanding of Taylor's entire developmental progress to date. From a trust vs. mistrust standpoint, it appears as if Taylor has been able to develop a reasonably secure sense of the world in general. She has been an excellent student in elementary school, she's been able to develop some good friendships thus far in her life, and she has gotten along reasonably well with her family and society in general.

But Taylor is anxious and worries a great deal. Although this may be a constitutional predisposition in her personality structure, that anxious predisposition may have affected her ability to interpret the world as a relatively safe place even from birth. From a neuroscience standpoint, one might argue that Taylor has an overactive amygdala. She may be constitutionally predisposed, like her mother, toward experiencing the world as a more dangerous place than others might see it. This possibly inherited factor would shape Taylor's view of the world, interactions with others, as well as the extent to which she can successfully negotiate Erikson's first stage. One might even suggest that Taylor's mildly oppositional, independent, and somewhat avoidant style is a result of that more anxious predisposition and the way in which she negotiated that very first stage of emotional development.

The autonomy vs. shame and doubt stage is generally understood to represent the child's first efforts to gain control of his physical self (particularly related to toilet training), as well as his incorporation of the emotional elements of those tasks into the rudimentary beginnings of identity and independence. From Taylor's obsessive, worried thoughts, one might speculate that she controls her world through anxious rumination. Even her anxious tics might in some way be related to her physical need to control her anxiety about the world. On the other hand, Taylor seems able to assert her independence with her family. She is quick to argue about almost everything with her parents and insists, like her grandmother before her, on having things her way. Taylor's sense of autonomy has not been thwarted, but she seems to have developed an anxious/avoidant style of asserting herself in her world. One has to question as well what function her self-injury has served as a bodily means of managing the anxiety of identity formation during adolescence. Taylor seems to have resorted to physical control and pain as a mechanism with which to manage the thoughts and emotions she is experiencing. This may be reminiscent of the struggle for physical control during that second stage of emotional development. The sense of control a child is able to achieve over her body is directly proportionate to her sense of emotional autonomy. Remember Freud's statement: "The ego is first and foremost a body ego." Taylor's physical anxiety may be a remnant of that earlier time period, reawakened in the second individuation of adolescence.

Initiative vs. guilt, Erikson's third stage of development, marks the beginnings of idealization and the internalization of the other that shape a sense of confidence in one's identity. The child can feel a sense of worth only if she feels attractive to and loved and valued by those most important to her. The end result of this process is the capacity for initiative. Failure to develop initiative results in insecurity and guilt. Taylor's ability to move ahead in the development of her identity is contingent upon the successful internalization of a sense of goodness as well as confidence.

Most adolescents struggle with self-esteem and self-confidence. Taylor is no exception. Her possible anxious predisposition has certainly compounded her difficulties. Her early relationship with her grandmother seems to have been a pivotal factor in shaping at least a relative sense of self-esteem and self-confidence. But her grandmother's death just a few years prior to adolescence has no doubt shaken Taylor's already anxious sense of self. Taylor, nonetheless, is able to function reasonably well in school and with her friends and her family. She seems to be in a crisis of identity right now as evidenced by her tendency to self-injure and her extreme moodiness, but she has been capable of more confident functioning in the very recent past.

Industry vs. inferiority, Erikson's fourth stage, is as much about the development of the emotional self and relationships as it is about the development of interests and skills. It rests upon the relative success with which the child has negotiated the first three stages in life and developed trust, autonomy, initiative, self-confidence, and self esteem. During the industry vs. inferiority stage, the elementary-school-aged child also develops more sophisticated emotional defenses, as well as adaptive social skills that will help them in their relationships with adults and especially their peers.

Taylor, although probably an anxious little girl, was able to manage this stage of development quite well, it seems. She had no trouble developing friendships, did well in elementary and middle school, and became a very good violinist. Taylor is also an avid reader and enjoys poetry. She was able to find subliminal outlets for her emotions that served her well prior to the onset of adolescence.

Chronologically Taylor is struggling with Erikson's stage of identity vs. role confusion. Although her difficulties negotiating the stages mentioned above have certainly tainted her ability to deal with her adolescence, Taylor does not appear to be fixated in them or to have regressed significantly to these earlier stages in order to cope with the demands of this present stage. But Taylor is having some trouble in dealing with her adolescence. She is clearly not comfortable with her identity. Her cutting behaviors indicate that she feels the need to hurt herself in order to experience and express emotion. These behaviors probably reflect at least a very ambivalent sense of self-esteem, if not a significantly negative sense of self in general. Taylor worries and ruminates excessively. Although it appears that this tendency may be inherited, it still exacerbates the normal adolescent soul searching that is part of identity formation. Taylor needs to be in therapy right now in order to help her find herself and begin to feel good about the self she will become.

3. *What type of attachment did the adolescent have with her primary caretakers, and how did these early developmental periods affect her present relationships with family, peers, and significant others, especially the therapist?* The answer to this question is a key element to understanding Taylor. Before I began meeting with Taylor individually for therapy, I met with her parents. Taylor had just been released from an inpatient psychiatric facility that specialized in working with adolescents who self-injure. I came highly recommended to work with their daughter, but Taylor's parents were understandably concerned and wanted to be sure I could be helpful to them. Besides, meeting with parents before seeing an adolescent for therapy should be a normal part of most clinical work with that population.

I was told that Taylor had been in three unsuccessful therapy relationships prior to her hospitalization. Taylor's father was quick to point out that she seemed to engage quickly in therapy but eventually became bored with her therapist, felt that the counseling was doing no good, and wanted to stop coming. I was a bit surprised that Taylor's parents did not encourage her to continue when she began to feel that way, but they both seemed to feel that once Taylor made up her mind, there was no changing it. This was a feature of her personality that was pervasive throughout her life.

Taylor's parents informed me that she had always been a stubborn child. Her father told me that even when Taylor was born, he remembered the scowl on her face when she came out of her mother. He acted out for me the dramatic grimace he saw on her face as she emerged from her mother. He told me that Taylor has been that way ever since. His wife agreed and said that Taylor was just like her mother, Taylor's grandmother. She had a will of her own and was not a very cooperative child in any shape or form.

Her father told me two other stories that help to get a picture of Taylor's personality style. When she was about four or five, he tried to get Taylor to hold his hand so that they could cross a busy intersection. Taylor refused, folded her arms around herself, and said, "I'm going to hold my own hand!" She then proceeded to cross the intersection, "hugging herself" all the way. Her father also remembered another interesting story. The family was scheduled to go to the doctor for a regular checkup but had other social plans. Taylor's father told the family that he was going to call and reschedule the doctor's appointment. Taylor, who was around five or six years old, said, "No, you are not canceling the appointment; we are going to the doctor!" Her father insisted and proceeded to get on the phone to the doctor. He was in the middle of telling the doctor that the kids were too sick to come to their appointment, a little white lie of convenience, when Taylor picked up another phone in the house and told the doctor, "We are not sick!" and hung up.

What do these two vignettes have to do with attachment issues? I believe they are clear representations of Taylor's avoidant attachment style. John Bowlby (1969) can be credited with developing the continuum of attachment styles used to understand human development throughout the life cycle. There are secure, anxious, avoidant, and disorganized styles of attachment that are present from early infancy and influence relationships throughout life. These styles can be constitutional as well as developmental. There can also be combinations of these attachment styles such as an anxious/avoidant child. Taylor, it seems, has been an avoidant child since birth. She has probably also been extremely anxious in her relationships with others. This attachment style has influenced her development in some very crucial ways. Whether Taylor's attachment style was inherited, or whether it developed through her relationships with her primary caretakers, we cannot know for certain. What we do know is that this style has become a problem for her and her family.

From an object relations standpoint, Taylor appears to have some difficulty in a number of areas. Her cutting behaviors clearly indicate that she has not achieved a healthy sense of object constancy. Taylor uses self-injury to relieve her anxiety as well as reconfirm the bad or ambivalent aspects of self that she has internalized. One might speculate that owing to her avoidant and anxious attachment style in infancy and early childhood, Taylor may not have had a strong emotional connection to her primary caretakers. This avoidant attachment style, whether of constitutional origin or developmentally influenced, may have contributed to Taylor's lack of ability to internalize soothing interactions with others. As a result, she has been left with a deficiency in the ability to self-soothe. The onset of adolescence reawakens the separation-individuation process. If the child has been able to become relatively object constant in early development, the emotional move toward autonomy in adolescence will not be as daunting. In Taylor's case, her cutting behaviors may be a signal that she is having problems in that area.

The acquisition of an observing ego is also a developmental ability that is influenced by a variety of factors. Taylor, like most adolescents her age, is very self-centered. Narcissism is a part of the adolescent search for identity. For Taylor, however, her extremely avoidant and anxious style has interfered in her ability to assume the role of the other. Taylor's avoidant manner contributes to her self-centered view of the world and has also made it quite difficult for her to see things from another's point of view. This has exacerbated her oppositional defiant traits, particularly in her relationship with her parents.

Taylor's self constancy has probably also been negatively influenced by her early relationships with primary caregivers. Although it is true that most teenagers do not achieve a healthy sense of self constancy until later in adolescence, Taylor's self-injury behaviors would suggest that she is having difficulty coping with aspects of her good and bad self. The conflicts from earlier developmental stages may have led her to rely on more physically self-destructive ways of managing emotions. Her anxious/avoidant personality style has further inhibited her from engaging with significant others to help her develop a more positive sense of self. As a result, when she is feeling bad about herself, Taylor isolates and cuts, rather than reaching out to others for temporary soothing. This is the crux of her developmental difficulty at the present time.

Self psychology would argue that Taylor has been unable to internalize sufficient mirroring and idealizing of self-objects. This difficulty may be due to the constitutional and/or developmentally derived avoidant attachment style that she has had since infancy. As a result, Taylor may have been ambivalent about accepting mirroring from primary caregivers. In addition, this ambivalence may have influenced her ability to accept primary caretakers as a source of welcome soothing through an idealized merger. Taylor may be both mirror and merger hungry but unable to incorporate those necessary self-objects owing to her avoidant style. This may have resulted in her reliance on self rather than others. The cutting behaviors are perhaps Taylor's best attempt to manage the depleted sense of self that she has continually experienced during this pivotal time in her adolescence.

Finally, one must take into account the impact of her early relationship with primary caregivers. Taylor's mother admits to having a very anxious disposition. That character style may have contributed to her worry about and overinvolvement with her daughter. Taylor's avoidant attachment style no doubt contributed further to her mother's worry about her and probably exacerbated that vicious cycle. Mom's worry led to overinvolvement, which was experienced by Taylor as intrusive, and she avoided her mother even further. This avoidance perhaps fueled mom's anxiety, and the dance intensified. Taylor's normal and natural push toward physical and emotional autonomy brought on by the onset of adolescence has intensified this dynamic even further. Her parents, especially her mother, are struggling with Taylor's emerging independence. In this sense, Taylor's difficulties are also a family issue.

I experience this same type of ambivalence in the therapeutic relationship with Taylor. She can at times seem eager to engage in conversation about almost anything. During these times I feel quite connected with her and get a sense that she wants to explore thoughts, feelings, and emotions related to all areas of her life. She seems invested in the therapy. At other times, however, Taylor can seem distant and even resistant to therapy. At those times, even the simplest question can be experienced by her as intrusive. As a result I am continually hypervigilant in my relationship with her. This is an example of a complex transference/countertransference dynamic. I experience Taylor's need to have distance and respect it, but at the same time I feel a tremendous need to reengage with her in therapy. I sense her ambivalence and don't know how to be connected with her and at the same time allow her to be separate. This is a normal part of most adolescents' struggle with dependency, but for Taylor the dynamic is much more extreme and influenced by her avoidant attachment style.

4. *Why is the adolescent in need of service right now? Is she self-referred, or does someone else believe she needs help?* Taylor is in a somewhat unusual position because she agreed to therapy. Apparently she was disturbed by her cutting behaviors and was a fairly cooperative psychiatric patient. Taylor would say that she needs therapy in order to learn to control her worried thoughts, which can spiral and lead to cutting. She feels that she got a lot out of the CBT that she received while in the psychiatric hospital. She wants to continue that work in outpatient therapy with me.

Taylor's parents are also worried about her cutting, but in addition, as I have already discussed, they feel that she has some longstanding problems related to her oppositional behavior and defiant attitude. They are particularly concerned about Taylor's drop in grades and her argumentative attitude with them over virtually everything, and they worry about her future.

I agree with both Taylor and her parents regarding the reasons for treatment, but in addition recognize that she may have some longstanding constitutional/developmental deficits that are complicating her ability to negotiate her adolescence at the present time. I believe that a strong therapeutic alliance may help Taylor develop the emotional, cognitive, and behavioral skills necessary to move toward adulthood.

5. *Does the adolescent see herself as being conflicted or in need of help, despite the fact that she may not be self-referred? To what extent can she see her part in the situation? Does the adolescent have the capacity to be introspective and/or to view herself objectively? What is the extent of her observing ego?* Although Taylor is willing to enter treatment, she is still a very oppositional and avoidant adolescent. I do not believe that Taylor is capable of much introspection regarding her situation, except that which is highly narcissistic in nature. By that I mean that her insights will be distorted and defended in order to justify and protect her fragile sense of self. Taylor tends to project and blame others, especially her parents, for her difficulties. Until she can begin to feel more confidence in herself she will not be able to explore her part in any scenario to any great extent. Her observing ego is extremely limited at this point in her development. Counseling will have to help her develop this ability, first in the therapeutic relationship, then in other areas of her life.

6. *Is the adolescent's defensive structure adaptive or maladaptive?* Taylor's ego defenses are not entirely maladaptive. She has been able to sublimate a great deal of her nervous energy into playing the violin. She is certainly capable of adaptive regression in the service of the ego, a helpful ego defense, as demonstrated by her ability to play with her friends, nap when she's stressed, and resort to childlike behavior when she's bored. Taylor is also very bright and can utilize intellectualization as well as rationalization in both positive and negative ways depending on the situation at hand.

As I have mentioned earlier, however, Taylor also utilizes some very primitive defenses when she feels controlled or intruded upon, particularly by her family. She denies her part in many things and blames others for her difficulties. This immature style is reminiscent of the emotional temper tantrum that a parent might experience with a two-year-old who doesn't get her way. Not surprisingly, adolescence is the revisiting of that same developmental struggle years later. Taylor's defenses come from her failure to resolve this emotional crisis years earlier.

7. *How would you assess the adolescent's family system, and how does it affect her present situation?* Taylor is the oldest in a sibship of two. Her mother is admittedly a very anxious person. She acknowledges that this anxious style may have contributed to Taylor's oppositional behavior. Taylor's father is almost the complete opposite of his wife. Although he agrees that

Taylor's behavior is troubling, he is not really worried about it and tends to cut her a bit more slack than her mother. Two interesting family systems concepts might help to explain how these dynamics have affected Taylor in her family.

Salvador Minuchin's concept of the family scapegoat might help to explain Taylor's strong tendency to defy her parents (Nichols & Schwartz, 2006). By becoming the symptom bearer in her family, Taylor unconsciously places the focus and blame on her own behavior and personality rather than on her parents'. Her mother can focus on Taylor rather than on the frustrations she might be experiencing in her marriage or the isolation she may anticipate when Taylor leaves the family nest. Bowenian family theory would describe the complementary but potentially conflicted style of Taylor's parents as a ripe relationship for triangulation. Taylor's mother worries to excess, while her husband seems almost unmoved by tensions in the family. A Bowenian family systems therapist might speculate that early in their married life, Taylor's mother turned to her husband to help in her worries about life (Nichols & Schwartz, 2006). We don't know how helpful he may have been, but it does seem clear that once Taylor came along, her mother focused a great deal of her worry on her. This may have taken the pressure off her husband to ease her worries and triangulated it upon Taylor.

Many parents are guilty of this dynamic, as I have discussed earlier in this text. A rigid, exclusive, and chronic triangulation, however, can lead to severe family difficulties. Tensions may arise in the family as Taylor moves into her adolescence. Although she probably never relished this triangulated role, Taylor was probably less resistant to it in her early childhood. Adolescence thrust Taylor into a more oppositional position in her relationship with her mother and father. She now defies her mother in stronger ways than ever before. Her cutting behaviors may signal her ambivalence about rejecting this role, but her ambivalence fortunately does not stop her from insisting on her independence from her parents.

I believe that this family dynamic, if it exists, is unconscious. But that does not mean that the clinician should not take it into consideration when assessing and working with the family.

8. *Are the adolescent's parents/caretakers invested and willing to recognize there might be a problem and help work on it?* One of the most positive factors in working with this case is the level of motivation and cooperation of the parents. It is obvious that Taylor's mother and father love her a great deal. They have invested a tremendous amount of time, money, and energy already in her treatment over the years. In my work with them I have witnessed their willingness to do whatever it takes to help their daughter. Both of them recognize that Taylor has had some longstanding developmental difficulties that are now having an impact on her adolescent development. Engaging their support will not be a problem. What may be difficult,

however, is helping them recognize the ways in which they may have contributed to Taylor's difficulties. It would appear that her parents would be willing to help in any way they can. This is an indication of this family's strength.

9. *Are there particular issues of diversity that heavily influence the adolescent's situation?* Taylor comes from a white, suburban, upper-middle-class metropolitan community. There do not appear to be any obvious issues of diversity that affect her developmental or presenting concern. One can imagine the complexities of this case if Taylor were living in an extremely dangerous environment or one in which she did not have the resources to assist her with her problems.

10. *What environmental factors are relevant to this situation?* Taylor lives in an extremely enriched environment. Both her parents work outside the home in prestigious positions. Taylor's family has almost limitless resources with which to help her. They have excellent insurance that will cover both her inpatient psychiatric care and her outpatient therapy. Her mother works very close to home and can be available to Taylor in a moment's notice. Taylor has good friends, as well as teachers and other supportive adults who care about her.

11. *What resources are available to the adolescent in dealing with this situation? What are the adolescent's strengths?* Taylor lives in an enriched environment that can provide almost limitless educational, medical, recreational, and mental health services. She attends one of the most prestigious high schools in the area that is also rich in educational and supportive services. Once a need has been identified for Taylor, it can be met through the resources of her community.

Despite her limitations and difficulties, Taylor has some obvious strengths. She is bright and creative. Taylor is also very independent. She has strong motivation once she decides upon a course of action. She has a wonderful sense of humor, is an attractive young teenager, and is able to be social and engaging when she decides it is in her best interests. Once Taylor decides to invest in her therapy, she will be successful. She seems to possess a strong sense of determination.

12. *Based upon all of the factors above, what is your intervention plan, and what do you think the outcome might be?* Taylor's initial assessment would seem to indicate that she is struggling with developmental difficulties that have been shaped by hereditary as well as parental and familial dynamics. She is an anxious/avoidant adolescent, who is both worried and rebellious in most areas of her life. Her recent cutting behaviors suggest that she has difficulty self-soothing and may also have some problems with her self concept and confidence. Her family dynamics seem to play a part in her difficulties. Given all these factors, it would seem that Taylor and her family

could benefit from treatment aimed at helping her develop a more stable and positive sense of self as well as assisting her family in helping her separate from them.

DSM-IV-TR *FIVE AXES DIAGNOSIS*

Any attempt to understand or work with Taylor can be further enhanced by examining her situation through a diagnostic assessment utilizing the *DSM-IV-TR*.

Axis I

Of the conditions listed by the *DSM-IV-TR* under axis I, oppositional defiant disorder, obsessive-compulsive disorder, and bipolar disorder are possible diagnoses for Taylor. Part of the reason for treatment is Taylor's parents' concerns about her defiant attitude. But oppositional defiant disorder does not explain her cutting or the thoughts and emotions that precipitated that behavior. Oppositional defiant disorder, is therefore probably not entirely correct. Taylor worries excessively, and the content and quality of her thoughts fit the diagnosis of obsessive-compulsive disorder. But her ruminative thoughts alone do not account for her cutting behaviors. Taylor seems to vacillate between extreme moods. The time when she is most likely to self-injure is when she is feeling very low, usually when she is alone. Although she doesn't fit the full criteria for bipolar I or II, she does seem to be having some chronic mood swings that fit a bipolar condition. The provisional diagnosis is given for a bipolar disorder not otherwise specified because it is assumed she will eventually meet the full criteria for a bipolar diagnosis. Because those criteria have not been fully met yet, bipolar cannot be listed as the primary diagnosis.

Axis II

Of the disorders listed under axis II, borderline personality disorder and narcissistic personality disorder are possible diagnoses for Taylor. Typically in the *DSM-IV-TR,* a patient is not given a personality disorder diagnosis unless she is at least eighteen years of age. In certain circumstances, however, especially when the symptoms are pervasive and have existed for several years, a personality disorder may be warranted and diagnostically helpful. Taylor does not yet clearly demonstrate enough of the full range of symptoms of either borderline or narcissistic personality disorder. But she has for some time evidenced clear and pervasive traits of these diagnostic disorders. The problem in assigning a full diagnosis of either of these two personality disorders to Taylor is that she may progress enough in her emotional development or treatment that she no longer fits the diagnosis.

Most adolescents are narcissistic, and many of them may demonstrate the kind of emotional instability inherent in a borderline condition. But many of these teens move ahead in their development and do not fit these diagnoses in adulthood. Unfortunately, Taylor's early development seems to have made her more prone to the rigid personality traits evident in these two disorders. Her cutting behaviors in particular are similar to coping mechanisms utilized by patients who fit the diagnosis of borderline personality disorder. Taylor also experiences chronic feelings of emptiness, has a variety of unstable friendships, and is unstable in her sense of identity. From a narcissistic personality standpoint, she displays an exaggerated sense of entitlement, often lacks empathy, and shows arrogant and haughty behaviors (*DSM-IV-TR,* 2000). These behaviors are excessive, rigid, and pervasive in her personality at the present time. They have also been present for several years. These axis II traits are red flags for Taylor. She may not carry them into her adult life, but it is important from a diagnostic standpoint to understand their prominence in her present adolescent development.

Axis III

Taylor has no traits of an axis III disorder. Aside from the physical scars that have resulted from her cutting, Taylor appears to be a normal, healthy adolescent female. As I mentioned earlier, she has some mild facial and bodily tics, but these seem to be related not to a physical condition but rather to her anxiety.

Axis IV

Axis IV is concerned with problems with the primary support group. Although I would argue that the main focus of Taylor's difficulties lies in her internalized sense of self and her ability to manage her emotions, her relationship with her family is the mechanism through which she demonstrates difficulties in those areas. Besides that, her parents are quite concerned with her defiance and abrasive attitude in general.

Axis V

Axis V contains the Global Assessment of Functioning Scale (GAF). The GAF is a highly subjective measure of an individual's overall emotional competence. But it can provide a snapshot of functioning at a particular point in time, which can be used to examine progress in the future. Taylor's grades have significantly decreased since middle school, she is extremely defiant with her parents, she worries excessively, and she has recently been hospitalized for cutting herself. These are more than mild symptoms and concerns.

I would assign her a GAF score of 62 (out of 100). Taylor is at risk in her life right now and definitely needs therapeutic help.

COURSE OF TREATMENT

Given the comprehensive diagnostic assessment above, it is clear that Taylor needs clinical treatment. There are any number of treatment models that could be utilized with her, given our understanding of her background and condition. This text has demonstrated that there are a variety of treatment approaches that can be successful with adolescents and their families. The differential decision to use any of them depends upon the type of client involved, her developmental history, the family makeup and dynamics, and the knowledge and skill of the clinician.

In my work with Taylor, I decided to use a combination of psychodynamic, CBT, and Bowenian family therapy. Taylor initially needed to be able to manage her intrusive and ruminative thoughts. While she was in the psychiatric hospital, she was taught CBT to learn techniques to recognize and manage troublesome thoughts and emotions. Taylor worked in groups with her peers to develop alternative behaviors to cutting herself. She learned to recognize the triggers to these compulsive and self-destructive acts. She also was put on medications that helped curb the rumination as well as the anxiety and depression that coincide with the impulses to cut. This was a very effective treatment strategy for Taylor while she was in the hospital. Unfortunately, as is the case in many hospitalizations, once she left the secure environment of the setting, her behaviors resumed.

In my first few sessions with Taylor, she seemed to want to work on eliminating her obsessive thoughts, as well as on improving her mood. Taylor and I consistently worked on measuring her mood, identifying key triggers that might send her into a ruminative downward spiral, and reinforcing the skills and techniques that kept her from cutting (Beck, 1995). Over the next few weeks, Taylor's medications seemed to curb her obsessive thinking and improve her mood significantly. As a result, she did not feel the need to work on maintaining her CBT techniques. Instead, she wanted to talk about her family, friends, and future.

Our therapy sessions began to shift in focus. Taylor started to discuss her friends and interests, as well as her relationship with her family. I began to sense that she had a need to be validated for what she thought, felt, and did in life. She was resistant to discussing any of these issues with her family, particularly her mother, but she seemed willing to talk about such things with me. I quickly realized that Taylor was ambivalent about these discussions with me. If she sensed for a moment that I was becoming too inquiring or intrusive, she would immediately change the subject and spend the remainder of the session in very trivial conversation. But if she allowed herself to become immersed in an area of true interest, she opened up, shared feelings and ideas, and didn't want to stop talking. These moments were wonderful, and I knew they were helping Taylor feel mirrored and validated.

I understood these interactions to be reminiscent of early child development. Taylor needed me to be the approving and mirroring parent but not the imposing or controlling one. If she suspected that my attention wasn't focused exclusively on her, she would distance herself in the conversation. This little dance was all nonverbal and very impulsive. I wondered whether it might also reflect a mild form of bipolar disorder, but it seemed much more closely related to her anxious/avoidant attachment style and her implicit interpretation of our interaction as a threat. As I have mentioned earlier, I will never know for sure whether Taylor's avoidant manner was due to her inherited constitution or a result of awkward attunement. What I do know is that my attempts at allowing her the space and distance she needed in order to decide whether or not to continue to engage in session were a very important part of my work with her. I came to realize that so much of Taylor's anxiety came from what she perceived to be intrusive interactions. I could clearly visualize how it must have been for her parents to find a comfortable manner in which to relate to their daughter.

Taylor's parents, especially her mother, may have exacerbated her tendency to avoid emotionally smothering interactions, but I suspect that Taylor was born with this attachment style. I imagine that even the best good enough parenting may not have kept Taylor from forming this interactive style.

My individual work with Taylor continued for many months. We were able to negotiate a fairly comfortable yet cautious therapeutic relationship. Our sessions usually started with making tea and gradually developed into some discussion that Taylor needed to feel ownership of if it were to continue. I failed as much as I succeeded in these endeavors, but I believe that overall they were helpful to Taylor. She began to seem less anxious and less compelled to avoid conversation in session. I believe that Taylor will always be a little distant and defensive in her interactions, but this will not interfere dramatically in her overall functioning in life.

Another key element in Taylor's successful therapy was the family work I did with her parents. One might consider this counseling technically couples therapy, except that my main focus was on their parenting of Taylor and only peripherally emphasized their coupling dynamics. Taylor's parents, as I mentioned above, were extremely devoted to her and conscientious in their therapy work. With Taylor's permission I gave them periodic updates about our progress in therapy. I touched base with them to get a sense of how Taylor was progressing at home and in school.

In as tactful a way as possible, I slowly began to help Taylor's parents ease up on their worries and concerns about her defiance of them and her insistence on autonomy. Taylor's mother in particular was able to do this as she realized how much Taylor was like her mother. She was able to get in touch with her own ambivalent feelings about her mother. This enabled her to have greater empathy for Taylor, as well as ease off in her own worries and need to monitor and control Taylor's life. Her husband was very supportive in this process. I educated them about the normal process of adolescent rebellion and autonomy as well as most adolescents' need to spend less time with family as they get older. This was reassuring to Taylor's mother, who had been feeling abandoned by Taylor's increased avoidance. I tried to explain that it really didn't have to do with her but that it reflected Taylor's developmental need for autonomy and individuation.

My family work was probably a form of Bowenian therapy. I did a good deal of developmental and parenting education as well as family-of-origin work, exploring the emotional conflicts and family dynamics that originated from past family relationships. This helped Taylor's parents feel less responsible and at the same time allowed Taylor to develop a greater degree of autonomy from them. I encouraged them to let Taylor spend more time with friends and in her room when she was home. I told her mother this didn't mean she couldn't go to Taylor's room, tell her she loved her, and even (God forbid) hug her once in a while, but not to expect Taylor to reciprocate on a regular basis or ever while she was going through this tough developmental time period. Her husband was supportive of her in her loss of Taylor, and the therapy seemed to help them adjust to the approaching empty nest.

NECESSITY OF AN INTEGRATIVE APPROACH

Like many of the cases in this text, Taylor's is an example of the necessity to understand and treat adolescents from a comprehensive integrative perspective. This client can be best understood when the clinician takes into consideration factors related to constitution, development, and environment. Neuroscience theory is pivotal to understanding the cognitive and emotional constitutional predispositions of many adolescents. As in Taylor's case, understanding that an adolescent may have an inherent avoidant attachment style helps the clinician not only understand the etiology of the condition but also devise the most suitable clinical intervention. In Taylor's case, a combination of cognitive and psychodynamic therapy was a helpful approach. Each of those two theories alone would not have fully addressed Taylor's problems. She initially needed the CBT in order to understand her cognitive and emotional triggers and develop structured coping mechanisms to deal with them. Neuroscience and psychopharmacology help the clinician understand the crucial role of medication in targeting the essential neurotransmitters responsible for the client's difficulties. After her symptoms were successfully managed through medication and CBT techniques, Taylor was ready to develop an ability to emotionally interact in a more attuned way in order to feel better about herself as well as feel more emotionally connected in life. The psychodynamic therapy subtly helped Taylor feel a greater sense of validation and confidence while at the same time maintaining a sense of interactive control. Work in any of these areas alone would probably have left Taylor vulnerable to further problems in the future.

Finally, family therapy modified Taylor's environment in such a way as to help both her and her parents experience a more satisfying relationship together. Even if Taylor had benefited from the individually integrative approach discussed above, she probably would have still been at risk if her therapist had not worked with her parents. Skillful work with adolescents requires this kind of diagnostic scrutiny and clinical approach.

BASIS OF PRACTICE

The recent development of so-called integrative and eclectic approaches to clinical practice is both promising and daunting. The reader is encouraged to review James O. Prochaska and John C. Norcross's cutting-edge text *Systems of Psychotherapy: A Transtheoretical Analysis* (2003). The authors extensively examine all the major clinical paradigms from a variety of perspectives, which includes a contemporary review of the research literature. Transtheoretical models of practice are also examined. From a practice wisdom standpoint, there is no question that experienced clinicians utilize a variety of interrelated theories and skills in their practice with adolescents. But this integrated approach has not yet achieved the status of validated knowledge.

SUMMARY

This chapter has once again focused on the necessity for comprehensive integrative and eclectic therapy with adolescents and their families. Throughout this text, the reader has been encouraged to become familiar with the wide range of theories of and approaches to work with adolescents. Developmental understanding, comprehensive clinical diagnosis, flexible styles of therapeutic engagement, traditional and nontraditional approaches to treatment, and family, group, and community work are all necessary. The competent practitioner must continue to expand and integrate her knowledge of comprehensive clinical practice.

RECOMMENDED RESOURCES
Readings

R. J. Barrnett, J. P. Docherty, & G. M. Frommelt, "A Review of Psychotherapy Research since 1963," *Journal of the Academy of Child and Adolescent Psychiatry* 30 (1991): 1–14. This is a good overview of the research on psychotherapy.

L. E. Beutler, "Manualizing Flexibility: The Training of Eclectic Therapists," *Journal of Clinical Psychology* 55 (1999): 399–404. This is an interesting article on eclectic practice.

Michael S. Kolevson & Jacqueline Maykranz, "Theoretical Orientation and Clinical Practice: Uniformity versus Eclecticism?" *Social Service Review* 58, no.1 (1982): 120–129. This study explores an important variable in practice.

Donald F. Krill, *Practice Wisdom: A Guide for the Helping Professionals* (Newbury Park, CA: Sage, 1990). This text provides some solid empirical information for practitioners.

Stephen Palmer & Ray Woolfe, *Integrative and Eclectic Counselling and Psychotherapy* (Newbury Park, CA: Sage, 2000). This is a good source for integrative practice.

James O. Prochaska & John C. Norcross, *Systems of Psychotherapy: A Transtheoretical Analysis,* 5th ed. (Pacific Grove, CA: Thomson-Brooks/Cole, 2003). This is a classic text on integrative practice.

David G. Roseborough, "Psychodynamic Psychotherapy: An Effectiveness Study," *Research on Social Work Practice* 16, no. 2 (Newbury Park, CA: Sage, 2006). This study provides important information on psychodynamic practice.

Film/Television/Media

Equus (1977). This film is a classic depiction of severe psychological disturbance in adolescence.

Appendix:
The Practice Formulation for Biopsychosocial Assessment and Intervention Planning

1. Is there any evidence of constitutional factors that may have contributed to the present situation? If so, how have they affected the adolescent?

2. What level of psychosocial development do you believe the adolescent has achieved? Do you believe the adolescent is fixated or regressed at all? What factors lead you to believe this may be the case?

3. What type of attachment did the adolescent have with her primary caretakers, and how did these early developmental periods affect her present relationships with family, peers, and significant others, especially the therapist?

4. Why is the adolescent in need of service right now? Is he self-referred, or does someone else believe he needs help?

5. Does the adolescent see herself as being conflicted or in need of help, despite the fact that she may not be self-referred? To what extent can she see her part in the situation? Does the adolescent have the capacity to be introspective and/or to view herself objectively? What is the extent of her observing ego?

6. Is the adolescent's defensive structure adaptive or maladaptive?

7. How would you assess the adolescent's family system, and how does it affect her present situation?

8. Are the adolescent's parents/caretakers invested and willing to recognize there might be a problem and help work on it?

9. Are there particular issues of diversity that heavily influence the adolescent's situation?

10. What environmental factors are relevant to this situation?

11. What resources are available to the adolescent in dealing with this situation? What are the adolescent's strengths?

12. Based upon all of the factors above, what is your intervention plan, and what do you think the outcome might be?

References

Adler, A. (1963). *The practice and theory of individual psychology.* Paterson, NJ: Littlefield Adams.

Applegate, J. (1984). Transitional phenomena in adolescence: Tools for negotiating the second individuation. *Clinical Social Work Journal, 12*(3), 233–243.

Applegate, J. (1989). Transitional object reconsidered: Some sociocultural variations and their implications. *Child and Adolescent Social Work, 6*(1), 38–51.

Austrian, S. G. (2000). *Mental disorders, medications, and clinical social work.* New York: Columbia University Press.

Bandura, A. (1977). *Social learning theory.* Englewood Cliffs, NJ: Prentice Hall.

Barrnett, R. J., Docherty J. P., & Frommelt, G. M. (1991). A review of psychotherapy research since 1963. *Journal of the Academy of Child and Adolescent Psychiatry, 30,* 1–14.

Beasley, M., Thompson, T., & Davidson, J. (2003). Resilience in response to life stress: The effects of coping style and cognitive hardiness. *Personality and Individual Differences, 34,* 77–95.

Beck, A. (1976). *Cognitive theory and the emotional disorders.* New York: International Universities Press.

Beck, J. S. (1995). *Cognitive therapy.* New York: Guilford Press.

Beutler, L. E. (1999). Manualizing flexibility: The training of eclectic therapists. *Journal of Clinical Psychology, 55,* 399–404.

Bieschke, K. J., Perez, R. M., & DeBord, K. A. (Eds.). (2007). *Handbook of counseling and psychotherapy with lesbian, gay, bisexual and transgender clients* (2nd ed.). Washington, DC: American Psychological Association.

Blos, P. (1967). The second individuation process of adolescence. In *The psychoanalytic study of the child* (Vol. 20, pp. 162–186). New York: International Universities Press.

Blos, P. (1979). *The adolescent passage: Developmental issues.* New York: International Universities Press.

Bowlby, J. (1969). *Attachment.* New York: Basic Books.

Bowlby, J. (1973). *Separation.* New York: Basic Books.

Bowlby, J. (1980). *Loss.* New York: Basic Books.

Boyle, D. P., and Springer, S. A. (2001). Toward a cultural competence measure for social work with specific populations. *Journal of Ethnic and Cultural Diversity in Social Work, 9,* 53–71.

Bratton, S., & Ray, D. (2000). What research shows about play therapy. *International Journal of Play Therapy, 9*(1), 47–88.

Brent, D. A., Kolko, D. J., Birmaher, B., Baugher, M., & Bridge, J. (1999). A clinical trial for adolescent depression: Predictors of additional treatment in the acute and follow-up phases of the trial. *Journal of the Academy of Child and Adolescent Psychiatry, 38,* 263–270.

Brestan, E. V., & Eyberg, S. (1998). Effective psychosocial treatments of conduct-disordered children and adolescents: 29 years, 82 studies, and 5,272 kids. *Journal of Clinical Child Psychology, 27,* 180–189.

Brown, L. N. (1993). Groupwork and the environment: A systems approach. *Social Work in Groups, 16*(1/2), 83–95.

Canino, I. A., & Spurlock, J. (1994). *Culturally diverse children and adolescents: Assessment, diagnosis and treatment.* New York: Guilford Press.

Cheung, M. (2006). *Therapeutic games and guided imagery.* Chicago: Lyceum Books.

Chung, R.C.-Y., & Bemak, F. (2002). The relationship of culture and empathy in cross-cultural counseling. *Journal of Counseling and Development, 80,* 154–159.

Congress, E. P. (1994). The use of culturagrams to assess and empower culturally diverse families. *Families in Society, 75,* 531–540.

Constable, R., & Lee, D. B. (2004). *Social work with families: Content and process.* Chicago: Lyceum Books.

Corey, M. S., & Corey, G. (2002). *Groups: Process and practice.* Pacific Grove, CA: Brooks/Cole.

Cozolino, L. (2002). *The neuroscience of psychotherapy.* New York: W. W. Norton.

Cozolino, L. (2004). *The making of a therapist: A practice guide for the inner journey.* New York: W. W. Norton.

De Shazer, S., & Berg, I. K. (1997). *Interviewing for solutions.* Pacific Grove, CA: Brooks/Cole.

Diagnostic and statistical manual of mental disorders (4th ed., text revision [DSM-IV-TR]). (2000). Washington, DC: American Psychiatric Association.

Dobson, K. S. (Ed.). (2000). *Handbook of cognitive-behavioral therapies* (2nd ed.). New York: Guilford Press.

Doweiko, H. E. (2002). *Concepts of chemical dependency.* Pacific Grove, CA: Thomson-Brooks/Cole.

Elias, L. J., & Saucier, D. M. (2006). *Neuropsychology.* Boston: Pearson.

Ellis, A. (1973). *Humanistic psychotherapy: The rational-emotive approach.* New York: Julian Press.

Elson, M. (1986). *Self psychology in clinical social work.* New York: W. W. Norton.

Erikson, E. (1950). *Childhood and society.* New York: W. W. Norton.

Evans, D. L., Foa, E. B., Gur, R. E., Hendin, H., O'Brien, C. P., Seligman, M. E. P., & Walsh, T. (Eds.). (2005). *Treating and preventing adolescent mental health disorders.* New York: Oxford University Press.

Fairchild, B., & Hayward, N. (1998). *Now that you know: A parent's guide to understanding their gay and lesbian children.* New York: Harcourt.

Floyd, F. J., Stein, T. S., Harter, K. S., Allison, A., & Nye, C. (1999). Gay, lesbian, and bisexual youths: Separation-individuation, parental attitudes, identity consolidation, and well-being. *Journal of Youth and Adolescence, 28*(6), 719–734.

Franklin, C., Harris, M. B., & Allen-Meares, P. (Eds.). (2006). *The school services sourcebook: A guide for school-based professionals.* New York: Oxford University Press.

Franklin, C., & Jordan, C. (2003). An integrative skills assessment approach. In C. Jordan & C. Franklin (Eds.), *Clinical assessment for social workers: Quantitative and qualitative methods* (2nd ed., pp. 1–52). Chicago: Lyceum Books.

Franz, C. & White, K. (1985). Individuation and attachment in personality development: Extending Erikson's theory. *Journal of Personality, 52*(2), 224–256.

Freud, S. (1938). *The basic writings of Sigmund Freud.* New York: Random House.

Freud, S. (1960). *The ego and the id* (J. Strachey, Trans.). New York: W. W. Norton.

Freud, S. (1966). *Introductory lectures on psychoanalysis* (J. Strachey, Trans.). New York: W. W. Norton.

Gambrill, E., & Mason, M. A. (Eds.). (1994). *Debating children's lives: Current controversies on children and adolescents.* Newbury Park, CA: Sage.

Garber, J., Little, S., Hilsman, R., & Weaver, K. R. (1998). Family predictors of suicidal symptoms in young adolescents. *Journal of Adolescence, 21,* 445–457.

Garmezy, N. (1991). Resilience and vulnerability to adverse developmental outcomes associated with poverty. *American Behavioral Scientist, 34,* 416–430.

Gendlin, E. T. (1969). Focusing. *Psychotherapy: Theory, Research, and Practice, 6,* 14–15.

Gendlin, E. T. (1978). *Focusing.* New York: Everest House.

Gilgun, J. F. (1996). Human development and adversity in ecological perspective, part 1: A conceptual framework. *Families in Society, 77,* 395–402.

Goldstein, E. G. (1995). *Ego psychology and social work practice.* New York: Free Press.

Goldstein, E. G. (2001). *Object relations theory and self psychology in social work practice.* New York: Free Press.

Greenspan, S. I., & Shankar, S. G. (2006). A developmental framework for depth psychology and a definition of healthy emotional functioning. In *Psychodynamic Diagnostic Manual (PDM),* pp. 431–482. Silver Springs, MD: Alliance of Psychoanalytic Organizations.

Gurman, A. S. (1977). The patient's perception of the therapeutic relationship. In A. S. Gurman & A. M. Razin (Eds.), *Effective psychotherapy: A handbook of research* (pp. 503–546). New York: Oxford University Press.

Heineman, M. B. (1981). The obsolete scientific imperative in social work research. *Social Service Review, 55*(3), 371–397.

Hoag, M. J., & Burlingame, G. M. (1997). Evaluating the effectiveness of child and adolescent group treatment: A meta–analytic review. *Journal of Clinical Child Psychology, 26,* 234–246.

Holinger, P. C., Offer, D., Barter, J. T., & Bell, C. C. (1994). *Suicide and homicide among adolescents.* New York: Guilford Press.

Hubble, M. A., Duncan, B. L., & Miller, S. D. (1999). *The heart and soul of change: What works in psychotherapy.* Washington, DC: American Psychological Association.

Jaynes, J. (1976). *The origins of consciousness in the breakdown of the bicameral mind.* Boston: Houghton Mifflin.

Johnson, J. (2004). *Fundamentals of substance abuse practice.* Pacific Grove, CA: Thomson-Brooks/Cole.

Johnson, S. M., & Whiffen, V. E. (2003). *Attachment processes in couple and family therapy.* New York: Guilford Press.

Journal of the American Academy of Child and Adolescent Psychiatry. (2001).

Kendall, P. C. (Ed.). (2000). *Child and adolescent therapy: Cognitive-behavioral procedures* (2nd ed.). New York: Guilford Press.

Kohut, H. (1971). *Analysis of the self.* New York: International Universities Press.

Kolb, D. A. (1984). *Experiential learning: Experience as the source of learning and development.* Englewood Cliffs, NJ: Prentice-Hall.

Kolb, D. A., & Fry, R. (1975). Toward an applied theory of experiential learning. In C. Cooper (Ed.), *Theories of group process* (pp. 27–56). London: John Wiley.

Kolevson, M. S., & Maykranz, J. (1982). Theoretical orientation and clinical practice: Uniformity versus eclecticism? *Social Service Review, 58*(1), 120–129.

Krill, D. F. (1990). *Practice wisdom: A guide for the helping professionals.* Newbury Park, CA: Sage.

Kurtines, W. M., & Szapocznik, J. (1996). Family interaction patterns: Structural family therapy in contexts of cultural diversity. In E. Hibbs & P. Jensen (Eds.), *Psychosocial treatment research of child and adolescent disorders: Empirically based strategies for clinical practice* (pp. 671–697). Washington, DC: American Psychological Association.

Lev, A. I. (2004). *Transgender emergence: Therapeutic guidelines for working with gender-variant people and their families.* New York: Haworth Press.

Levin, J. D. (1987). *Treatment of alcoholism and other addictions: A self-psychology approach.* New York: Jason Aronson.

Li, X., Stanton, B., Pack, R., Harris, C., Cottrell, L., & Burns, J. (2002). Risk and protective factors associated with gang involvement among urban African American adolescents. *Youth and Society, 34,* 172–194.

Luborsky, L., Crits-Christoph, P., Mintz, J., & Auerbach, A. (1988). *Who will benefit from psychotherapy?* New York: Basic Books.

Lyons, R. (1991). Rapproachement on approachment: Mahler's theory reconsidered from the vantage point of recent research on early attachment relationships. *Psychoanalytic Psychology, 8*(1), 1–23.

Mahler, M. S., Pine, F., & Bergman, A. (1975). *The psychological birth of the human infant.* New York: Basic Books.

Malekoff, A. (2004). *Group work with adolescents: Practice and principles.* New York: Guilford Press.

Marcia, J. E. (1966). Development and validation of ego identity status. *Journal of Personality and Social Psychology, 3,* 551–558.

Mays, V. M., Chatters, L. M., & Cochran, S. D. (1998). African American families in diversity: Gay men and lesbians as participants in family networks. *Journal of Comparative Family Studies, 29*(1), 73–87.

McEachin, J. J., Smith, T., & Lovaas, O. I. (1993). Outcome in adolescence of autistic children receiving early intensive behavioral treatment. *American Journal of Mental Retardation, 97,* 359–372.

McGoldrick, M., Giordano, J., & Garcia-Preto, N. (Eds.). (2006). *Ethnicity and family therapy* (3rd ed.). New York: Guilford Press.

McKenzie, F. R. (1995). A study of clinical social workers' recognition and use of countertransference with adult borderline clients. (UMI No. 9543475).

McKenzie, F. R. (1999, June). *The clinical validation method: Use of self in the therapeutic relationship.* Paper and conference publication presented at the International Conference for the Advancement of Private Practice of Clinical Social Work, Charleston, SC.

McNamee, S., & Gergen, K. (Eds.). (2002). *Therapy as social construction.* Newbury Park, CA: Sage.

Meeks, J. E., & Bernet, W. (2001). *The fragile alliance* (5th ed.). Malabar, FL: Krieger.

Meenaghan, T. M. (2005). *Generalist practice in larger settings.* Chicago: Lyceum Books.

Miller, D. (1994). *Attack on the self.* New York: Jason Aronson.

Mitchell, S. A. (1988). *Relational concepts in psychoanalysis: An integration.* Cambridge: Harvard University Press.

Monk, G., Winslade, J., Crocket, K., & Epston, D. (1997). *Narrative therapy in practice: The archaeology of hope.* San Francisco: Jossey-Bass.

Moreno, J. L. (1970). The triadic system: Psychodrama—sociometry—group psychotherapy. *Group Psychotherapy and Psychodrama, 23,* 16.

Morrow, D. F. (2004). Social work practice with gay, lesbian, bisexual, and transgender adolescents. *Families in Society, 85*(1), 91–99.

Muuss, R. (1996). *Theories of adolescence.* New York: McGraw-Hill.

Nichols, M. P., & Schwartz, R. C. (2006). *Family therapy: Concepts and methods* (7th ed.). New York: Allyn & Bacon/Pearson.

O'Hare, T. (2005). *Evidence-based practices for social workers.* Chicago: Lyceum Books.

Palmer, S., & Woolfe, R. (2000). *Integrative and eclectic counselling and psychotherapy.* Newbury Park, CA: Sage.

Pavlov, I. P. (1927). *Conditioned reflexes.* London: Oxford University Press.

Payne, M. (1997). *Modern social work theory.* Chicago: Lyceum Books.

Perez, R. M., DeBord, K. A., & Bieschke, K. J. (2000). *Handbook of counseling and psychotherapy with lesbian, gay, and bisexual clients.* Washington, DC: American Psychological Association.

Perls, F. (1969). *Gestalt therapy verbatim.* Moab, UT: Real Person Press.

Phinney, J. S. (1991). Ethnic identity and self–esteem: A review and integration. *Hispanic Journal of Behavioral Sciences, 13*(2), 193–208.

Pinderhughes, E. B. (1995). Empowering diverse populations: Family practice in the twenty-first century. *Families in Society, 76*(3), 131–140.

Pinel, J. P. J. (2006). *Biopsychology.* Boston: Pearson.

Powers, G. T., Meenaghan, T. M., & Toomey, B. G. (1985). *Practice focused research.* Englewood Cliffs, NJ: Prentice–Hall.

Prochaska, J. O., & Norcross, J. C. (2003). *Systems of psychotherapy: A transtheoretical analysis* (5th ed.). Pacific Grove, CA: Thomson-Brooks/Cole.

Psychodynamic diagnostic manual (PDM). (2006). Silver Springs, MD: Alliance of Psychoanalytic Organizations.

Racker, H. (1968). *Transference and countertransference.* London: Hogarth Press.

Rice, P. F., & Dolgin, G. K. (2005). *The adolescent: Developmental, relationships and culture* (11th ed.). Boston: Allyn & Bacon/Pearson.

Rodgers, K. B., & Rose, H. A. (2002). Risk and resilience factors among adolescents who experience marital transitions. *Journal of Marriage and Family, 64,* 1024–1037.

Rogers, C. R. (1957). The necessary and sufficient conditions of therapeutic personality change. *Journal of Consulting Psychology, 21,* 95–103.

Rogers, C. R. (1961). *On becoming a person.* Boston: Houghton Mifflin.

Rogers, C. R. (1965). *Client-centered therapy.* Boston: Houghton Mifflin.

Roseborough, D. G. (2006). Psychodynamic psychotherapy: An effectiveness study. *Research on Social Work Practice, 16*(2). Newbury Park, CA: Sage.

Roth, A., & Fonagy, P. (1996). *What works for whom? A critical review of psychotherapy research.* New York: Guilford Press.

Ryan, C. C., & Futterman, D. (1998). *Lesbian and gay youth: Care and counseling.* New York: Columbia University Press.

Saari, C. (1986). The created relationship: Transference and countertransference and the therapeutic culture. *Clinical Social Work Journal, 14*(1), 39–51.

Saleebey, D. (1997a). Is it feasible to teach HBSE from a strengths perspective, in contrast to one emphasizing limitations or weaknesses? (Yes). In M. Bloom & W. C. Klein (Eds.), *Controversial issues in human behavior in the social environment* (pp. 16–23). Boston: Allyn & Bacon.

Saleebey, D. (Ed.). (1997b). *The strengths perspective in social work practice.* Boston: Allyn & Bacon.

Santrock, J. W. (2006). *Life-span development* (10th ed.). New York: McGraw-Hill.

Schaefer, C. E., & Cangelosi, D. M. (1993). *Play therapy techniques.* Northvale, NJ: Jason Aronson.

Searles, H. F. (1959). Oedipal love in the countertransference. *International Journal of Psycho-Analysis, 40,* 180–190.

Searles, H. F. (1979). *Countertransference.* New York: International Universities Press.

Shulman, L. (2006). *The skills of helping individuals, families, groups, and communities.* Pacific Grove, CA: Thomson-Brooks/Cole.

Siegel, D. J. (1999). *The developing brain.* New York: Guilford Press.

Skinner, B. F. (1953). *Science and human behavior.* New York: Macmillan.

Smith, T. (1985). Group work with adolescent drug users. *Social Work with Groups, 8*(1), 369–376.

Stampley, C., & Slaght, E. (2004). *Cultural competence as a clinical obstacle. Smith College Studies in Social Work, 74*(2).

Stern, D. N. (2004). *The present moment in psychotherapy and everyday life.* New York: W. W. Norton.

Stolorow, R. D. (1992). Subjectivity and self psychology: A personal odyssey. In A. Goldberg (Ed.), *New therapeutic visions: Progress in self psychology* (Vol. 8, pp. 241–250). Hillsdale, NJ: Analytic Press.

Sue, D. W., Ivey, A. E., & Pedersen, P. B. (1996). *A theory of multicultural counseling and therapy.* Pacific Grove, CA: Brooks/Cole.

Sullivan, H. S. (1953). *The interpersonal theory of psychiatry.* New York: W. W. Norton.

Tansey, M. J., & Burke, W. F. (1989). *Understanding countertransference: From projective identification to empathy.* Hillsdale, NJ: Analytic Press.

Turner, F. J. (1996). *Social work treatment* (4th ed.). New York: Free Press.

Verono, A. (2004). *Counseling children and adolescents.* Denver: Love Publishing.

Walsh, J. (2000). *Clinical case management with persons having mental illness: A relationship-based perspective.* Belmont, CA: Brooks/Cole.

Weaver, H. N. (2005). *Explorations in cultural competence.* Belmont, CA: Thomson.

White, M., & Epston, D. (1990). *Narrative means to therapeutic ends.* New York: W. W. Norton.

Winnicott, D. W. (1953). Transitional objects and transitional phenomena: A study of the first not-me possession. *International Journal of Psychoanalysis, 34,* 89–97.

Winnicott, D. W. (1971). *Playing and reality.* New York: Routledge.

Winnicott, D. W. (1992). *Deprivation and delinquency.* New York: Routledge.

Yalom, I. D. (1985). *The theory and practice of group psychotherapy.* New York: Basic Books.

Zayas, L. H. (2001). Incorporating struggles with racism and ethnic identity in therapy with adolescents. *Clinical Social Work Journal, 29,* 361–373.

Index